Scorched Worth

Also By Joel Engel

L.A. '56: A Devil in the City of Angels

The Oldest Rookie

*By Duty Bound: Survival and Redemption
in a Time of War*

What Would Martin Say

*Rod Serling: The Dreams and Nightmares
of Life in the Twilight Zone*
(reissued as *Last Stop, The Twilight Zone*)

Screenwriters on Screenwriting

Oscar-Winning Screenwriters on Screenwriting

By George: The Autobiography of George Foreman

Gene Roddenberry: The Myth and the Man Behind Star Trek

Addicted

Scorched Worth

A True Story of Destruction, Deceit, and Government Corruption

Joel Engel

Encounter Books

New York   London

© 2018 by Joel Engel

First American edition published in 2018 by Encounter Books, an activity of Encounter for Culture and Education, Inc., a nonprofit, tax exempt corporation. Encounter Books website address: www.encounterbooks.com

Manufactured in the United States and printed on acid-free paper. The paper used in this publication meets the minimum requirements of ANSI/NISO Z39.48–1992 (R 1997) (*Permanence of Paper*).

Jacket images: background © Stuart McCall/Photographer's Choice/ Getty Images; sparks and burnt texture © photka/Shutterstock.com, © Bernatskaya Oxana/Shutterstock.com, and © Angelina Babii/ Shutterstock.com; seal © Ilyashenko Oleksiy/Shutterstock.com

FIRST AMERICAN EDITION

LIBRARY OF CONGRESS CATALOGING-IN-PUBLICATION DATA
Names: Engel, Joel, 1952-author.
Title: Scorched worth : a true story of destruction, deceit, and government corruption / by Joel Engel.
Description: New York : Encounter Books, 2018. |
Includes bibliographical references and index.
Identifiers: LCCN 2017039033 (print) | LCCN 2017040455 (ebook) |
ISBN 9781594039829 (Ebook) | ISBN 9781594039812 (hardback : alk. paper)
Subjects: LCSH: United States. Department of Justice—Corrupt practices. |
Justice, Administration of—Corrupt practices—United States. |
Misconduct in office—United States. | Political corruption—United States.
Classification: LCC KF5107 (ebook) | LCC KF5107 .E54 2018 (print) |
DDC 347.73—dc23
LC record available at https://lccn.loc.gov/2017039033

To every law enforcement officer, investigator, and prosecutor motivated by justice. That you are the overwhelming majority is a great comfort. That there is a small minority motivated by something else is cause for eternal vigilance.

"The United States wins its point whenever justice is done its citizens in the courts."

—INSCRIPTION ON THE WALLS OF
THE U.S. DEPARTMENT OF JUSTICE

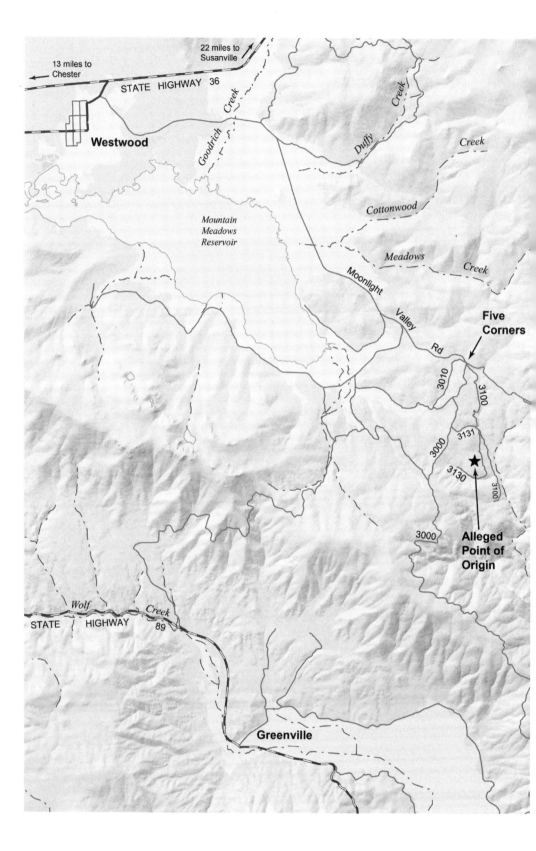

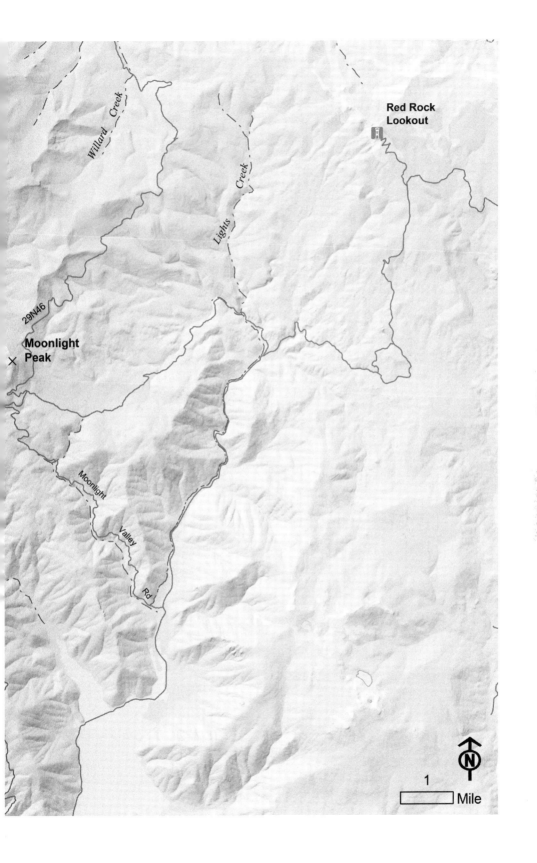

Scorched Worth

Introduction

The Moonlight Fire, as it would come to be called, began September 3, 2007—Labor Day—two and a quarter miles from Moonlight Peak in the Plumas National Forest of California's eastern Sierra Nevada, "southeast of the town of Westwood and northeast of the town of Greenville," as the fire's official report later put it. Though the precise time the fire broke out at this mile-high elevation on a hot, windy day would become the subject of much serious debate, with significant ramifications, it was reported at 2:25 P.M. by the fire prevention technician from a truck parked below the Moonlight Peak lookout tower.

The apparent point of origin was not on land owned by the U.S. Forest Service (USFS) but on adjacent private lands—reported as an "east-facing slope in the Cooks Creek drainage" area—for which the owners had sold temporary logging rights to Sierra Pacific Industries (SPI), one of the country's largest lumber companies. In turn, SPI had contracted with a long-established mom-and-pop company, Howell's Forest Harvesting, to cut the timber and manage the harvest before snows began in November.

Firefighters arrived quickly and fire suppression aircraft began dropping borate, a retardant, just before 3:00 P.M. Southerly winds pushed the fire north-northeast, angling down-slope in this mountainous area covered with tinder-dry terrain that hadn't burned or been thinned by man for decades. It advanced as a crowning fire, meaning that the tops of the conifer trees were so close together that they easily ignited, sometimes independently of what the fire was doing on the ground.

By nine o'clock that night, when darkness halted flights, only about 250 acres had burned, and there was hope a complete conflagration might be averted. But in the morning, a cold front brought erratic winds and downdrafts from thunder-cloud cells, making any effective containment measures impossible. By noon nearly two thousand acres had burned or were burning, and for several hours that afternoon the firefighters had to cease their work because the winds and meteorological conditions were too unpredictable. That night the firefighters were prevented from going out by lightning strikes, some of which may have sparked more blazes. Winds reached twenty-five miles an hour.

The third morning brought more of the same, then worse. Winds from the northeast pushed the fire toward populated areas in Indian Valley, where rugged terrain, wind gusts, and variable meteorology hampered all firefighting. By late afternoon on September 5, the blaze had burned more than twenty-two thousand acres.

Another six thousand acres went up the next day when firefighters were prevented from accessing huge portions of the steep perimeter. From there the fire burned uninterrupted from Indicator Peak in the north to Rattlesnake Peak in the south; and on the following day it began pushing eastward into areas that had been recently thinned, where the fuel load was less dense.

On September 8 the fire detoured in almost a circle around the firefighters, rendering them impotent, though fortunately unharmed.

By afternoon, wind speeds moved into the high teens, but there was good news: except for years' worth of pine needles on the forest floor, the fuel load consisted of fewer trees with greater spacing between them, making the fire less hot and angry. The bad news was that spot fires began breaking out, some of them with the potential to become large enough to earn their own names.

The seventh day brought weather conditions that allowed firefighters to build a fire line up Wildcat Ridge, and the intentional burnout continued downhill until the fire line stopped the fire's eastward progression. There was nothing now left to burn in front of it. The fire had gotten as big as it was going to get, spreading from Taylor Lake in the south nearly to the Diamond Mountain Motorway in the north.

Eight more days of intensive firefighting would be needed, aided by lower winds and higher humidity, before the Moonlight Fire was, at 9:15 P.M. on September 15, declared officially contained. Fighting it had required 707 firefighters, 42 fire engines, 11 fire crews, 6 airplanes, 11 bulldozers, and 34 water tenders—at a cost to California of $31 million.

There had also been 34 injuries and 2 homes and 5 outbuildings destroyed—and 65,000 acres of wilderness burned, 42,000 of them on lands owned by the federal government.

Nearly two years later, on June 30, 2009, the California Department of Forestry (Cal Fire) and the USFS issued their joint origin and cause investigation report, which had been compiled and written by lead Cal Fire investigator Joshua White. Five weeks later, on August 4, White also sent a letter to SPI and the owners of the land on which the fire had broken out, as well as to Howell's Forest Harvesting and two Caterpillar drivers who worked for Howell's, demanding payment of $8.1 million as reimbursement for suppressing and investigating the fire that he'd deemed the result of the dozer drivers' negligence. If payment wasn't received immediately, said the letter, the state would file a lawsuit. Payment was to be issued in two separate checks. The first, for $7.7 million, should be made payable to the State of California; the second, for $400,000, to the California District Attorneys' Association (CDAA) Wildland Fire Training and Equipment Fund (WiFITER).

Payment was not made. And so, on August 7, 2009, the State of California filed suit against all those named in the letters. Three weeks later the United States of America filed a separate suit against the same defendants for the loss of the forest lands, which had already begun to grow back.

Over the next few months, the two governments filed amended complaints, and for the most part the prosecution of this case by U.S. Department of Justice attorneys working out of the Eastern District of California and by the Deputy Attorney General of California in Sacramento was conducted simultaneously, with most of the same percipient and expert witnesses and exhibits for both. They were, in fact, nearly congruent cases relying on identical facts uncovered by the same two investigators: one from Cal Fire, one from the USFS.

Over the following three years, it became an increasingly reasonable inference that neither suit would have been filed if not for the fire's fragile connection to Sierra Pacific Industries—the only defendant whose pockets could conceivably accommodate the sums being sought in reparation.

With interest, the amount the United States sought would eventually reach more than $1 billion.

W hat the California attorney general and the U.S. Department of Justice knew about Sierra Pacific Industries at the time they filed their lawsuits was probably little more than this: SPI was one of the largest lumber providers in the country, and the Emmerson family who controlled the privately held company were the third largest private land owners in the United States, with some two million acres of forest lands in California and Washington used to supply most of the timber that Sierra Pacific's mills turn into lumber. What's unlikely was that any of the attorneys involved knew much, if anything, about billionaire Archie Aldis "Red" Emmerson, the man who'd founded the company fifty years earlier.

Red Emmerson had always kept a low profile, refusing to grant interviews even to *Forbes* and *Fortune*, on whose billionaires' lists he's ranked annually. It's possible that if the prosecutors had known more about the man and his humble beginnings—if, for example, they'd hired investigators to construct a personality profile of their legal opponent, as major corporations do before filing or defending substantial lawsuits—they would have known that Red Emmerson had earned every penny of his fortune the hard way and was entirely disinclined to pay monetary damages for something he knew he hadn't done wrong. So they might not have set a high damages figure designed to make him spend millions fighting back, hammer and tong, to protect the company he'd built by himself.

2

September 3, 2009. Bill Warne rose from his office chair, unfolding his lanky frame to stretch his back and legs. He was looking forward to a long Labor Day weekend with his wife and children, even though a "long weekend" to this complex litigation attorney meant only taking off some of Saturday and half of Sunday. Monday he'd be back at work but get out early—five o'clock—and meet his family at his brother's barbecue. That's all right, he told himself. The next summer was his scheduled three-month sabbatical, given every ten years to Downey Brand partners who worked as hard as Warne had for twice that long, and no one in the firm, at least in the Sacramento headquarters office, had worked harder. His plan was to take everyone to Europe for all three months. It was the carrot on a stick that kept him going, and he'd just given himself permission to Google images of places they'd told him they most wanted to see. Two minutes, no more, and then he'd finish the brief on his desk. A page on Aix-en-Provence was loading when his cell phone rang.

The caller ID said David Dun, general counsel to SPI, headquartered near Redding, about a three-hour drive north of Sacramento. SPI, Warne knew, had been founded in the mid-1950s by Archie Aldis "Red" Emmerson, who'd returned from the Korean War and opened his first small mill on the Northern California coast with pretty much nothing but an insatiable desire to succeed and the capacity to outwork anyone, both of those characteristics products of his Dickensian childhood. (SPI's headquarters and primary mill had long ago moved from Arcata, the site of the company's original mill, to Redding.)

At eighty, Emmerson was still one of the most fascinating men Warne knew or had ever known. Completely self-made and disarmingly modest, he was up there on the *Forbes* billionaires list because of the two million acres of forest lands in the Northwest he'd begun buying thirty years ago, after correctly foreseeing that ever-more-restrictive environmental laws and regulations would compel the USFS to sell fewer cutting permits on national forest parcels, which ordinary mill owners had for decades relied on as their primary source of trees. Thanks to purchases large and small, Emmerson was the country's third largest individual landowner, behind only media tycoons John Malone and Ted Turner—which was ironic because Emmerson would do anything to avoid the limelight, even if he was known in the industry as "the last timber baron." Each time Warne received Emmerson in his office, Warne had to remind himself that the man hadn't ridden the 160 miles from Redding on horseback; he'd flown in his private plane. On the short list of people whose word and handshake Warne considered more rock-solid than a written contract, Red Emmerson was first.

Emmerson's general counsel wouldn't be calling if it weren't important. "Hi, Dave," Warne said.

"Do you remember the Moonlight Fire a couple of years ago?" Dun asked. "Two years ago today, actually."

"Sure," Warne said. "It was big news up and down the valley. Fifty thousand acres, or something like that."

"Sixty-five," Dun said. "The feds and state are suing us for it. We just finished reading the suit."

"Wait, they're accusing you of starting it?"

"Yep."

"Whoa," Warne said. He didn't have to ask what damages the governments were seeking to know that SPI's future could be on the line. This recession that felt like a depression had hit the lumber market particularly hard.

"The damages aren't stated," Dun says, "but no one will be surprised if it reaches a billion or more."

"Jesus."

"Of course," Dun says dryly, "that's with interest."

In his spare time between the hours of midnight and four, Dun had established a decent little career as a thriller novelist and had a modest bestseller to his credit. This was the kind of line the hero in three of his novels would have spit out.

"You want to know how ridiculous this is?" he said. "If you nuked the forest land where the fire was so it could never be used again, the total assessed value would be about twenty-five million. It's insane."

"Sounds like extortion."

"That's Red's take, too. The land's already recovering. So this is either just punitive or a money play. Or both."

"In terms of liability, what are they saying you did? Or didn't do?"

"Their theory, so far as it can be said to be a theory, is that a Caterpillar tractor drove over a rock, and the friction between the granite and the metal grousers threw a spark that landed in a pile of dry brush."

"An SPI tractor?"

"No, a subcontractor SPI hired to log a parcel on some private land where we had a permit."

"Is that even possible, a spark from a tractor setting a fire?"

"That's why I say it's a theory in search of a fact. Red said we'll discover when we get into this that a bulldozer driving a few miles an hour over these rocks can't start a fire. All I know is, he said it didn't and couldn't happen, and I believe him. People say they've heard of dozers starting fires, but no one's ever actually seen it happen. It's kind of a rural fable. Not that it's stopped Cal Fire from pinning it on defendants before. That's why I'm calling."

Dun had gotten the go-ahead from Red Emmerson and his two sons, who now mostly ran the company, president George Emmerson and CFO Mark Emmerson.

Three times before, twice as defendant and once as plaintiff, Sierra Pacific had come to Bill Warne, and all three times he'd effected excellent outcomes. Never, though, had the opposing party been a government entity. Yes, as a logging company SPI was required to have frequent contact with government agencies, but those contacts were regulatory and bureaucratic. And because of his wealth, Red Emmerson had his share of contact with presidents, governors, and congresspersons, all of them eager to demonstrate their friendship. Yet for all the donations—including allowing California governor Jerry Brown to honeymoon at his 2500-acre retreat in the California redwoods—Red Emmerson couldn't think of a tangible benefit he'd ever received beyond a sympathetic ear when he called to complain that one regulation or another didn't make sense on either an environmental or economic level.

"The case is between you guys and Morrison Foerster," Dun said, referring to a San Francisco–based law firm, "but you've got no chance of getting it unless you tell me you'll make it number one on your desk."

"Oh, I'll make it number one," Warne said. "My whole team will. But before we go any further, I have to tell you, in the interest of full disclosure: I'm scheduled to go on my sabbatical next summer. I get three months off, so the girls and I are going to Europe."

Dun wasn't pleased. He said, "This is really the knife's edge for us, Bill. My clients really like you, and I'm sure you're their first choice. But if I call them up and say you're leaving next summer for three months, I don't have to guess how they'll respond."

What Dun didn't know, because Warne had never thought to tell him, was why Warne had become a lawyer twenty years ago. For a moment he considered revealing it now on grounds of pertinence: Warne had grown up with four siblings, one of them an older sister with Prader-Willi syndrome, a rare disease that stunted her height, making her about four ten, not tall like the others, and gave her the countenance of someone with Down syndrome. Yet the cruelly debilitating aspect of the syndrome was the way enzymes secreted in her hypothalamus caused her to feel constant starvation pangs, even after devouring a full meal. Lacking an ordinary internal appetite suppressant, she couldn't control herself around food. To see it was to eat it, and not to see it was to need it. Held back in elementary school, she'd ended up in the same high school as Warne. He often agonized at the sight of other kids teasing her without conscience, like the time he walked into the cafeteria where some football players had laid a trail of Peanut M&Ms and were laughing as she got down on hands and knees to pick up each one. Mercy and justice became his animating principles, Atticus Finch his role model.

"Look, Dave," Warne said, "I want this case. I want it bad. So how about if I cut my sabbatical in half—if I take six weeks instead of twelve? Hell, everyone takes three or four weeks anyway, so this isn't that much longer. Plus, I promise you I'll have everything teed up here before I go. You'll hardly even know I'm gone. But in the event you need me, I'll have an email address for you alone that I'll check every day no matter where I am."

Dun was quiet for a moment. "Back during the fire," he said, "there was a lot of talk, rumors, in and around Westwood"—the eastern Sierra Nevada town adjacent to where the forest fire began—"about someone who may have had something to do with maybe starting it—by accident or not."

"Okay," Warne said.

"So when you get on this case," Dun said, "we need a full-blown investigation. Do you understand?"

"Of course."

"Full-blown, Bill, full-blown. No rock unturned, especially the rock they say started this thing."

"Got it," Warne said.

They hung up. The job was Warne's.

One day—five years in the future and $40 million worth of investigation and discovery behind them—the two men would recount this conversation and laugh about how accidentally fitting Dun's metaphor had been. And Warne would remember, less fondly, how naïve he was to believe, after meticulously dissecting the report by Cal Fire investigator Josh White, that this case was so blatantly without merit and riddled with factual elisions that it would be dropped as soon government lawyers saw the kind of evidence it was based on.

Even after 2,700 hours of depositions taken from 232 witnesses and a mountain of otherwise dispositive physical evidence, the prosecutors never relented.

3

September 3, 2007. On this sweltering Labor Day at the end of a scorching summer during the state's driest year on record to date, Caleb Lief had one of the most important jobs in California. The argument could've been made that, with the windy season due any moment, there may not have been a more vital job than manning the Red Rock lookout station, watching for fire across tens of thousands of acres of conifer timberland in the Plumas National Forest of the northern Sierra Nevada mountains. The sooner a lookout spots smoke in the distance, the faster he can call it in and get borate-dropping airplanes aloft and firefighting trucks to the site. Mere moments often make the difference between a fire that can be put down quickly and one that reaches critical mass, which was, after all, the reason the job of fire lookout was originally created and funded by the U.S. Forest Service.

Lief was in his early forties, the divorced father of a teenage boy. He'd grown up in New England before coming west and had fought wildfires before catching on with the USFS. He may well have learned at some point that the Red Rock lookout was originally built in 1941 on this 7,600-foot peak two miles south of Diamond Mountain to prevent catastrophes on the mostly federal-owned lands in the Moonlight Peak, Lights Creek, and Lone Rock areas. Over the years, with vigilant eyes continually scanning for the first sign of any smoke and pinpointing its location via radio for firefighters on the ground, small fires— whether started accidentally or intentionally, by man or nature—had often been squashed before becoming destructive and deadly conflagrations. It's tedious being a fire lookout. In a best-case scenario, nearly every moment is uneventful.

It's also a lonely job. Fifty years before, novelist and poet Jack Kerouac had spent a summer as a lookout in the North Cascades of Washington State, confined to a fourteen-square-foot shack eight thousand
feet atop Desolation Peak, intentionally inviting the loneliness as a way
of compelling him to write. And write he did. "It was all mine," he described in *Desolation Angels*. "Not another human pair of eyes in the
world were looking at this immense cycloramic universe of matter,"
where "the sunsets are mad orange fools raging in the gloom."

Caleb Lief had not produced work that would inspire backpackers to
set off on literary pilgrimages to the Red Rock lookout station, as they
do to Desolation Peak. On the other hand, Lief, unlike Kerouac, hadn't
had to tough out three days by truck, tugboat, and mule to get to his
comfortably appointed Cape Cod structure with a four-sided catwalk
whose views stretch into tomorrow. He had driven from his home in
nearby Greenville, population a thousand and something, along a meandering fire road that kicks up clouds of dust visible fifteen minutes
before someone arrives for a visit. It's a foolproof early warning system.

But shortly after two this particular afternoon, when the wind had
begun to blow, the temperature was above 100 degrees, and the humidity was in single digits, the forest service may or may not have issued
a red flag warning, meaning perfect conditions for wildfires. That day,
USFS lookout Caleb Lief somehow had *not* noticed the clouds of dust
that should have alerted him he'd soon have a visitor. Because when
fire prevention technician Karen Juska noisily climbed the stairs after
noisily ascending the road and noisily parking her truck, there stood
Caleb Lief, blithely urinating on his feet.

He was stunned and surprised by Juska's presence, a reaction that
stunned and surprised her, too, given that she had all but sounded a
bullhorn. For that matter, an hour earlier she had signaled her im-
minent arrival by radioing her superiors in Plumas that she'd begun
driving from Antelope Lake to Red Rock lookout—a communication
transmitted over their standard frequency and 10–4'ed by Lief. Yet
knowing that Juska would soon be arriving had not made him more
attentive. Either that or he'd since forgotten.

As Juska learned and would later document in two reports, one of
them sanitized per the order of her superior, Diane Welton, and one of
them factual, Lief did have an excuse for his stunned surprise. She inadvertently stumbled on it when they came in from the catwalk (Lief's

feet still wet with the urine intended, he said, to cure his athlete's foot): a marijuana pipe lying on the counter by the sink, in plain sight.

"Oops," Lief said, snatching it away and hiding it behind his back. "You weren't supposed to see that."

No, she wasn't, but it explained a lot. Still, she'd have to decide whether to say something to someone about what she'd seen. Even on Labor Day, fire lookouts who preferred to be at their neighbor's barbecue beer bash down in town weren't supposed to toke on the job—something about how being high tends to interfere with one's ability to remain alert and focused.

Lief handed Juska a USFS radio in need of repair, which was more or less the reason she'd come in the first place. Both the radio and his hand smelled strongly of pot.

When she was later compelled to write down what had transpired, Juska would note that she had decided at this point to scan the landscape herself by taking a quick 360 around the catwalk. She saw nothing, she said, which, if true, would be helpful to her bosses at the USFS and therefore to the Department of Justice and the California Department of Forestry. Because if, at 2:15 P.M., no smoke was visible even to the attentive lookout, the forest service could be absolved of any financial responsibility for not spotting a fire at the earliest possible moment—when it might have been put out before spreading.

Now Juska was ready to leave and agreed to port out a bag of garbage Lief had accumulated. He carried it down to her truck.

According to her story, it was at this point that Juska noticed something in the distance above the trees, where mere moments before there had been nothing.

"Caleb," she shouted, "we got smoke right there. I think it's in Moonlight Valley."

She had already called it in on her truck's radio by the time Lief ran back up the stairs.

4

The first Emmerson ancestor to come to the United States was David W. Emmerson, who was born in New Brunswick, Canada, in 1843. Sixteen years later he headed south to the new state of Minnesota and soon married Eliza Richardson, six years younger and a native of the territory. They had three daughters before their son George was born in 1877.

At twenty George grew tired of farming their forty acres. The United States was still pulling itself out of the Panic of 1893, the country's worst economic crisis, brought on by the overbuilding of railroads financed with funny money. Many of those railroads ran through Wisconsin, carrying products out of factories that had sprung up alongside new dairy farms, and lumber and paper from mills supplied by the state's ample forests.

In Wisconsin George Emmerson met Ida Hume, daughter of Aldis Hume—originally from New York state—and Mary Margaret Barclay, a Wisconsin native. The Humes were a strict Seventh-Day Adventist family. George was irreligious, but to marry Ida he agreed that they'd raise their children as Adventists. As far as he was concerned, that meant taking Saturdays off instead of Sundays, and abstaining from alcohol and tobacco and unhealthy foods—all of which he either did anyway or tried to do for the good sense of it.

When George decided he didn't like working in Milwaukee's factories, Ida's family told them about a large Adventist community in Newberg, Oregon, near the Willamette River just outside of Portland. George bought fifty acres there, and he and Ida and their three boys arrived in Newberg in spring 1906. A summer of hard work followed. Raleigh was six years older than George and Ida's second son, Marlin, but both boys worked full-time in the fields. Chet, their younger brother, was still a toddler.

When he reached eighth grade, Raleigh was sent to a Seventh-Day Adventist boarding school half a day's travel away. The headmaster was renowned for helping young men reach their full academic potential, but Raleigh could not be persuaded that reaching his full academic potential was worth the effort. And what was he supposed to do with it? Work behind a desk? He quit and came home at about the same time his grandfather David bought the fifty-acre lot adjacent to George's and then died. Now George Emmerson owned all hundred acres. But money was short. He sold off twenty acres and set up a small logging operation that could, with luck, be a source of constant, if modest, income. The property was near enough to the coastal forest to harvest and mill Douglas fir.

It was Raleigh who was most responsible for setting up a small mill. He bought salvage parts from here and there and assembled them, Frankenstein-like, into a workable operation. He even skidded (dragged) the logs by horse from the logging sites to the mill and then got the lumber to town, where it was sold.

And when George decided to set up a second mill and sell rough-sawn lumber, it was Raleigh who figured out the logistics and Raleigh who peddled the merchandise. On one of his sales trips to Portland, he passed through Sherwood, where he fell for Emily Aebischer, the third of Chris and Emma Aebischer's eight children. Chris had arrived from Switzerland in 1875 and saved every penny he earned as a carpenter, so when property values collapsed after the Panic of 1893, he was able to buy 120 timber-covered acres on Chehalem Mountain, about ten miles south of Sherwood, near the Tillamook Forest. He built his own home on the land, planted fruit trees, and established a small dairy, keeping a dozen or so cows, as well as pigs that he butchered himself.

Emily blushed the first time Raleigh Emmerson smiled at her in church, where he'd gone specifically to meet girls, both because there weren't a lot of girls around who didn't go to church and because he knew that it would send a good message to their parents. The two married in 1923.

Between the small dowry he received from the Aebischers and the money he'd saved working with his father, Raleigh put a down payment

on forty acres of his parents' farm and planted strawberries and raspberries. But farming was not a good fit for Raleigh. It was something
that measured progress by the seasons, not hour to hour or even day to
day. Nothing satisfied him like transforming fallen timber into something else in mere minutes. He missed the mill. He missed everything
about logging and skidding and the grind of the saws. As long as he
had to work, which he would've preferred not to do, timber and lumber
were better than strawberries and raspberries. True, he could've gone
back to labor for his father, but he hated working for the old man (or
with him) only slightly less than he would have hated working for anyone else.

5

By 3:30 on the afternoon of September 3, 2007, personnel from the California Department of Forestry, the U.S. Forest Service, and local law enforcement had begun to assemble on the mountain below Moonlight Peak at an area called Five Corners—the intersection of several maintained dirt roads, all bearing four-digit numbers, that split off here from the main road, Moonlight Valley Road. Some of the personnel were charged with keeping any locals who might want a closer peek at the flames from driving past the checkpoint. Already, several people from Westwood who could see the smoke plumes from town had gathered there to enjoy, if that's the word, the sight of the angry cloud billows.

The fire's origin appeared to be about a dozen miles southeast of Westwood and northeast of Greenville, off roads 3131 and 3100, not far from Moonlight Peak. Lake Almanor was about four miles to the west and Honey Lake five miles east, so the water bombers, if it came to that, wouldn't have to travel far to load and reload.

Karen Juska had arrived from the Red Rock lookout station at 3:17 and spoken to a grizzled man, two months shy of his fifty-third birthday but older looking than that, who'd just made it safely back from the fire area. In his silver pickup, he had guided the first group of fire trucks toward where he believed the fire was burning. Covered in soot and shaken by the experience, he identified himself as J.W. Bush and said he drove a Caterpillar dozer for Howell's Forest Harvesting, the logging subcontractor on the Cook's Creek job for Sierra Pacific Industries, which had outbid other lumber companies for the rights to harvest trees on the privately owned parcel. Once upon a time, companies like SPI did most of their logging on U.S. forest lands, but in the last few decades the federal government had acceded to the demands of environmentalists and was now holding many fewer auctions for the rights to cut trees on smaller and smaller USFS parcels. This required lumber companies that wanted to remain in business—and over the last twenty years a majority of the smaller operations had either been bought out or gone bankrupt—to buy logging rights on private lands. Some, like SPI, had seen the writing on the wall in the 1980s and begun buying their own timberlands. By 2007 SPI owned nearly 2 million acres, but company policy, called "long-term sustained yield," is to cut in any given year only the amount of timber grown that year. That year, SPI lands could supply only half of what SPI's mills needed to meet demand.

Bush told Juska that he and his coworker Kelly Crismon had begun working at about six that morning, constructing water bars—small berms that help prevent erosion during rains—in the areas where the logging crew had cut the previous week or so. Because of the winds, which began picking up as the day wore on, they'd treated it as a red flag warning day, knocking off at about 1 P.M. and returning the dozers to the yard several hundred yards west of where they'd been working. Once there, they had checked the machines for damage, greased them, and filled them with fuel from the tender that was the only other piece of equipment in the yard. Then Crismon drove his own pickup truck down the hill to go home to an RV park. Bush, meanwhile, drove his pickup to his trailer near the logging camp where he was staying to pick up the cell phone he'd forgotten that morning. It was about a fifteen-minute drive one way, but it had to be done before he began his fire walk, a visual inspection of the site for any hot spots that might have theoretically been left by the dozers. (Dozers have hot engines and manifolds that can pick up woody debris, which will smolder until it's knocked off.) Though fire walks are not legally required for water barring, only for logging activities, Bush was heading back because Howell's company policy required fire walks within ninety minutes of every dozer operation. Normally, it's the job of the side rod—foreman—to perform the fire walk, but as it was only Bush and Crismon working that holiday, Bush had drawn the short straw. He'd planned to return and clear out the draw where they kept the slash pile—mounds of extraneous limbs that are essentially green trash but that can also be used to slow erosion during heavy rains—by spreading the contents across the area. Then, while looking for hot spots, he would keep an eye out for arrowheads to add to his collection.

Bush told Juska that he was driving back on the uphill side of Road 3130 when he noticed thick black smoke. He didn't see flames, he said, but there was no way to get to his destination, no way to save the Caterpillars, if indeed they were in the fire's path. As he drove out of the smoky area, he said, he nearly ran over someone riding an ATV fast toward him. The two men stopped and spoke, and Bush asked him to alert the authorities about a fire, since his own cell phone didn't have service at that spot on the mountain. He said the guy told him he'd already called it in. Minutes later, Bush saw a red Cal Fire truck heading up the hill. The firefighter driving it asked him where the fire was, and Bush had led him as far as he could up the 3130 road before having to turn back because of smoke.

Hearing Bush say there had been logging going on in the area struck Juska as consequential. That he hadn't said he'd been cutting logs but rather had been putting in water bars on the logging roads was irrelevant. The federal government was about to settle a huge lawsuit against Union Pacific Railroad for a fire seven years ago near the Feather River Canyon. Union Pacific workers repairing a track had used a high-speed rail saw and grinder capable of throwing sparks and chunks of red-hot metal up to forty feet. Some of them did go that far, landing in a bed of dry leaves before growing into what became known as the Storrie fire, which over the following weeks destroyed fifty thousand acres in both the Plumas and Lassen National Forests. Word from the top at USFS was that the settlement would be California's largest ever for a forest fire—at least $100 million—and that the agency's bigwigs were getting pats on the back from Washington and already scoping out some of the latest firefighting tools to buy with their percentage of the award.

On her way out, Juska passed USFS investigator Dave Reynolds, who was just arriving, and recommended that Reynolds talk to Bush, whom she described so that Reynolds could recognize him. When Reynolds reached Five Corners, there were still few enough people gathered that it wasn't difficult to identify Bush as the man leaning against his pickup. Reynolds approached and asked if he could speak to him. Bush agreed to talk to the man in the USFS uniform. If Reynolds had a voice recorder with him, he either didn't turn it on or didn't later provide a transcript and copy of their conversation. He entered into evidence only a U.S. Forest Service statement sheet with his notes: "Started using Cat to waterbar on sale at 0600. Worked until 1300. Went back to camp. Came back to sale. Saw fire. Could not call out. Stayed at Moonlight sale to direct resources. Kelly (——) [Reynolds left a space for the last name] new cat operator, was working in (lives in chester RV park) the area waterbarring also. Believes Kelly was operating closest to the fire area. Believes Cat tracks scraped rock to cause fire."

Reynolds wrote 3:36 P.M., September 3, 2007, as the starting time of the interview and, as the end time, 3:46 P.M. on September 13, 2007, which he would later, under oath, call a simple error. He also claimed that he'd read aloud the completed notes to Bush before having Bush sign the sheet, though printing his notes in block letters rather than writing in cursive, inserting a parenthetical into the middle of a sentence, and using "believes" instead of "says" would seem counterintuitive for notes taken in real time.

If Bush had indeed told Reynolds what Reynolds had written on the statement sheet, Reynolds might have considered calling an assistant U.S. attorney to inquire about holding Bush as an accessory to a felony, instead of letting him walk away. At 3:46 P.M., little more than an hour after the fire had been called in, for Caterpillar driver J.W. Bush to already blame the ignition on a rock strike implied that he had (a) seen the strike, the spark, and the smoke; (b) watched the flame grow; and (c) done nothing to prevent its spread. And if he'd known that Crismon's dozer was closer to the fire's apparent point of origin, the necessary implication is that Bush had (a) said nothing to Crismon about what he'd seen Crismon's dozer do, (b) abandoned the fire to get his cell phone before returning later to do a fire walk for a fire he would've already known was burning, and (c) driven intentionally into the mouth of an inferno.

At 4:42 that afternoon, less than an hour after Bush walked away, USFS investigator Dave Reynolds determined that the fire which had begun on privately owned land had now spread into national forest. He radioed in a request for a Cal Fire wildlands fire investigator to lead the investigation.

6

Raleigh Emmerson, whom everyone called "Curly" for the bright shock of hair that was as conspicuous as his smile, began assembling his first sawmill on Chehalem Mountain using spare and salvaged parts.

In an old flatbed truck, he drove down Front Street in Portland, picking up every discarded component he found, offering to take off owners' hands something they might otherwise have to pay to haul away, and buying, for a song, anything else he needed. What he ended up with was a workable circular saw, driven by an old car engine and capable of cutting at most a few thousand railroad ties. He or the buyer could buck the ties into the appropriate length and add the tie bolts. The work was as exhausting as it was dangerous. With mounds of sawdust on the mill floor, fires were common.

Oregon, like Northern California and coastal Washington State, had dozens, if not hundreds, of such portable sawmills. Many were three- or four-man operations that often lacked a permanent roof to protect against the rain, and the majority failed in a season. But Curly Emmerson's mill was profitable—until it burned down.

Within weeks, though, he got a second mill up and running and licensed a substantial timber patch near Carlton, west of Newberg and south of Beaverton. He'd negotiated a good deal, but the location was too far and too remote to make it home most nights.

His mill was no longer cutting just railroad ties. Curly had worked a deal with a Portland lumber company that agreed to pay him half of the contract price in advance instead of paying solely on delivery. As long as he doled out the advance wisely on labor and supplies—and, of course, groceries and rent—he could eke through the winter with the lumber stacked and waiting for delivery in the spring. It was a life-saving arrangement. Given how distant the mill was from the lumber supply, he'd have had to close up shop otherwise.

Every day the stack of lumber grew higher, eventually exceeding the contract amount. No matter. Even if the company didn't want what remained, someone else would when spring 1928 arrived.

Before then, though, another fire destroyed both the mill and almost every board foot of lumber. There was no inventory to deliver and no way to remill the lumber he owed. Not only would he not earn the rest of the money, but he also owed the lumber company every cent he'd been advanced. Plus interest.

To pay it back, he got a cutting job and moved with his wife and two children into one of the company's mill shacks. It had four walls and a wood-burning stove. But at least he was bringing home a paycheck that managed to cover weekly expenses to the penny.

The last thing he needed was yet another mouth to feed, so at first he didn't take the news well. Not that it mattered: on April 10, 1929, his son Archie Aldis "Red" Emmerson was born.

7

Only thirty-seven at the time of the Moonlight Fire, Joshua White was considered a golden boy in the California Department of Forestry. As battalion chief for fire prevention in Lassen County, he commanded a number of men who were older than he.

White had grown up in Boise, Idaho, graduating from Boise High School in 1988. The next two years he spent in California as a Cal Fire seasonal firefighter before enrolling in Boise State University, graduating five years later with a degree in criminal justice instead of his first love, forestry. As he later explained under oath, after a few weeks of studying botany he'd changed from forestry to criminal justice but had spent his college summers fighting fires in Butte County, California.

During his junior year he'd earned class credits for a semester-long internship with Cal Fire, working out of Butte's fire prevention bureau. He insisted that the internship had not been arranged by his uncle, Jack White, the agency's chief for the region. Nepotism, he said, had nothing to do with the hire. But internships were few and fiercely sought, and he was, after all, an Idahoan, not a Californian, so suspicions would have been unavoidable. As it happened, in fact, he also had a cousin—Jack White's son—who was a Cal Fire battalion chief. Those circumstances do not necessarily imply White didn't begin at the bottom. He did, though somewhat more in the way that the boss's son sweeps floors before becoming assistant to the finance manager. For White to move up at Cal Fire, he would not need to labor in obscurity, rising on wits and talent alone—though he may have had both in abundance. What he certainly had plenty of were looks and charm and the self-confidence that comes with believing that others think of you as good-looking and charming. When enough people tell you that blue-gray eyes and a killer smile are powerful weapons, you learn to use them well.

Josh White returned to California after graduating college and again worked as a seasonal firefighter before being promoted in 1996 to fire apparatus engineer in Butte County—a job he described as the "mid-step between firefighter and captain. You learn to operate the fire engine, drive the fire engine, operate the pumping systems. First-line supervisor, if you will."

By 1998 White was an acting fire captain during the fire season. In the winter he went back to working as a fire apparatus engineer on the coast in Mendocino, before taking and passing the civil service test that entitled him to become a fire captain. From there his career advanced on a steep trajectory.

On the day of the Moonlight Fire, White had every reason to believe he was on a career roll. Just weeks before he had arrested a serial arsonist named Jim Hough.

Hough was a fifty-six-year-old soft-drink distribution manager, the father of two boys—one a high school senior, one a professional corrections officer—and a devoted husband to his wife of twenty-nine years. For reasons inexplicable to himself and anyone else who studied the case, three summers before, he'd begun buying firecrackers around the Fourth of July, and instead of setting them off in a safe and sane fashion, as the saying goes, he'd been tossing them out of his car window into dry grass and brush. And he stopped each summer only after running out of his stash, usually around the time snow covered the ground. Some of these explosions sparked wildland fires that grew to hundreds of acres, and many were kept from doing so only by the rapid response from local fire agencies. In all, the fires Hough caused burned nearly eight thousand acres and cost tens of millions of dollars to fight.

What made this particular arsonist such an enigma—and so difficult to catch—was that nothing about him fit any of the classic profiles of a serial arsonist. He never missed his boys' soccer games. He volunteered his time for charitable causes. He remained a loving and devoted husband. He was adored at work by his employees and colleagues and clients. He had never evinced the least interest—so far as anyone had noticed—in either becoming a firefighter or watching fires burn, not even the campfires he set when the family went camping. He struck everyone who knew him as being happy and well-adjusted, with an infectious passion for life.

Statistics show that arrests are eventually made in fewer than two out of ten arson incidents, so the odds were against catching Hough. But two weeks before his last day of freedom, investigators caught a lucky break. Someone had spotted his late-model Toyota 4Runner leaving a forested area where several fires had burned the previous two years. Based on that sighting, Cal Fire investigators got a warrant, sent out an undercover team to secretly tag his truck with a GPS device, and began following him according to the coordinates that the device beamed.

For three days, Josh White and other Cal Fire investigators surreptitiously trailed Hough, waiting and watching for the moment when he did something that would convince first a prosecutor and then a jury that they had indeed found their arsonist. Some of the cars drove ahead of him, and some followed at a safe, unsuspecting distance. When he would turn off the road, leaving the cars in front with no one behind, other cars shifted to fill in the rotating formation, all of them communicating via a secure network.

On the fateful morning, Hough returned home from work at about 10 A.M., changed into a T-shirt, loaded the family's dogs into the 4Runner, and drove north on Highway 99 toward Chico. He turned onto Highway 162 toward Oroville, headed north on Highway 70, cut back to 99 toward Chico, and finally took Highway 32 toward Chester. Just the zigzag route he took was suspicious, since it was anything but the shortest distance between points. White and the other investigators believed he was looking for somewhere to toss his ordnance. Either that or Hough suspected he was being followed.

This went on for five hours, until about 3 P.M., by which point they were twenty miles north of Forest Ranch, south of Lassen National Park, on the boundary of the Plumas National Forest. Hough suddenly pulled to the shoulder of the highway in Deer Creek, outside Chester, by a heavily forested draw. The cars behind had been caught in a road construction stop, so by the time they were free, they couldn't blow their cover by stopping, too. They were forced to pass and meet up with the cars ahead that had also pulled over to see what Hough was doing. Soon, though, Hough approached, and the Cal Fire investigators prepared to fall back into formation. Just then he made an abrupt U-turn, nearly colliding with White's car coming the other way. Not wanting to spook him, White waited a while before making his own U-turn and giving chase. By then, Hough had turned around again and was headed their way fast.

Again the investigators had to pull discreetly ahead and find somewhere to make their own U-turn—and in so doing they came upon a fire that had already begun its destructive path up a hillside. Apparently, that was the point at which Hough, too, had chosen to turn around after throwing a firecracker out the window. (What would come to be called the Colby Fire burned 168 acres, closed Highway 32 for three days, and cost over $1 million to fight.)

The investigative brigade resumed the chase. White phoned Alan Carlson in his Redding office. Carlson, thirty years his senior, was White's superior (deputy chief of the fire prevention unit) and, in many ways, his mentor, seeing in the younger man natural talent and potential. Both agreed that the risk of allowing Hough to remain at large until they could catch him in the act was too great; he needed to be picked up. Carlson joined them for the arrest, made at 6 P.M. that night on a Forest Service Road, a few miles east of Chester. It went well but could have ended badly, as White realized when they found on Hough's front seat a loaded nine-millimeter pistol, which in retrospect may have been intended for a different purpose than the one White inferred.

Later that night, Hough sat with White and Carlson in the Butte County district attorney's office. As happens sometimes when opportunity smiles, White would not have been in the room with Hough if the official case officer, Shannon Garrett, had not gone on vacation; it would've been Garrett conducting the interview with Carlson instead of White. This being the largest, most important investigation of White's career, comporting himself well and getting results might further his career.

Hough was read his Miranda rights. He said he wanted to wait for an attorney, at which point he was supposed to have been left alone in order to comply with the "right to remain silent" protocol established forty years before by the Supreme Court's *Miranda* ruling. But he did not, apparently, clam up, adding instead that there wouldn't be much he could tell them until his attorney arrived. Had his case gone to trial, that might have been enough for a clever defense attorney to get what-ever Hough said from that point forward thrown out from evidence. (Three years later, in *Berghuis v. Thompkins*, the court amended and clarified *Miranda v. Arizona*, ruling that whatever a defendant volun-tarily says to law enforcement at any time after being Mirandized, even if he's previously invoked his right to remain silent, is admissible and can be used against him.)

White and Carlson were both surprised by how calm Hough seemed under the circumstances. "We know you were responsible for this fire," Carlson said.

"And how do you know that?" Hough asked.

White explained that they had been following him all day, handing him a sheet that detailed every movement, down to the speed of his truck—including when Hough had pulled off for the second time near Deer Creek.

"That's when you threw out something to start that fire," White said.

Hough didn't deny it. Instead, he asked whether anyone had seen him throw something out.

"Yes," White said, describing a fisherman who happened to see Hough toss the firecracker as he was walking from the creek to the highway. "He described your vehicle. He described you. And he saw it."

This was a lie. Defensible, perhaps, under the circumstances—and not illegal—but still a lie. A necessary one. Because even after chasing their suspect all day, the investigators still had no hard evidence that Hough had intentionally set this or any other fires.

Carlson handed him a photo of the burned firework found at the scene and said it was already at the crime lab being analyzed for DNA and other forensic evidence.

White added that they had no doubt the results would tie Hough not only to this fire but to several others and exaggerated the length of time that the GPS device had been attached to the car. (In 2012 the Supreme Court, in *United States v. Jones*, ruled that installing GPS devices on cars without a warrant violates the Fourth Amendment against unrea-sonable searches and seizures.)

For a while White and Carlson weren't sure whether they were deal-ing with a psychopath or a sociopath as opposed to a garden-variety sicko. That Hough was a family man, good at his work, and evidently loved by all didn't eliminate the possibility of a pathology marked by

lack of remorse and absence of conscience over unconscionable be-
haviors. But as the interview went on, Hough's body language, tone of
voice, and increasingly distant gaze demonstrated to the investigators
that he was an otherwise normal man at the mercy of a dangerous fe-
tish. Once they understood that, they began appealing to the better angels of his nature by insinuating that the crimes he'd committed weren't
necessarily serious, and trying to convince him that confession would
be good not only for his soul but for his legal situation.

From what they could gather, the soft spot to poke and prod was his
family—especially his older son, the one he was so proud of. The corrections officer.

His name was Ryan.

"What would Ryan want you to do?" Carlson asked.

The answer was on Hough's face, and White pressed the point. "It's
not the crime of the century," he said in a calming voice. And now both
men took turns massaging the point that the judge and prosecutor
would surely take into account Hough's cooperation.

That did it. Hough assumed that because no lives were lost or struc-
tures burned in any of his blazes, his crimes were merely misdemeanors.

"Well," he said, "I guess I'm guilty."

From that moment on, he cooperated fully, trying to garner the
greatest break from the authorities by poring over maps and pointing
to all the places where he had tossed fireworks. It was always in the
daytime, always the same kind of firecracker lit with a burning ciga-
rette, always tossed out the passenger window, always while he was
alone.

There was little left to discuss, except White's curiosity over what
made him do it, which Hough said he didn't understand and couldn't
explain, and Hough's curiosity over what he now faced.

They told him he couldn't be released on his own recognizance. It
was up to the judge at his arraignment to set bail. According to California's penal code, the sentencing options were two, four, or six years.

Only now did Hough realize that he could never again go back to
the life he'd known. He stared at the handcuffs, rubbed his shoulder,
looked like he wanted to cry, and said, "I'd just as soon shoot myself."

White and Carlson ignored him. Carlson, in his many years, had
heard a similar line any number of times. It didn't mean anything. It
was a non sequitur, the anguished rhetoric of a guy who suddenly regretted doing the crime and didn't want to do the time.

What White and Carlson hadn't explained was that two to six years applied to *each* count—and there were nearly fifty of them. So as Hough later learned from his attorney, who was angry about the confession, the arsonist faced a possible life sentence.

Life was unthinkable, undoable, unbearable. To the judge who set bail at $675,000, an amount Hough and his family would be unable to make, he announced he'd rather commit suicide than go to jail. The judge, too, had heard that before.

Over the next two weeks, as Josh White and Alan Carlson received kudos from Cal Fire for catching a maniac; Carlson celebrated one of the best gets of his career by counting the months until his retirement; White began counting the weeks to another promotion; Jim Hough's wife visited him in jail every few days, separated from him by a glass partition—both of them unable to do much more than cry; and Jim Hough plotted his exit.

Had he made bail, he would have had nearly limitless choices for that exit, maybe even one of the firearms kept in his home. But with the county jail providing few resources, it would not be easy to prove that he meant what he'd said about preferring death.

No fixture dangled from the ceiling of his cell, so he could not hang himself and enjoy a quick death. Instead, late one night, after knotting his bed sheet into a crude noose, this man who had come clean to White and Carlson in part because he thought he was doing right by his son Ryan, mustered the gumption to suffer the slow, agonizing process of strangling himself. The mechanics of it are horrifying to contemplate. With a length of the sheet wrapped around his neck and the other two ends fastened to the bars, he willed himself to lean in a way that tightened the pressure—and even used his legs to push backward until he lost consciousness.

Guards discovered him at 3:45 A.M. He was rushed to Oroville Hospital and placed on life support until his wife consented to pull the plug.

Joshua White received a call the next morning informing him of the suicide of Ryan Hough's father.

It was August 24, 2007. Ten days later, he received another call informing him that a fire had broken out in the Plumas National Forest, and as new battalion chief it would be his job to investigate and determine the cause.

8

In the late fall of 1929, just after Aldis's birth, Emily Emmerson presented her husband, Curly, with a small roll of cash she'd been squirreling away from her household money without telling him. She'd kept it a surprise because she knew that if he knew she could live on less than he was giving her, he'd have given her less and spent the remainder. Which would have defeated the whole purpose of her saving it in the first place. She'd done it because it was miserable living with a man who was miserable, a man who believed he was a better mill operator than the men he worked for.

With the money, Curly Emmerson assembled a new mill and licensed another timber plot outside Newberg. He envisioned someday building a mill beside a railroad spur so that the lumber could be loaded on freight cars and delivered far and wide. Transport was what separated small-time operators delivering only to nearby lumberyards from the big boys who could fulfill orders to Southern California, which had not only a building boom going on but mills waiting for product to plane and finish.

Curly recruited his brother Chet, who had briefly owned his own mill—and had managed to save a bit of money he was now willing to invest in this mill in Springbrook, a few miles northeast of Newberg.

One of his first memories as a boy, Red Emmerson says, is accompanying his father to the mill and watching the two circular saws—the bottom sixty inches and the top thirty-six inches—cut dimension lumber (two-by-fours) used in construction. He remembers the tiny roof and the mill floor that didn't even have a cement foundation. He remembers the basic, almost primitive, conveyor beneath the saws that carried out the sawdust. He remembers the adjacent one-acre pond on which logs floated. He remembers that whenever the equipment stopped working for one reason or another, it was his father who fixed it while the two or three other employees sat and watched—their idleness making as much of an impression on him as his father's skill.

From the beginning, the mill was just profitable enough to pay its and the Emmerson family's bills. Everything left was put back into operations. So there was no margin for error—for instance, the bottom dropping out of the home-building market, thanks to the Depression.

Still, Curly refused to give up. Even as other mills in the area closed for lack of business, he kept hanging on. Until there was nothing left to hang on to.

9

At 7 P.M. on September 3, Josh White received a call from Cal Fire division chief Joe Waterman with orders to respond immediately to the Moonlight Fire; his federal counterpart would be Investigator David Reynolds. White drove from his home in Ravendale, about ninety miles north and east of Westwood, and arrived there a little after 9 P.M.

His first stop was the Cal Fire station on the main drag. There, Leo Whitlock, a private patrol officer for the logging companies, explained that loggers had been working in the fire's general area. Whitlock told White that he'd been on the mountain that day and seen three people. The first was George Bullard, a logger who was driving down the mountain when Whitlock was driving up, looking for the fire he'd heard about over the radio after it was called in by the Red Rock lookout.

Numbers two and three were a couple Whitlock recognized as Eddy Bauer and his wife Jennifer. The Bauers, he said, had told him they were looking for their son, who they thought was falling timber around there. A little later, Whitlock explained, a Plumas County sheriff's deputy named Benny Wallace had seen the Bauers' son speeding down the mountain, away from the fire, in a green Toyota pickup. The son's name was Ryan.

Whitlock introduced White to John Forno, a state-licensed forester working for SPI, and explained that the loggers were subcontractors, not directly in SPI's employ. White, of course, knew of SPI. Everyone in logging did. SPI was California's five-hundred-pound logging gorilla, the third largest lumber producer in the country.

White was eager to see the fire for himself. There is a terrible beauty to the spectacle of a forest burning at night. A ragged wall of yellow flames stretches across the horizon, and the dancing light reflects on the faces of those watching. Even professional investigators are not immune from this guilty pleasure that may not be mixed in equal parts.

Driving south on Moonlight Valley Road, following the fire's glow behind the peaks ahead, White reached the clearing known as Five Corners and was met by Reynolds. It was now nearly 10 P.M. White insisted on getting closer to the action. So against Reynolds's advice and better judgment, they continued on Road 3100 to Road 3131 from which, in daylight, Reynolds had seen what he identified as the heel of the fire. Twice that day he'd been there—once after interviewing bulldozer driver J.W. Bush, and once to help direct the U.S. Forest Service bulldozers as they cut suppression lines.

Up ahead, White could see, in the reflected glow, damage consistent with a crown fire. But how had it grown from the forest floor to the tree crowns? Answering that would have to wait till the morning. Even White had to agree that the danger and smoke were not to be ignored. They would leave—White to his motel, Reynolds to his home in Susanville—and return in the daylight to begin their work in earnest.

10

Curly and Emily Emmerson and their three children moved to Milwaukie, Oregon, twenty-five miles northeast of Newberg, and lived in a small rental. Archie began the first grade. Curly had begun felling trees and selling the logs to mills up and down the Willamette, rafting the goods to the buyers—and feeling hemmed in by his family obligations. All that changed when the other four Emmersons came down with scarlet fever, and health authorities posted a quarantine sign out in front of the house. It applied to him, too.

Yet even after the sign was removed and all had recovered, Curly Emmerson didn't come home except on rare occasions to check in and say hello. For whatever reason, Curly's only son didn't feel angry or embittered.

"Somewhere inside I must have just understood it for what it was," Red Emmerson says. "And it was what it was. I never held it against him or felt sorry for myself. And I still don't think of my father as bad for leaving. Mom never said a bad word about him, so I figured that whatever happened was between them. And whenever I did see him, which wasn't that often—just whenever he'd be in town and stop by for a quick visit—he never said anything bad about Mom. He'd even ask if I had remembered her birthday."

Financial circumstances forced Emily Emmerson to move frequently and rely on the kindness of family, including Curly's brothers, Marlin and Chet, as well as her parents. Archie Emmerson attended first grade in Milwaukie, then second and third grades in Dundee, three miles southwest of Newberg.

Like his father, Archie was smart about numbers, good with mechanical things, and indifferent to general learning. Yet even before he could read, he could hear a story once and recite it from memory. School bored him. He loved being outside, especially if he could tinker with a piece of machinery or drive a tractor.

In summer he picked cherries and berries for modest wages, working from sunup till last light, and gave most of what he earned to his mother. Even as a young boy, Archie Emmerson always aspired to be the hardest worker, whether the others were kids or adults.

"I don't remember a time," he says, "when I didn't think that I could keep up with everyone else. Hard work never bothered me. Never. I just kind of took it for granted that whatever it took to do the job, I'd do it."

After two years the Emmersons moved again, this time to Rose Lodge, about forty miles to the southwest, where Emily had been hired to teach school—and where Harry Thorpe owned a home, sold real estate, and sometimes preached on the side. Once Emily had accepted that Curly was never coming back to her, she had agreed to the introduction made by common friends in the church. Each had something the other needed.

Of course, Emily also had something that Harry didn't need: three kids.

Archie was in the eighth grade now, and school still hadn't caught on with him. Not only was Rose Lodge's curriculum strictly Adventist, he was being taught by his own mother. Still, he endured it until fire destroyed the school in April of that school year. Without her job, Emily no longer had the money to support her son, which she had agreed to continue doing before marrying Harry.

Archie was first sent to live with his father's parents, which he didn't like, then with his uncle Marlin and aunt Bernice. Marlin operated a stud mill and put Archie to work pushing logs on the pond. Archie begged Marlin to let him work inside, but state and federal law would've shut the place down for employing a minor under the age of fourteen. So Archie spent ten hours a day learning through trial and error how best to maneuver a wooden pole sixteen feet long and two inches in diameter—a heavy thing and unwieldy to use—to get the logs pushed from the pond into the mill.

II

The California Department of Forestry and Fire Protection expects its investigators to follow prescribed protocols when searching for the causes of wildland fires. These protocols were developed over time to minimize the possibility of error, and the agency publishes manuals and booklets describing them in exactitude.

Before receiving their certifications as state-licensed investigators—and long before reaching the level of battalion chief—Cal Fire field personnel must demonstrate an intimate knowledge of these procedures through both experience and written exams. It would be impossible to pass these tests without complete familiarity with the state's booklet FI-210 on determining wildland fire origins and causes.

The protocol is built expressly, according to FI-210, on "Use of the Scientific Method," which is outlined on an entire page, with explanatory paragraphs for each step. First comes recognizing the need, followed by defining the problem, collecting data, analyzing the data, developing a hypothesis, testing that hypothesis, and selecting the final hypothesis.

To a layman, traipsing through a burned forest and locating the exact spot where and why a fire began may seem impossible. But, just as with structure fires, forest fires often but not always leave telltale clues for those trained in where to look. That's why classrooms are filled with men and women who pay or are paid to learn how to properly and accurately locate what's called a general origin area, then to refine the search from there to find the specific origin area, and then—after systematically, methodically gridding that area—to ascertain the specific point of origin. Finding the former two requires training; finding the latter requires both patience and an open mind, uncluttered by expectation bias.

In many cases, the general origin area of a forest fire is found by searching for a burned-out inverted V-pattern. As the fire progresses from the specific origin area forward and to the sides, it creates a triangle whose shape and path are determined by topography, fuel load (amount of vegetation, in this case mostly conifer trees), and wind direction and speed.

Forest fires often start slowly and creep along the ground, where the wind is less of a factor, until they achieve critical mass and begin crowning—that is, reach a height and ferocity that allow the flames to consume an entire tree at once. Once that happens, progress is self-sustaining, aided by currents that the fire itself creates and atmospheric winds that may be ten miles an hour faster than those on the ground.

Picture an enormous traffic cone lying on its side. The head of the cone is where the fire began, and the remainder of the cone, shaped like an arrow, points in the direction the fire burned. The perimeter of the cone will be a line of trees that weren't damaged on the side away from the fire.

Protocol is clear that once the cone is located, the investigators are to proceed slowly across it, with a practiced eye, in a zigzag pattern. Alert to clues, they can ascertain the general area of origin.

The sooner that area is outlined, the more likely it is that the fire's true cause will be determined. Because just the way homicide investigators rope off the crime scene inside a home before it is accidentally contaminated, fire investigators secure and protect a fire's area of origin. The reason is only common sense. During the first stages of a forest fire, hundreds of firefighters and bulldozers and other machines creating firebreaks may inadvertently disturb, displace, or destroy evidence on the ground. Something as simple as boot prints can contaminate the clue-gathering process, which, after all, may actually be a crime investigation if the fire's cause is revealed to be arson.

FI-210 mandates that after outlining the general origin area, the investigators are then to grid the specific origin area, the space at the top of the virtual cone. To find that area, they locate the fire's micro-indicators—anything from a twig burned on only one side to soot.

These clues will be used to determine where, exactly, to place the grid lanes that will surround the specific point of origin.

To begin the gridding process, investigators locate each lateral edge of the fire at the head of the virtual cone (or V). Then they drive small nails into the ground at points along the perimeter and connect the nails with string. The result is a series of parallel strata eighteen inches wide. A grid.

Now comes the search for the specific point of origin, a painstaking, tedious process. If done well and correctly, it can establish what started the fire and track the precise route from the original flame to what becomes the main fire vector—the point at which the fire achieved critical mass and became a giant blowtorch.

The investigators are to get down on their hands and knees in the space just below the bottom stratum of the grid line (marked by the tow string) and conduct a slow, excruciatingly systematic search. They are to use the naked eye, then a magnifying glass and a hairpin to turn over leaves, pine needles, and other small objects—all in search of, possibly, a tiny match head, a piece of charred paper, even a bottle or shard of glass that might have acted as a lens.

Following the eyeball examination, the first lane is then passed over with a metal detector and a magnet for fragments possibly hiding below the surface.

Once the first lane is searched thoroughly and any evidence photographed, documented, and securely stored, the investigator must disturb that lane, crawling through it as he inspects the next lane above it with the same studious care. Then comes the third lane, and so on.

Eventually, as he works his way to the tip of the V, if there is indeed something to find, the careful investigator will have found the cause of the fire. Of course, if the fire was hot set—that is, with an arsonist's lighter—or if he can't find traces of any accelerant that might have been used, the investigator may be left with no better than an informed theory about what started the conflagration. But at least he will have located its point of origin.

On the FI-210 page detailing the scientific method, the final paragraph warns expressly against expectation bias—that is, the tendency to let expected or preferred outcomes influence the methodology and therefore the result. Unlike a physics or chemistry lab, where experiments are repeatable and conditions controlled, a burned forest offers only one chance to get it right.

"Until all the data has been collected and analyzed," the paragraph says, "no specific hypothesis can be reasonably formed. An investigator must not make assumptions about the cause of a fire until this process is completed."

12

For a time, even the young Curly Emmerson had attended Laurelwood Academy in Gaston, near Portland. In fact, the school had been operating for about forty years when Archie Aldis Emmerson enrolled in 1943 during the height of World War II. Of the few dozen students studying the strict Seventh-Day Adventist curriculum, none of them was more uninterested in learning it than Archie was. Except for the handful of classes offered in the manual arts, he disliked school so much that he spent as much time as he could working the farm that Harry and Emily had bought outside Boardman, east of Portland.

Archie was not surprised to find that Harry was a less than diligent farmer. Often, Emmerson says, the two of them could have completed a major task if only they had pushed through until dark—and thereby save all the time of getting the tractor and other machinery out of the barn the next morning. But if Harry felt at all tired and hungry, he would insist on knocking off before the job was done. So Archie would stay out by himself.

To the degree Emily saw anything wrong with Harry, she was more troubled by reports of Archie's "unruly" behavior at school. It was un-Adventist. He had threatened to run away, lie about his age, and enlist. And he sometimes snuck off to Portland, where he walked the streets and saw how many of the men were away at war.

As rebellions go, this was minor. But in the Adventist world, little allowance was made for a young man whose father had abandoned him and who, in any event, didn't understand how book learning could put food on a table and a roof overhead. What he wanted to learn was how to grow his own food and build the roof that would shelter the table at which the food would be eaten.

The Laurelwood administrators convinced Emily that the evil could be coaxed out of Archie Aldis Emmerson—something they couldn't do themselves—by sending him to a new Adventist boarding school south of Spokane.

In Washington.

Far from home.

Where his mother, stepfather, sisters, uncles, grandparents, and everyone else he knew would have zero influence on him.

To Emily, her son's being a good Adventist was more important even than his being alive—or so it seemed to Archie. Even in 2017 Red Emmerson suspected that his death as a teenager would have caused his mother less grief than his abandoning the faith.

"All you had to do was look at her to know that," he says. "She loved me. I believe she did. But her world had to be ordered just right, and I think it hurt her and embarrassed her that I didn't fit into or accept that world the way she and all the rest of her family did. That meant more to her than anything else."

13

The idea that the Moonlight Fire had been the result of a tractor's metal grouser striking a rock and throwing a spark seems already to have become fixed in Josh White's mind by the time he awoke on the morning of September 4, 2007. Soon after sunrise, fewer than eighteen hours after the Moonlight Fire had begun, White asked Scott Packwood, a Cal Fire forestry inspector from Westwood, to lead him onto the mountain. The two men drove south on Road 3130 past the perimeter of the fire but not to the general area of origin or to the area White had approached the night before with Reynolds. The first thing White wanted to see that morning was a point due west of what he'd seen the night before, beside a trickling creek and green meadow: the "yard," as it's called in the logging trade, where the two Howell's Caterpillar tractors and a fuel truck had been parked.

It was a revealing choice, one he may very well not have made if he had stopped to consider that his visit to the Caterpillars before anywhere else would come to light, thanks to discovery in the lawsuit and time code on his camera, and be interpreted as evidence of expectation bias. He'd ignored the investigation protocols established in FI-210.

As far as Josh White knew, firefighters and other personnel coming on duty at this moment were trampling the general area of origin, which hadn't yet been secured and wouldn't be until he, as the ranking investigator, protected it with do-not-disturb-or-trespass tape. If the fresh personnel were at the site, it would be useless for a detailed, scientific investigation.

So why did he make the Caterpillars his first stop instead of securing the general area of origin from possible contamination? The big

Cats weren't going anywhere that day, so inspecting them later on Tuesday or even the following day would have changed nothing. To be sure, White's naked eye could not have detected what he might have been looking for on their grousers unless what was missing from them was a substantial chunk, in which case he would have done well to follow FI-210 by beginning his search from the ground up at the place where such a chunk might be found.

Josh White examined the tractors and took photos of them before driving back out on the road he came in on for a short distance; then he turned left up the hill to the beginning of a goat trail, no more than four hundred yards long, that was often used by firewood cutters in the area. The end of this trail connected to another road on which private patrol officer Leo Whitlock had stopped Jennifer and Edwin Bauer in their truck when they were looking for their son Ryan, as Whitlock had recounted to White the night before.

White had arranged to meet Dave Reynolds along this trail at an old rusty barrel locals used for a landmark. The barrel, Whitlock had explained, was where he'd seen the fire in front of him, to the east, burning "in a draw"—that is, an area where the ground slopes upward in three directions and downward in the other direction.

Reynolds had suggested meeting there for its proximity to a ridge that paralleled the western lateral of the initial main fire vector, not far from the general area of origin. White and Reynolds walked south on the ridge before starting down. They could see the burned-out V below. The wind was still blowing from the south, more or less in their faces, as it had the day before; it was clear that the wind, topography, and fuel load had conspired to create something of a blowtorch that knocked out a swath of forest. The word "nuked" came to mind. Gray ash and pathetic sticks that used to be proud conifers were surrounded by trees burned on one side only, marking out the V. Clearly, somewhere up ahead and at the head of that cone-shaped torch lay ground zero. Their task was to find it.

White and Reynolds walked on the ridgetop to their right—south—for a while, without making the zigzag pattern from one side of the cone to the other. Instead, they walked straight down, even after reaching the southernmost edge of the fire—another FI-210 violation.

They hiked down the crest of the hill toward the apex of the V, then turned left and walked easily down a skid trail, approximately 250 feet, before reaching a stand of still-green trees that represented one edge of the seventy-five-foot by fifty-foot general origin area. By choosing to walk down the skid trail rather than follow protocol, they overlooked clues and passed through what would have ultimately been the bottom of the fire's heel.

The two investigators may have recognized the fifteen-foot-wide skid trail as one on which Bush said Crismon had been building water bars, which may have been correct, given that the yard where the Howell's dozers were parked was about fifteen minutes west in a Caterpillar. Was this the last trail Crismon had worked before leaving for the day? Down the skid trail from the ridge top—past where the trail intersected a spur trail—was a fresh water bar, though with a tractor mark on it. In the middle of that mark lay a granite rock about the size of two basketballs.

Which of the men found that rock is not known, but whoever it was must have excitedly noted that there was a strike mark on the rock, presumably made by a Caterpillar's grouser bar. Farther toward the fire's heel was a small patch of burned ground cover that could, they theorized, have been the fuel source from the thrown spark—*if* the spark from the rock had been thrown that far.

Yes, they agreed: this was the specific origin area—about ten feet by ten feet. Inside it lay the specific point of origin, the rock that the Cat grouser had struck. That the rock did not lie in the point of the V didn't matter. This was it, they concluded, and it wasn't a coincidence. They'd found it. The Caterpillar had started the fire by driving over the rock and throwing a spark into the ground cover, which ignited before the fire continued to burn north and east. Plenty of micro-indicators verified this, they told themselves, though of course they couldn't have known whether Crismon's dozer or a firefighting dozer had made this mark on what was the logging equivalent of a highway.

There was now no need, they apparently thought, to go back and follow procedure or search for another ignition source by gridding the general area. Later on they could mark the ground with the appropriate blue, yellow, and red flags to indicate the advancing indicators that they'd now obviously find—blue for a backing fire, yellow for a lateral fire, red for an advancing fire, white for the point of origin. Right now they needed to resolve the only weak link in their theory.

If Bush was right about the time that he and Crismon had knocked off; and if, as the investigators hypothesized, the rock was struck while Crismon was building that particular water bar; and if, as they hoped, the water bar was the last one he built that day, the fire would have had to smolder for more than an hour after ignition before becoming the blaze that Karen Juska spotted from the Red Rock lookout.

But an hour is a long time for a flame to smolder in a clump of brittle twigs on a dry, windy summer day (assuming, of course, that a fleck of metal from a slow-moving dozer could reach and sustain a hot enough temperature to ignite the patch). From that they concluded that Bush had been off with his estimates about the time when the two Cat drivers had quit work that day. They would have to check with both him and Crismon.

White planted a small white flag in the ground next to the rock and snapped dozens of photos, the flag appearing small in the foreground— small enough to be near invisible in the camera's two-inch LCD viewfinder when he later decided which photos to keep and which to trash.

14

Until its conversion to a school, Upper Columbia Academy had been either a clinic or a hospital. Upstairs were the boys' dorm rooms, which weren't exactly rooms; they were spaces demarcated by movable barriers placed at strategic places for minimum privacy in what had been an open room. Classes were held downstairs to serve the 120 students. Archie Emmerson was the only student responsible for paying his own tuition, room, and board: about thirty dollars a month.

When he showed up for his first semester, he had in his pocket most of the proceeds from selling his watermelons that summer, when he'd carted them from shop to shop, town to town, for sale. Whatever was left after he'd paid his school expenses he spent parsimoniously on himself, maybe purchasing a soda or candy bar if he happened to be in town. But he often loaned small amounts to other students at low interest rates, so long as they collateralized the debt with any personal property he deemed worthy, from marbles to knives to fountain pens.

These transactions put him in an interesting and awkward position because they made him more visible than he would've been otherwise.

"I guess you could say I had something of a complex," Emmerson remembers. "I was bothered by the feeling I wasn't as good as the other kids. I had only one sweater and wore it to classes every day. That's why I really looked forward to warmer days, so I didn't have to wear that old thing. But this was Washington, and it was cold. In my mind, everybody was looking at the sweater and thinking I was some boxcar kid. I didn't even have a suitcase for my clothes. I just put everything I owned into a paper bag or pillowcase. I was sure everybody thought worse of me. Eventually I just learned to live with it."

The only thing that made him feel better about having one sweater and a pillowcase suitcase, he says, was working harder and longer and signing up to do every job that offered pay, so he'd always have money in his pocket.

Bob Christiansen, the school's farm manager, took an interest in and a liking to Archie after he noticed how hard and long the kid was willing to work, even at thirty cents an hour. The school's curriculum required that every student work a few hours a week in the dining hall or kitchen or somewhere else. The point was for them to learn the value of hard work. But most of them complained, and several found ways to get out of it. That benefited Archie. He gladly picked up whatever needed doing, especially on the farm. So he and Christiansen got along well.

As it happened, Archie was the only student with a bona fide driver's license, which he'd gotten in order to drive Harry's truck. The school administrators soon trusted him with the keys to the academy's vehicle and sent him on errand runs into town. While there he'd buy small items that he knew students either liked or craved and bring them back to sell at a small profit. Any kid who resented having to pay him that little extra didn't have to do business with him, but eventually almost everyone bought from his little makeshift canteen—especially after he began stocking up on sodas that went great with the hamburgers he was capable of grilling on the hot plate he'd brought back, too.

The fact that he was breaking school rules by doing this didn't deter him. But from the school's perspective, his capitalist initiative was yet one more symptom of his rebellion against the strictures of the Adventist faith. A hot plate was one thing; it was clearly against the rules. But to cook hamburgers—that is, meat—on one was to add injury to what they already considered spiritual insult.

Still, for a while the administration ignored Archie's canteen. They did not take away his privileges with the school vehicle or prohibit him from going into town, maybe because the errands he ran freed the staff to do other things.

Besides, a few teachers couldn't help noticing his potential, even if that potential was nothing more than a rare determination to succeed. Like Bob Christiansen, they spoke up for him behind closed doors, pointing out that he was liked enough by his classmates to be voted school treasurer and that thanks to his hair, other students had begun calling him by an affectionate nickname: "Red."

15

Westwood, California, population two-thousand-something, abuts the vast Plumas National Forest some two hundred miles south of the Oregon border, just north of Greenville, east of Chester, and southeast of Susanville. The town reaches for about a mile just below Highway 36 and averages about six hundred meters wide, with Lassen County Road A21 on the eastern border serving as the main commercial drag. Among other establishments, in 2007 Westwood supported a True Value Hardware, an equipment rental store, an auto parts shop, a Buffalo Chips and Pizza, an Assembly of God church, a tanning salon, a bank, Captain Andy's Mountain Market, a Cal Fire field office, and a watering hole or four.

Not to be overlooked in any discussion of the town's character in the mid-aughts, fair or not, was Westwood High School's drug testing program, in which students were tested for alcohol, marijuana, amphetamines, cocaine, opiates, barbiturates, and benzodiazepines. Among the 125 students, random testing was mandatory only for anyone who engaged in extracurricular activities like sports and music. So one can be forgiven for inferring that this school provided disincentives to students who occasionally smoked pot but who might have liked to do more with their lives than spend six hours a day in classes that produced test results far below California's dismal averages in English, math, and science. A stoner who had zero chance of being flagged for a random test when he did little more than show up to class had a high probability of being kicked out of school entirely for trying to join chess club and failing the mandatory drug test.

That Westwood has always been a logging town proud of its logging past accounts for the public display of statues and monuments to history's most famous lumberjack. And in fact, when Ryan Bauer—Westwood High School class of '05—was growing up there, he aspired to be Paul Bunyan.

By age twenty, the best lumber job Bauer had been able to manage was knot bumper, which is to logging what orderlies are to neurosurgery. Fallers cut down trees. Knot bumpers slice off the extraneous limbs once the trees have been felled.

Bauer was lucky in September 2007 to have recently landed the knot-bumping job with Howell's Forest Harvesting Company, contracted by SPI to clear a parcel of privately owned land near Moonlight Peak, a twenty-minute drive from his parents' home in Westwood, where he still lived. Howell's was headquartered nearly one hundred miles away in Shingletown, closer to SPI's offices in Redding, so Eunice Howell hadn't heard anything that might have dissuaded her from hiring Ryan Bauer. He came across well enough on the informal phone interview he'd managed to land. If she had spent more time in Westwood or asked around about him, Bauer may not even have had his call returned, given his reputation in town. But he'd come across as ingenuous and enthusiastic, and this was just a knot bumper's gig. He began work a few weeks before the fire.

For better and worse, Westwood is a place where locals tend to know the other locals, know their family and friends, know their reputation. That can be a good thing when you're the kind of person everyone would like to know but not so good when you're the kind of person people prefer to avoid. By most accounts, Ryan Bauer was the latter.

He did best with those who knew him least. The more Eunice Howell's crew got to know him, the more they disliked and distrusted him. In just the short time they worked together, even J.W. Bush and Kelly Crismon—middle-aged Cat drivers who for the most part don't work side by side with logging crews and who would have had little contact with a knot bumper except for shooting the shit at base camp—considered Ryan Bauer bad news. Crismon, among others, refused even to speak to him.

"His elevator didn't go all the way to the top floor," was how Crismon later put it.

There was, for example, the time Bauer spread the word about his girlfriend's getting pregnant—the girlfriend no one had seen and whose name they still didn't know. He'd met her during a visit to Portland, he claimed, and both were overjoyed by the unexpected but still welcome news and had decided to marry as soon as possible. Probably to his surprise, the announcement brought an unsolicited slew of baby clothes and other gifts from the good people of Westwood, who were later shocked and surprised—and also neither shocked nor surprised— to hear that the poor girl, who may or may not have existed, whose phone number he could no longer find, who may or may not have had an abortion, had "lost the baby."

Then there was the time, months later, when Bauer descended the mountain where he'd been cutting and flagged down Deputy Sheriff Benny Wallace, who knew Ryan Bauer and Bauer's parents, Eddy and Jennifer, well from several otherwise unpleasant encounters with Ryan.

"Boy, I'm having a bad day," Bauer said.

"What's going on?"

Bauer said he'd been cutting up on the mountain with Dan "Hippie Dan" Voth, one of the area's beloved old-time fallers, when he realized that he hadn't heard Voth's saw in quite a while. So he went over to see what had happened and found Voth pinned under a fallen tree with a severe cut on his thigh from an accidentally self-inflicted chainsaw wound. Though he did everything he could to save the man, Bauer said, Hippie Dan ultimately bled out and died.

Wallace was shocked. He wondered whether this was one of Ryan Bauer's tall tales. After all, femoral arteries severed with a chainsaw tend to spout like geysers or gush like fire hoses, and while Bauer's clothes were dirty, sure, the way clothes get from working trees with chainsaws, there wasn't a spot of red anywhere. Still, not even Ryan Bauer would make up something like that, Wallace decided. As he would later explain, Bauer seemed so sincere that Wallace had no choice but to believe him.

This was the kind of tragedy that shakes up a town dependent on men willing to cut timber for a living. So while Wallace didn't personally know Voth, he passed on what he'd heard to others, including Steve Goodwin, who owned the local Shell station with his wife, Susan, and to Rod Theobald, a former faller who owned the Mill Café. Theobald, Wallace remembered, went "ballistic" at the news.

So a few days later, when Voth pulled into the Shell station to fill up his truck, Susan Goodwin ran over to hug him. He was of course startled by her sudden affection, but not nearly as much as she'd been to see a dead man pumping gas.

She explained what she'd heard from her husband, Steve, and others. The report of his death was too incredible not to believe. Word had spread so quickly after someone checked his home and found it empty that Voth's own relatives in Tehama County, a few hundred miles northwest, had called around to find out more. A search party had even converged on the mountain to find his body, since Bauer hadn't brought it back with him.

Voth explained that he'd been out of town on a minivacation and couldn't imagine why Ryan Bauer would choose him to make up a story about. He had no idea how Bauer would've known he was out of town in the first place. Voth would later testify that he never brought up the incident with Bauer, but in the following months he had other encounters with Bauer that led him to believe the young man was quite possibly mentally ill.

And Deputy Wallace had other encounters with Bauer that led him to believe the young man deserved to be jailed.

16

Red Emmerson endured his junior year at Upper Columbia Academy and now had the summer to work and put away more cash.

It would've been convenient to return from near Spokane, Washington, to his mother's home in Oregon and tend to his watermelon patch on Harry's farm (among other paying jobs) for the summer, but Harry and Emily were now living in Alaska, where Harry had bought a fish cannery. So Red Emmerson accepted an offer from Sam Smith, a cattle rancher in nearby Omak, whom he'd met through a friend at school. It was Sam, Emmerson remembers, who had first called him "Red" in a way that made the nickname stick.

"Sam," says Emmerson, "was a big, tall, skinny Indian—very good-natured. His wife, May, was a really pleasant lady and a wonderful cook. And they had a son named Dave, who was probably about five years younger than me. We all got on well."

Being a ranch hand was hard work, but as Smith saw, there was no amount of work that could draw even a groan out of Emmerson, at least not where anyone else could hear. He liked the job so much he hated to see the summer end. But Emmerson was delighted to begin his final nine months of schooling. They would, he vowed, be his last.

The school administration hired him full-time to work the school farm and help with construction on a new dorm. His wages on the crew were a buck an hour, an amount he thought reasonable for learning a new trade. Besides, at quitting time he got a chance to sneak an occasional beer with the crew.

The school continued paying him to drive the truck, deducting from his wages the amount of his room, board, and tuition. That still left him a bit with which to wheel and deal.

But his entrepreneurial activities didn't leave him much time to socialize with other students, around whom he still felt self-conscious. Most of them came from intact families and charming homes, and their parents visited. For Red Emmerson, the school was his legal residence. Other kids' closets held enough clothes that they could wear a clean set every day. He was forced to rinse out and wear the same ones.

Ten weeks before graduation, Red Emmerson convinced a classmate that it might be hilarious to hang a condom on the school bulletin board. His classmate actually did it, and the practical joke was pretty darn funny—until an administrator rushed into his room at eleven o'clock that night and dragged him before a disciplinary committee. He'd been accused of being the condom culprit. Emmerson told them the truth—that he'd contrived the joke but hadn't himself pinned the condom on the board. Then he went back to bed, not thinking too much about what the consequences might be.

The next morning Upper Columbia's dean showed up at his door and told him he was being expelled on the spot, no questions asked, no explanation solicited or accepted, and no allowance made for the fact that he had literally nowhere else to go.

"He told me I had to leave," Emmerson says. "I said I didn't have a home to go to, that my parents weren't anywhere around for me. He said, 'Well, too bad. You're out of here.' By then I was crying, so I don't remember what I said. The only thing I remember clearly is, he definitely wanted me gone right that second. So I gathered up everything I owned—some rubber boots, my clothes, the hot plate—and put it all in a cardboard box."

By then Red Emmerson had reached the conclusion that crying and feeling bad weren't going to solve his problem. "I had to pull myself together," he says. "What choice did I have?"

At a pay phone, Red Emmerson called Bob Christiansen, the farm manager who'd quit a year earlier because of differences with the administration's policies and philosophy. Christiansen told Emmerson to come right over. Emmerson hitchhiked to Omak, just northwest of Spokane, about eighty miles away. It took about eight hours.

By the time Emmerson walked in, Christiansen had already called the academy and tried to talk the dean into taking the kid back. "Bob said, 'Boy, they really don't want you there.' I said, 'I know.'"

There was, Emmerson remembers, something oddly comforting about knowing that whatever happened to him from then on would be entirely in his hands.

"I felt self-sufficient, and I felt good about that," he says. "I had some money in my pocket, the energy to work as hard as I needed to, and the confidence that I could always handle my own affairs."

Red Emmerson spent the summer as a hand on Smith's cattle ranch. The job helped him pay for Omak High School, which accepted him on the condition that he redo his entire second semester of that year. Until he graduated in spring 1948, he lived with Bob Christiansen and his family. As a way of earning his keep, he volunteered to build a fieldstone retaining wall on the property, taking the rocks from the property and assembling them into a two-hundred-foot long wall that, in Emmerson's words, "got a lot better near the end than it was at the beginning. The last time I went by there, not that long ago, it was still standing."

17

Josh White and Dave Reynolds spent the morning and early afternoon of September 4 investigating the area where Kelly Crismon had been making water bars in his dozer the day before. By one o'clock, they had found the general origin area, a plot they estimated at seventy-five feet by fifty feet, and within the hour had determined to their satisfaction the ten-by-ten-foot specific origin area.

They left the area unguarded, climbed into White's Cal Fire truck, and made their way to the Howell's camp in the hope of re-interviewing Bush, intending to ask again about the apparent timing discrepancies between when he left the landing a bit after 1:00, according to his memory, and the fire's being spotted closer to 2:30.

On their way to Bush's trailer, White called Crismon's cell and left a voicemail with a request that he return the call. They found Bush at his trailer. The air was smoky, and ash rained down, but the direction that the fire was burning meant the logging camp was otherwise safe. Bush was home. He had nothing else to do with his time now, since there would be no more work on the Cook's Creek job until the fire was out. By the looks of things, that might be weeks. So unless Howell's was hired to work salvage on the fire, the cutting season might be over.

White had a voice recorder with him but either didn't turn it on or Bush said nothing noteworthy beyond repeating that he'd knocked off work at one o'clock the day before and left to get his phone and a soda before returning to the site.

Whatever else he may have told them (White would later admit to having destroyed or discarded his field notes), Bush didn't say that he believed a grouser strike had caused the fire, which he didn't know he'd allegedly said to Reynolds the afternoon before. Had he volunteered anything like that, White presumably would have recorded it for posterity.

As White and Reynolds returned to the area of origin, Crismon called White's cell. White asked him to meet them at the intersection of the 3130 and Moonlight Road, from which he'd drive them to the site.

Kelly Crismon was forty-four years old. He'd graduated from high school in 1981 and began working in the logging industry a year later, starting at the bottom as a knot bumper. Not until 1999 had he worked his way up to driving Caterpillars and skidders, though he'd never worked as a faller.

Crismon arrived soon after the investigators and parked his truck. White gave everyone protective fire gear, which he and Reynolds had not worn earlier that day. Reynolds drove himself in a USFS truck while Crismon rode with White. They talked on the way. White didn't turn on his voice recorder, even though he was unable to take notes.

Not till they reached the base of the last landing, where Crismon had finished up the day before, and got out to hike up to the skid trail beside the general origin area did White turn on the recorder and ask Crismon for permission to use it as they hiked. Crismon said he didn't mind, and they set out. He would later say that he felt intimidated, being with two "government agents."

Crismon explained that he had walked his dozer out after finishing the water barring, meaning that in essence he had satisfactorily performed the fire walk and didn't need to come back.

"Your partner's name?" White asked, having just come from interviewing Bush.

"J.W.," Crismon said.

"J.W. Bush," White said. "He was working a different section, is that right?"

"Yes."

"Was he there where you guys parked the dozers before you or after you?"

Crismon said he'd arrived after Bush.

"He was there before you?"

"Yes."

White called Crismon's attention to the sidearm on his belt in a way that suggested they had already had this conversation, perhaps when they'd stopped to put on the Nomex fireproof jumpsuits and White had chosen to wear the belt conspicuously on the outside of the suit instead of inside. "And you're not still nervous about the guns, right?"

"No," Crismon said.

"Okay."

"He wasn't there much before me, though."

"All right," White said. "I just want to make sure you're okay, you're comfortable. And by no means are you under arrest or anything, okay? I mean, this is a relaxed environment. I'm just, you know, the logging industry is all new to me."

"Is it?" Crismon asked politely.

"Absolutely," White said. "You know, I just don't deal with it that much, and that's why I was asking you vernacular on dozer versus skidder versus everything else—just to get the terminology right. All I know is, that's fire and that's why I'm here."

As they continued hiking to the landing near where Crismon had worked the day before, Crismon explained that he had driven home with his windows down and would therefore have smelled smoke if there'd been any in the air; that he'd driven out first, just ahead of Bush; and that it was hunting season, so on some days Moonlight Valley Road became a veritable thoroughfare with trucks, ATVs, and fishermen.

White pretended not to know what a fire walk was and asked Crismon to explain the concept. Then Crismon reiterated that both he and Bush, independently of each other, had knocked off at one o'clock.

So far, Crismon hadn't told White and Reynolds anything they didn't already believe they knew, with the exception of pointing to three stray logs that the Howell's skidders hadn't caught the previous Friday. He said that, in the morning, he'd grappled them and skidded them onto the landing.

"My schooling over with?" Crismon asked.

"What?" White said.

"My schooling over with?"

"Schooling?" White said.

"You're schooling me. Imagine if we'd have been logging."

Reynolds chimed in to say that he'd once bought a book at a garage sale called *Woods Words*, about loggers' terminology. "It gave defini-tions of all kinds of things," he said. "Everything goes on in logging and stuff. It was a pretty cool book."

"Huh," White said. "I need to find a copy of that to whip down some bad words and everybody'd be like, 'Whoa, he knows what he's talking about.'"

White's notes of this meeting (written years later) say that Crismon had skidded the logs near the end of the day, rather than in the morn-ing, and that the water bar White asked him about—the one near the rock—was indeed the last one he'd put in that day. The voice recording contains no such statement.

The recorder was not on when the investigators pointed at the rock they believed had sparked the fire, calling Crismon's attention to what they referred to as metal shavings on it from the grouser. Crismon couldn't see the metal. To him, the rock looked scratched—a single eight-by-ten-inch scratch more or less identical to any other rock over which a Caterpillar had driven. That particular mark had been made the day before, the investigators insisted, by his Caterpillar. How they knew that was unclear to Crimson. On that trail alone, his Cat had made up to a hundred trips a day for weeks. And as Crismon would later testify, there was no charred or burned matter near the rock. Only dirt surrounded it.

18

Just before graduating high school, Red Emmerson received an invitation from his father to move down to Arcata, California, and help him in the lumber business.

In the 1940s mills of all sizes—from two-man operations to giant factories—buzzed with activity in the Northwest. Curly Emmerson had made his way to the Northern California coastal logging town of Arcata, near Humboldt Bay. Arcata had been California's most productive logging center for almost a century since James Ryan and James Duff bought one of the steamers that captains were abandoning in San Francisco Bay after the gold rush, when they could no longer get enough passengers to make the trip back.

Curly had started small and leveraged his successes, eventually buying some acreage just north of Arcata on which to build a larger mill powered by a steam engine, which in 1946 he sold to build an even bigger one. One bigger than that followed just as the nine major redwood mills in the area were struck by their unionized employees, many of whom had just returned home from the war.

Curly and his partner pretty much sucked up all the business in the area. They were so profitable (and hated by the strikers) that in 1947 they sold the mill and some tracts for nearly $1 million to a co-op of smaller operators. Alas, the co-op soon went bankrupt, leaving Curly and his partner holding an unpaid mortgage.

In the previous two years, Red had visited for a day or two a couple of times, spending hours in Curly's shop practicing the welding skills he'd begun learning in high school. He got good enough quickly enough to believe that he was a far better and more knowledgeable welder than his high school instructor. Later Red Emmerson would help his father build a saw husk to hold circular saws.

Curly was intrigued by his son's inventiveness, industry, indefatigability, and willingness to try and to learn. He enjoyed hearing the boy recite all the little ways he'd managed to earn a living and pay his own way in the world. Since age eight, Red Emmerson told his own father, he hadn't taken a penny he hadn't earned with his own hands.

As Curly pointed out, with Red's sister Bernadine living with Emily and Harry in Alaska, and his other sister Margaret married in Portland, there was no good reason why Red shouldn't move to Arcata.

That good reason, for some children, might have been the father's sudden disappearance from their lives. Curly never offered an explanation or apology for having abandoned his children, but his son chose to put that behind him when he said yes, he'd be happy to move down there. Red Emmerson does, he says, remember Curly admitting that he hadn't been much of a father. But by then, Emmerson says, he had stopped caring. In fact, he says he considers the abandonment something of a gift. It had taught him at an early age that the world is a cruel place; that gravity doesn't care whether you believe in it; that the righteous fail, evil men prosper, things are the way they are, and the only way to get them to be the way you want them to be is by working harder than anyone else.

The day after his high school graduation, Red Emmerson jumped into the first car he ever owned, a yellow '37 Ford convertible that was "a real piece of junk"—though it had cost $800, which in 2017 dollars is about $7,500 (more than twice what a comparably old and decrepit car would cost now). This was Supply and Demand 101. During World War II, car factories had been retooled to fuel the war effort, so no new passenger cars had been built, meaning cars in existence before the war were (a) far more expensive than they otherwise would have been, and (b) were often still on the road long past their appointment with the scrap heap.

Emmerson's car sputtered for two days on its way south. When he got to Arcata, he knocked on the door of the home Curly shared with his new wife, Myrtle, and her youngest son, Larry, who was a year or two older than Emmerson.

Myrtle had nothing against Emmerson, but she didn't want him living with them. In those days, boardinghouses were common, many of them operated by widows catering to single men, young and old, who needed cheap, comfortable surroundings and decent food for a decent price as they and the country were getting themselves back on their feet after the war. Mrs. Thacker's was one such place. After a single night at Curly and Myrtle's, Emmerson installed himself there and stayed for much of the year, sleeping well and soundly after long, hard days of labor and eating heartily from Mrs. Thacker's starch-laden meals that tasted swell to a young man grateful to be eating any hot food at all.

The only surprise to Emmerson was that it would apparently be a while until he and Curly could work together on the mill that they'd daydreamed about. Curly, his son learned, was owed a lot of money, and that debt was just now being settled in bankruptcy court.

Emmerson soon found a job at a nearby mill but became disenchanted when he discovered that men working the green chain—that is, sorting the lumber according to required dimensions—were earning far more than he was. The mill manager, recognizing an unusually hard worker when he saw one, agreed to put Emmerson on the green chain. When he'd mastered that, he started clamoring for bigger jobs.

Weeks later the mill had an opening for ratchet setter, which paid better still because it required skill and was dangerous. The ratchet setter maintained the cutting equipment and selected the position of the log for initial cuts by adjusting the carriage on which the log was gripped, and riding it as it moved against the head saw. All day long the setter rode back and forth on a carriage that held the big logs, and each time a log neared the end, he came close to the blade. Fatalities among ratchet setters were not uncommon.

The mill's management skills weren't as good as its products, and when operations shut down five months later, Emmerson had to look for another job. He found one at Precision Lumber, starting as a ratchet setter before eventually learning each job above him in the mill hierarchy. He mastered all of them, in part by volunteering to fill in whenever someone didn't show up, day or night, whatever the job was, whether or not he'd done it before. And any free hour Emmerson had—again, day or night—he worked in Curly's shop, helping him build or repair mill equipment.

That experience soon paid off in a new way—he became his father's partner.

19

Soon after 7 A.M. on September 5, fewer than two full days into the fire, Cal Fire investigator Josh White and USFS investigator Dave Reynolds returned to the site they'd identified as the area of origin, now protected by pink do-not-disturb tape they'd set up after Kelly Crismon had left at four o'clock the previous afternoon. The rock that they believed had been struck by the grouser of Crismon's Caterpillar, sparking the fire, now had a short white plastic flag planted in front of it, indicating the specific point of origin. And red and blue flags were planted various places elsewhere.

White's first photo, taken at 8:18 A.M., was a close-up of the rock. Four more photos of it were taken in the following few minutes.

The two men walked through the area as if they were the fire itself, beginning at the rock before meandering west up the hill, then north. As far as they were concerned, they had solved the puzzle—even if they did have to step around some trees and rocks that the fire would've had to circumvent if their theory of its pathway were correct.

Reynolds had taken a GPS reading of the rock at 6:30 the previous evening. But White wanted one on the state's most up-to-date GPS device, which would eliminate several manual steps by uploading data directly to a computer whose software would then translate everything into English. He intended to borrow the device from Ivan Houser, the licensed Cal Fire forester he soon summoned to the site for counsel on the California Code of Regulations foresting practices requirements. Whatever Houser said would help White determine the exact liability of the lumber harvesting company for presumably failing to meet those requirements.

From his truck, White radioed the Cal Fire incident command center in Westwood and reached Houser at his desk. Houser, a few years older than White, worked in resource management. The two had been acquainted with each other since White's days as prevention battalion chief for the Modoc unit. Houser had spent nearly a decade at W. M. Beaty and Associates, the company that managed the land on which Howell's was harvesting, as a timber cruiser and assistant district forester before earning his registered professional forester's license. In 2004 he'd been hired by the State of California to work for Cal Fire.

White knew Houser had spent a lot of time in this particular area of the forest when he worked for Beaty and that Houser had been the Cal Fire forester who'd signed off on Beaty's timber harvest plan, the detailed document that must be given state approval before logging is allowed to commence legally even on private lands. White asked Houser if he'd agree to drive up to this particular landing on the 3130 road and discuss proper forest practices—and please bring the latest GPS unit.

Houser explained that at the moment he was finishing an incident report regarding the progress of the Moonlight Fire. He estimated he'd be able to meet them at the landing by 10 A.M. From there White could lead him on a hike to wherever they were going, and Houser would be happy to answer their questions.

White and Reynolds went back to work documenting the scene. White took another couple of dozen photos, as Reynolds sketched a diagram of the site with the rock as the point of origin. At about 9:25, satisfied that they had all the evidence they needed, White and Reynolds began pulling out the colored marking flags and untying the pink perimeter tape. By 9:50 they'd finished clearing the scene and made their way down the hill to White's truck for the meeting with Houser. There'd be no need to have Houser walk up to the site; they'd do their talking by the truck. Once Houser left, White would take the GPS unit and hike back to capture the rock's coordinates, just as Reynolds had the previous evening.

But Houser, still finishing his report, wasn't there at ten. And with no cell signal where White and Reynolds were, Houser couldn't warn them he'd be late.

Waiting for Houser, White snapped some shots of the metal fragments he'd collected in and on the ground at the site—shots he hadn't taken one by one at the time he'd collected the fragments; instead, he'd dropped them all into a small envelope.

On the hood of his truck he placed a sheet that Reynolds handed him, on top of which he slid a piece of light-colored paper. Onto that he poured out the contents of the envelope. For size comparison, he positioned a ruler near the bottom of the frame. Some of the dozen or so pieces appear no bigger than flecks. A few longer ones, at most half an inch, are ragged, twisted, and discolored.

Snapping the two photos and pouring the pieces back into the envelope took until five after ten. Still no Houser. Reynolds pulled out his notebook and began hand writing his incident report. White, he recorded for posterity, instructed him to "release" the scene at 10:15 A.M.—apparently that very moment—having concluded that the fire had been started by a rock strike.

In the section reserved for liability, Reynolds named SPI as the civil defendant for whatever damages and penalties would be incurred. Only two days in, there was no way yet to know how much they might total, but from the looks of things, this might exceed the amount contemplated by the powers that be in the Storrie fire—at least $100 million.

And now, "We were done," Reynolds would later testify he remembered thinking after finishing that report.

Houser still hadn't arrived.

White snapped a photo from above of the landing where a dozen pine and cedar logs, already bucked, lay side by side. Grouser tracks from the Caterpillar that had skidded them were visible in the dirt around the perimeter. The previous day they'd asked Crismon about the logs, but what White later wrote in his report about that conversation was contradicted by Crismon, who under oath claimed that he had said nothing about skidding them all; and though this did not appear in White's report, Crismon also testified that he had told White he'd finished skidding the two logs early that morning, several hours before leaving for the day. As far as Crismon was concerned, driving back to the landing over that same terrain at five miles an hour in his Caterpillar was the equivalent of a fire walk.

Another quarter hour passed. Houser had already kept them waiting almost an hour, so if he arrived anytime soon he'd have to wait for them while they drove to the landing where the Howell's dozers were parked. White wanted to take some photos of the grouser—specifically the left one, which they'd settled on as the offender.

From 10:46 to 10:59 A.M., White snapped five close-up photos of a dozer's left grouser. Just after arriving at the landing, at 10:43, he'd photographed the contents of an emergency fire kit in a rectangular wooden box that sat on the ground, its hinged top open. The box and its contents dominate most of the photographic real estate. Besides the ground, the only other objects in the photo are human legs and feet, White's not among them. In the lower left corner is a man's right leg, visible from the knee down, wearing work boots and yellow Nomex protective gear. Because of the gear—standard issue USFS—the leg presumably belonged to Reynolds. On the other side of the box are two other feet—men's, wearing the same boots. But there's no protective gear on the little that can be seen of his ankles. Whoever he was, neither White nor Reynolds named him in their reports. And he may or may not have had anything to do with what happened later.

When Ivan Houser finally arrived at 11:30, White and Reynolds were no longer behaving as though the case was closed.

Houser had seen White's truck parked by itself but failed to notice White's note on the windshield telling Houser where on the hill to find them. Houser had found them anyway by following their footsteps up a skid trail, hearing their voices as he drew near.

Both men were on their hands and knees, White waving a magnet in the white ash inside what appeared to be the burn area but not near that rock on the skid trail, which Houser later noted had a white flag in front of it. He also saw three or four small yellow flags to the north of where the men were.

In Houser's later retelling, White and Reynolds seemed sheepish, as though he'd surprised them. White asked whether Houser had found the note. Houser explained he'd located them on his own and indicated he wasn't sure which of the two men, White or Reynolds, was in charge of the investigation. White made it clear he was lead investigator.

For the next several minutes Houser watched White wave the magnet across the ground near rocks clustered inside the ashy area, but not in the skid trail where the rock lay. He ran the magnet along the surface and lifted it up to see what metallic fruit, if any, it bore. Houser asked what he was doing.

"Looking for metal fragments," White said, displaying those he'd already funneled into a small envelope. They had come from grousers on a dozer, he said, and pointed to the rocks he believed had caused the grouser to shed, though there was not a white flag in front of them.

This, White said, was where all the investigative work had led him. And while he did not declare expressly that this was the fire's point of origin, Houser inferred that that was his intended meaning. As a forester, not a fire investigator, Houser was suitably impressed. He watched White collect four more pieces of metal, one of which was larger than the others, nearly three-quarters of an inch long.

But why was White doing this? More than an hour before, he and Reynolds had released the scene where they believed the Moonlight Fire had started. They'd taken down the tape and most of the flags, and Reynolds soon composed his written report, having already completed a diagram of the scene that would be appended to it.

Then, sometime in the following seventy-five minutes, after visiting the landing where the two suspect dozers were parked, they returned to the scene and began searching the ground not on the skid trail where they'd declared the fire to have begun but on the intersecting spur trail.

It may have occurred to the investigators that the rock they'd fingered as the specific origin point was parked in the logger's equivalent of I-95. Crismon had told them that he'd skidded two logs early that morning, yet there were nearly a dozen more logs beside them. Any number of dozers might have been on that skid trail striking that rock, including possibly a government dozer—perhaps even after the fire began. And someone might know that. Which would make their collection of metal fragments irrelevant unless Crismon's dozer could be connected to an act that was done only on the day the fire began and only if those metal fragments were indisputably from Crismon's dozer.

Nearby, on the adjacent spur trail, was a fresh water bar that must've been constructed by Crismon on Monday. It bore no marks of having been driven over since its construction. Not far away were two adjacent rocks, each smaller than the original rock but together larger than it, that looked as though they may have been struck by a Caterpillar. True, one or the other of them might be too far from the water bar to argue that either was struck in the bar's construction—unless both rocks were deemed the specific point of origin, which they were.

That left the issue of metal fragments, which the investigators may have learned are commonly found in the soil wherever dozers run. Every fragment they found beyond the first fragment would logically undermine the persuasiveness of their theory of the fire's origin.

The physics of whether such a small piece of metal from a tractor grouser going no faster than five miles an hour could (a) reach a temperature hot enough to ignite dry brush and (b) maintain that temperature after flying through the air remained to be established, though it was conventional wisdom in logging communities that previous fires had been sparked that way. This was in part because fires whose cause could not be determined conclusively were often blamed on tractors if logging was going on anywhere in the area.

Assuming that a lone piece of metal could be credibly identified as the culprit, White and Reynolds may have reasoned that every additional fragment reduced the odds of their selected one having been the catalyst. Two pieces could be problematic, three a problem, and four plus might be considered grounds for finding a new theory at a time when their own actions had contaminated the investigation area, preventing them now from following FI-210 protocol. Any large number of metal pieces found in a given area's soil would unavoidably suggest that fragments from grousers are nearly as common as rocks and tractors themselves. Fires, however, are not. So if White had already found, collected, and photographed all of the offending fragments from the point of origin, any new ones would be exculpatory, not damning. New ones would prove how often Cats strike rocks without incident. It was therefore to the investigators' advantage that no additional fragments be found.

Three years later, Houser would testify that he remembered seeing tractor marks "in the vicinity of" but not necessarily right up to the rocks where White was collecting samples.

Houser had been there no longer than twenty minutes when White began preparing to leave by putting away the magnet, a clipboard, and the envelope. White asked Houser to accompany them to another landing for a look at the Howell dozers.

The three men walked down the hill and paused at the bottom for White to put the bag of metal fragments in his truck. He then pointed at some logs lying by the landing that had been skidded, and singled out one that had fresh drag marks behind it. He told Houser that those logs had been skidded on the day of the fire by one of the two dozer drivers and asked whether there were any specific regulations about how soon fire walks needed to be conducted after logging operations. Houser summarized from memory Title 14 of the California Code of Regulations for forest practices: a fire walk is mandated within two hours after logging operations cease. He was not asked about regulations pertaining to water barring, after which no fire walk is required.

White did inquire about Houser's expertise on how dozers construct water bars. Houser may never have driven a Caterpillar before and had never constructed a water bar, but he'd seen it done. He imagined that because the water bar sloped downhill, the dozer would have had to assume a ninety-degree angle to the bar, then turn to push it out. He agreed with White that it might move up and back several times over the same spot—and that if the grousers happened to pass over a rock, the driver probably wouldn't feel, hear, or see what was happening behind him. Houser watched as White silently wrote some notes in his small notebook.

The three men climbed into White's truck and drove farther south down Road 3130 to where the dozers were parked. From Houser's perspective White appeared to be looking for the vehicle identification numbers and focusing his attention on the left grousers of both dozers. White recorded his findings in his notebook.

While there the men also peeked inside a rectangular wooden box, resembling a narrow coffin, that lay on the ground of dead grass and straw. With its lid hinged open, they could see that this was the landing's emergency fire kit—shovels, picks, canteens, and other gear, neatly stacked. Houser told them that all operations on Beaty-managed lands are required to have such fire boxes readily accessible near logging operations.

Minutes later they drove back on the original road to observe a loader and a fire trailer. Whom they belonged to, Houser wasn't certain. But he checked to see whether the motor might have had an exhaust leak, potentially making it an ignition source. It didn't, so the point was moot whether it had been recently run, and from the looks of things, it hadn't.

The three men returned to the landing where Houser's truck was parked. White reminded him about the GPS unit, explaining he wanted to log locations and features of the investigation, and promised to return it soon. Houser didn't ask why, as the lead investigator, White hadn't brought his own unit with him. He handed White the GPS, shook hands with both men, and left for the station.

A day later White asked Houser to participate in an interview White conducted with two Sierra Pacific foresters, Mike Mitzel and John Forno. And two weeks after that, White asked Houser to prepare a supplemental report on the Moonlight Fire. Houser did so, submitting it to White.

Houser's report was inconveniently more detailed than White had anticipated. It noted with specificity Houser's arrival time on scene as 11:30 and even called attention to the time by offering a sort of apology for not arriving as promised at ten, calling it "a delay stemming from work needs of the Resources Unit I was assigned to."

Now, if anyone looked carefully enough, White's digital footprint in the camera and Reynolds's notation that the site was released early that morning would appear suspiciously contradictory. Why would White be on his hands and knees collecting metal fragments at 11:40 A.M., two hours after they'd released the site and determined the liable party? And why, at noon, would White need to ask about how water bars are constructed and whether a dozer constructing that particular water bar might have driven its left grouser over, say, that rock there?

Not only did White omit from his extensive origin and cause report the report he'd asked Houser to write, but he also failed to mention Houser's name anywhere, even when describing his second trip to the dozers that day, when he was accompanied by Houser: "Reynolds and I," White wrote, "drove .7 miles to the location Crismon parked his bulldozer. I photographed the identification plate on the bulldozer Crismon was operating (Photo CV) as well as identification markings on the left track (Photo CW) and front blade (Photo CZ)."

White referred passively to his search for metal fragments: "a handheld magnet was utilized to sweep in the area to identify ferrous metal. Within close proximity of two of the rocks, a ferrous material, consistent with that of metal shavings, were recovered." "[U]pon returning to [the] 3130 [road], I photographed the three logs Crismon had identified that he yarded prior to ceasing operations for the day."

It is not known how many photos of the original rock with the white flag in front of it White deleted. But as attorney Bill Warne would later discover, the number was at least one less than White had believed—the one taken at 9:16 that morning.

20

Curly Emmerson had his eye on a small mill near Jacoby Creek, just east of Arcata Bay and not far from vast forestlands, that the Olson family had had to shut down because it had become a money loser. He thought that he and his son could make a go of it by leasing the existing mill and making small adjustments here and there. Red Emmerson spent any spare time he had in Curly's shop tweaking equipment, and at last they were ready to make their play.

But they needed someone with the capital willing to back them. Mike Crook, who called his company Pacific Fir Sales, loaned them $10,000 with no collateral on the condition that, besides getting back his investment, he'd pick up a 5 percent commission for selling the lumber. It was a good deal all around.

Curly and his son signed a year's lease on the old Olson mill. Curly bought the logs from here and there, a time-consuming, tedious job, even back when there were few restrictions on cutting and loggers didn't have to file harvest plans with any governmental agency. Red Emmerson supervised operations, at which he seemed to be a natural. None of the older workers balked at taking orders from this young man whose only goal was efficient productivity.

As long as Curly acquired enough timber to cut, Red made sure that what came out of the mill at day's end was tens of thousands of board feet of lumber. The mill used a diesel generator, and it otherwise pulled only enough electric power to run a few light bulbs. In all, the mill managed to produce about twenty-five thousand board feet a day that were then sent by truck to a planing mill. Every time there was a carload of lumber, Crook paid promptly—minus his commission. It was a profitable arrangement for both sides.

Curly was fascinated by Red's ingenuity and industry. In his son, he'd found the ideal partner. As he could plainly see, the young man was not only capable of doing every job in the mill, but he'd never rest as long as there was work to be done. Just so he could be on-site all the time (and, among other things, watch for flames to prevent them from becoming conflagrations), Red had moved out of his boardinghouse and into a tiny shack located yards from the mill. It was barely large enough for a bed and a wood-burning stove that he fed with scrap, and its sanitary facilities were the outhouse that everyone at the mill used.

At the end of the year's lease, which just so happened to coincide with a downturn in the market, the two partners, Red and Curly, had cleared about $40,000. That was enough to stake and expand an ambitious young man's plans for the future. R. H. Emmerson and Son were in business.

In the fall of 1950 father and son began building their dream mill. They bought nearly twenty acres on Humboldt Bay, where they could raft and float the logs, then opened a planing mill with Mike Crook as their main customer.

Not till the following fall would the sawmill cut its first load of lumber.

"We built the mill out of a junk pile, I guess you could say," Emmerson remembers. "We bought a bunch of chain and rolls and machinery from the pile at Hammond Lumber Company. They'd been there for years and had stuff from old mills that they'd torn down and replaced. Pretty much everything there we built." Through trial and error, he even taught himself on a borrowed lathe how to transform thirteen-foot sections of steel tubing into a thirty-two-foot shotgun structure with a ten-inch piston in the middle to run the carriage.

"At the beginning," he says, "I didn't know beans, but I learned from my mistakes or I found help. Most people were willing to help."

The mill, he says, was profitable almost from its first day. Then Red Emmerson got his draft notice from Uncle Sam.

21

In his Cal Fire origin and cause investigation report, filed nearly a year after the fire, Josh White came to several conclusions.

He concluded that a "rock strike resulted in superheated metal fragments (Competent Ignition Source) separating from the blade or grouser and landing in the cured fuel bed."

He concluded that all other common ignition sources of forest fires— from lightning to cigarettes to campfires—should be excluded as possible causes, and he noted specifically that there had been no incendiary devices found nor a bottle capable of concentrating the sun's light if refracted just so.

He concluded that his investigation "in the origin area revealed a set of tracks consistent with that of a bulldozer. The bulldozer tracks continued through the origin and were in a direct path with multiple rocks that had recent damage consistent with coming in contact with a hard object."

He concluded that the visual examination he and Reynolds conducted of the specific origin area revealed "no competent ignition sources," but instead "there were six rocks with damage consistent with sustaining damage from heavy equipment such as a bulldozer. The grouser tracks were in line with four of the rock strikes."

He concluded that "evidence gathered within the specific area of origin included multiple metal fragments" that " had a shiny appearance with the larger shavings having a 'blued' color. The evidence was gathered by 'sweeping' the area with a magnet and excluding the natural occurring ferrous material."

He also noted that on the night of September 6, just before meeting with his recently arrived investigators, Dieter Schmitt and George
Gonzales, SPI's John Forno had informed him of the rumor around
Westwood: the fire's cause was arson. "I explained to Forno," White
wrote, "that we would be following all leads concerning the cause of
the fire."

Then there was Dave Reynolds. In his USFS origin and cause report,
Reynolds concluded that the fire's cause "was determined to be from
the friction created between metal dozer grousers on rock, defrag-
menting hot metal particles (Competent Ignition Source), to the Material First Ignited: cured forest litter, which created the Ignition Factor."

Reynolds and White had decided all that by September 5. September 5 was two days after the fire had begun. September 5 was the day
before a Sierra Pacific Employee was assured that all leads would be
pursued, especially the possibility of arson. And September 5 was
two days before his own investigators began interviewing witnesses—
witnesses like Ryan Bauer.

22

It was 1952. The war in Korea had waged in earnest for nearly two years and was not going well. During the Battle of Heartbreak Ridge just a few months before, almost four thousand American and French soldiers—and at least six times that many North Korean and Chinese soldiers—had been killed. All of the newspaper and radio attention about the four-week battle fought over a single ridge of little strategic importance had begun to turn public opinion. But the six-month-old armistice talks still mirrored the lack of progress around the thirty-eighth parallel, so the war raged on.

Red Emmerson, of course, had expected a letter from Washington someday. In the few weeks' time he was allowed before he had to report to an induction center in San Francisco, he did everything he could to prepare the mill and its staff for his absence. He was less worried for himself—that is, his own safety on the front line—than he was for the future of this enterprise into which he had invested so much of himself.

With other young men from the Eureka area who'd been called up, he boarded a bus for what was supposed to be an eight-hour overnight ride down Highway 101, near the coast but not on it, through the redwoods. At twenty-two, he was apparently the oldest of the recruits. Judging by the number of eighteen- and nineteen-year-olds, he figured the draft board had probably spared him until then on account of his productivity as a man of business. Some of these other young men, he could see, had never been away from home, and well beyond the fear of what the battlefields of Korea might hold for them, it seemed logical that they might be terrified of going to bed and waking up far from

Mom and Dad. Compared to them, Emmerson thought, he might as well have been a combat veteran. He wasn't afraid of anything except coming home to find that the mill had burned down or, worse, gone out of business for lack of leadership.

About ninety miles south of Eureka, first rain and then snow conspired against the 1930s model bus, which groaned pitifully, lacking the power to climb a steep grade near Leggett. Everyone had to get out and push the thing.

When the recruits reached the San Francisco induction center, joined by hundreds of others, Emmerson found that he'd been chosen to "volunteer" as a U.S. Marine.

"I was drafted into the Army," he explains, "but I guess there weren't enough guys enlisting in the Marines, so they took every tenth guy—or maybe it was every fifth, I can't remember anymore—and told us that we had volunteered to be Marines."

As it turned out, though, being a marine fit Red Emmerson better than the regular army would have. More was expected both physically and mentally of marines than soldiers, just as Red expected more of himself. The hard physical labor he'd been doing for years now put him way above the mean in terms of surviving boot camp at the Marine Corps recruits depot in San Diego, a bit south of the Miramar Air Station.

"I gained weight in boot camp," he says. "It was actually easier than my regular life. A lot of the guys, they got in there and couldn't take it. Some of them didn't like the mental stress. I remember a few who went goofy, probably from the abuse dished out by the drill instructors—big fat men who were always yelling. They'd take those guys off to sick bay, and you'd never see them again. But for me, it worked out fine."

His military occupational specialty was turret mechanic in a tank battalion. "I never fixed anything," he says. "I just changed parts. It wasn't a very efficient operation, and I just did what I was told."

A perk of being stationed at Camp Pendleton as opposed to other marine bases or camps around the country was that he could spend his three-day liberties driving home and back. True, that wouldn't give him more than twenty-four good hours out of the seventy-two, but there were good reasons to go.

One reason was to check on things at the mill. Though he loved his father and respected him, in matters of business Red didn't completely trust Curly to put the business itself above his personal needs—for instance, satisfying a sudden urge to take some time off.

The other reason was a girl he'd met a year earlier. Ida Mitchell was twenty, the youngest of five, fourth daughter of a former baker turned mill worker, and one of the prettiest girls around Eureka. She alternated between welcoming and deterring a steady stream of admirers who seemed always to vie for her attention and time. That meant she wasn't in the least interested in a blind date with this Red Emmerson fellow, set up by an older woman she knew—Zelma, whose husband just so happened to be Emmerson and Curly's bookkeeper, Arnie.

Emmerson, however, was distinctly interested in Ida. And it was he who had instigated the blind date. More than a year before he was drafted, he'd spotted Ida with her date for the night at Walt's, a small bar inside a restaurant in Eureka. He'd elbowed his friend and asked about the gorgeous young lady. His friend knew her name and that she worked as a secretary at Pacific Gas and Electric.

The intro lasted a few seconds. Emmerson never forgot it. But Ida would never admit remembering meeting Red Emmerson that night.

In the ensuing year, Emmerson tried several different tacks to woo Ida, but nothing worked until after he'd been assigned to Camp Pendleton. She found it hard to turn down a marine who might very well get called at any moment to go fight for their country.

As per Ida's expectations, dinner with this brash young man at Eureka's Ingomar Club, located in a beautiful old Victorian, was a mostly forgettable affair. Or it would have been forgettable and forgotten if Emmerson hadn't persisted.

In the morning he called and expected her to jump at the chance to go out again that night. She didn't jump. But he wouldn't take "no" for an answer. And even after that second reluctant date at Arcata's Bella Vista Inn, Ida didn't feel herself swept off her feet by this marine who owned a thriving sawmill in town.

But Emmerson kept calling from Camp Pendleton.

Those first few calls she felt obligated to stay on the line for at least the first three minutes, knowing that the exorbitant price of long distance from a payphone included that much; every minute afterward would cost extra. But eventually she was in no hurry to hang up. And a few months later, she even accompanied Curly and his wife, Myrtle, for a three-day trip to Pendleton, arriving just before Emmerson's liberty kicked in and leaving after it ended.

23

In 2006 Ryan Bauer enjoyed the company of a girl whom he could legitimately call "girlfriend." And she was, to be sure, a girl.

Andrea Terry was a fifteen-year-old high school sophomore when the nearly twenty-year-old Bauer accompanied her to the junior prom and they began dating. What finally ended their relationship was Bauer's two-week disappearance from Terry's life after the Moonlight Fire, while he was consumed, he told her, with fighting a massive wildfire in Graeagle, ninety minutes to the southeast of Westwood.

Months later Terry wasn't surprised to hear the truth from Jennifer Bauer, Ryan's mother, that during those two weeks Ryan had not been away fighting a fire; in fact, during those weeks he had rarely ventured outside the confines of his home and was, to Jennifer's chagrin, drinking himself into an alcoholic stupor or snorting a persuasive combination of Norco, OxyContin, and methadone.

As for Graeagle, it had been left untouched by fire, wild or otherwise. Ryan Bauer had lied about something for which the truth could be easily discovered.

Even so, it had been Bauer himself who broke up with Terry, apparently because he was angry she'd caught him in a lie.

A year later, after she announced her engagement to another classmate, Ryan Bauer told others that she was pregnant with his child. To Terry herself, he said, "I have liver cancer."

24

In early July 1953, Red Emmerson and his fellow marines exited a bus in San Diego and boarded a transport ship bound for Korea. The mood was somber on board, even fatalistic. Nearly forty thousand Americans had already died in the conflict, and at least twice that were badly wounded. For a long time both sides had been killing each other with neither side gaining enough ground to make it appear that victory—or defeat—was inevitable. This was a war that might go on forever.

And then, with Emmerson's ship one day away from its destination, came armistice. The shooting stopped, an agreement was signed, and the ship was redirected to peacekeeping duties in Japan, where the marines stayed for several months before returning to Treasure Island in San Francisco Bay.

By the time Red Emmerson was finally discharged in February 1954, eager to get back to the mill business, there wasn't much of a business left. In Emmerson's two-year absence, Curly had bought a ranch near Crescent City and had spent more time fooling around there than at the sawmill.

In a sense, that turned out to be fortuitous for Red Emmerson. The mill was essentially his now: his to rescue from the brink of insolvency, his to get running properly, and his to succeed—or fail—with.

25

On Thursday night September 6, two Cal Fire investigators arrived in Westwood at the request of Josh White, who wanted help interviewing percipient witnesses whose names he'd learned from others in town. One of those names was Ryan Bauer. SPI forester John Forno, who at the time was unaware White and Dave Reynolds had already identified SPI as the liable party, told White that rumors about Bauer's having started the fire, either accidentally or purposefully, appeared to be more than mere rumor-mongering.

White already knew Bauer's name. Plumas County sheriff's deputy Benny Wallace had seen the twenty-year-old speeding down the hill in a green Toyota pickup, away from where the fire was burning less than half an hour after it started. Wallace had stationed himself in a clearing on the mountain to do crowd and traffic control, if necessary, and recognized Bauer from previous unpleasant encounters. Bauer was dressed in work clothes and covered in sawdust and dirt, he said.

Stopping him, Wallace asked what he was doing. The young man seemed particularly distressed. He said he'd gone to collect his chainsaws, which he had left in the crook of a tree to avoid having to transport them every day to the job he was working, and was worried about losing them in the fire. Wallace glanced in back and saw two Stihl chainsaws in the bed of the truck—the ones a Cal Fire employee had led him up the hill to fetch, Bauer insisted. It was, as Wallace recognized, an implausible story—not atypical Ryan Bauer. A few minutes later Wallace's boss, Sheriff Steve Warren, a friend of Bauer's father, Eddy, had stopped to talk about the fire with Wallace. Meanwhile, Wallace had continued running traffic control, letting only a dozen or so authorized vehicles in. But when Ryan Bauer returned, claiming that he'd forgotten something at the landing, Wallace had let him pass both ways without Warren's objection.

Josh White assured Forno he'd heard the same about Ryan Bauer and guaranteed Forno his team would soon be conducting a thorough investigation, following every lead. Indeed, he said, two investigators had arrived in town for the sole purpose of interviewing witnesses, including Ryan Bauer.

Greg Dieter Schmitt had begun working for Cal Fire as a seasonal firefighter in 1982 and since then had held several jobs in firefighting, though not all for Cal Fire. On September 6, 2007, he was a fire captain specialist in Cal Fire's Fire Prevention Bureau out of Klamath. George Gonzales had been working for Cal Fire since 1993 and in September 2007 was a fire captain specialist stationed in Sonoma County. Both men had been well trained in fire investigation techniques and were considered law enforcement officers with the power to arrest people. Both understood that arson had to be ruled out for every wildland fire, particularly those started on windy days in the fall when there was no lightning to blame.

The two men, each driving from their respective homes, met with Josh White that Thursday night in White's office in Susanville, about twenty miles northeast of Westwood. White gave them a list of names and phone numbers of people he wanted them to begin interviewing the following day.

Schmitt and Gonzales's first interview, in the Westwood fire station, was with Leo Whitlock, the private forest guard who'd once worked for Cal Fire. Whitlock told them he'd been on the mountain in the area of the fire when he heard the dispatch from the Plumas National Forest at about 2:30 and began driving toward the Westwood station. Driving through a meadow he'd seen a silver Dodge pickup driven by an old-timer he recognized as George Bullard, who was looking to gather cedar logs. Whitlock said he asked Bullard if he knew where the fire was, but Bullard didn't, so he turned down the 3000 road and saw the fire down below the road in some vegetation. At one point, Whitlock said, he had to get out of the way of a small gray pickup driven by a couple he recognized as Edwin and Jennifer Bauer, who told him they were looking for their son Ryan, who had been cutting on the mountain near that area. Whitlock told them to flee, then hurried down the mountain to the Cal Fire station in Westwood.

Schmitt and Gonzales briefly interviewed two others before calling Edwin (Eddy) Bauer in to the Westwood station shortly before 2 P.M. Eddy said he and his wife had left home around noon to let his dog run on the mountain; they got back to town sometime later and stopped at the post office for their mail. At that point they saw the smoke, "So we just went cruising up there and got up to the trailer, and caught a lot of crap, you know. It's basically the crew my kid is working with."

"Do you know about what time that was?" Gonzales asked.

"Well, the fire started at two, didn't it?" Eddy Bauer said.

"Like somewhere around three," Gonzales corrected him.

Bauer continued, "I think the only one that was up there was one fire truck at the time, and then Leo Whitlock, when I was driving inward." He said Whitlock had warned him about continuing up the road, so he followed Whitlock's truck out, waiting behind him on the road when Whitlock stopped to talk to someone in a USFS green truck.

Gonzales asked a question predicated on conversation that must have occurred before either he or Schmitt had begun recording the interview: "And when did you run into the silver—"

"That was right while Leo was talking to that person, that guy flew out of there and then he stops and he was on like on a CB [radio] or something, trying to get somebody. So we're parked. . . . I go, 'Hey, you know how that fire started?' And he goes, 'A bulldozer hit a rock, started it.' He made it sound to me like he was right there."

Schmitt asked the man's name. Bauer said his son Ryan would prefer he not say. "I don't know why. I mean, accidents happen. And he just told me his name. I already forgot it."

"Okay," Gonzales said.

"So you might have to ask him, if you want," Eddy Bauer said. "Or I can call him up and ask him, if you want."

"And you said Ryan was down—Ryan's your son?"

"Yeah. He wasn't in there at the time."

"Okay."

"Matter of fact, we called him up and asked him if he knew anything about it, and he was driving—basically, when we were parked right there, he went by us. I told him not to go in there; I didn't want him in there. He's a twenty-year-old kid."

"Uh-huh," Gonzales said.

"And click, hung the phone up on me and went in anyways, because he had chainsaws up there and he didn't want to lose his chainsaws."

Neither interviewer interrupted to ask how he knew Ryan had hung up on them, as opposed to losing the call, since cell phones don't click. Eddy Bauer continued explaining that Ryan was worried about losing to the fire the chainsaws he'd stored on the mountain for the job he was working.

"Your son," Gonzales asked, "who does he work for?"

"I can't tell you that either," Eddy Bauer said, identifying the boss as "Bill out of Shingletown. And that's the crew that ended up starting the fire, according to the guy in that silver truck."

They talked about the kind of chainsaws Ryan used (Stihls) and the truck Ryan drove (red Ford pickup with extended cab) before Eddy Bauer asked how Schmitt and Gonzales had gotten his name. For some reason, he volunteered that he'd spoken with Lassen County Sheriff Steve Warren "that day and then I just talked to him within the last half hour"—presumably after Schmitt and Gonzales asked him in for an interview—"and I asked him, I go, 'Well, why do they keep saying it's under investigation? They don't know how it started?' And because I'd mentioned to him how it started, and so I didn't know if he called and let you guys know, or Leo, or whatever."

Gonzales mentioned that they had already talked with Whitlock, then Schmitt interrupted to explain that the two of them "are from nowhere in this area. We were called in, and there was a list of names and numbers, and we got started, and seeing who was there, who saw what."

Eddy Bauer kept talking.

"Well," he said, "I'll tell you what: If you talk to my wife, either this guy [in the silver pickup] was, like I say, he was there, okay? Now, he may not appreciate. He probably wishes he wouldn't have said anything, you know, but it was like it wasn't no secret. . . . I mean, he was pretty open with it, so I didn't think it was that big of a deal."

Gonzales asked if Ryan had been working that Monday, Labor Day.

"Far as what he told me," Eddy Bauer said, "that he cut some trees down lower. Matter of fact, he's been out there cutting trees every night, working, I guess, with CDF [Cal Fire had changed its informal acronym nine months earlier] on the fire line. He got home at four-thirty this morning."

Had twenty-year-old Ryan Bauer been hired on by Cal Fire, their employer and Josh White's employer, without any of them knowing about it?

Schmitt asked the name of the man who'd told Eddy Bauer about the fire's cause. Bauer said he didn't know, but he could get the name from his son.

"Maybe," Gonzales said, "we can just talk with Ryan and get it from him?"

"Do you think," Schmitt asked, "he'd be interested in meeting with us real quick, a little bit later?"

"I don't see any reason why you couldn't do it right now," Eddy Bauer said.

He picked up his cell and voice-dialed. "Hey, Ryan, I'm with these investigators, and they want to talk to you. Yeah. So I'm going to come and get you, okay?" Then: "Well, because you were up at the fire that morning. . . . I thought you said you went out there that morning and cut trees. . . . Well, they want to talk to you."

"It'll be real quick," Schmitt said, "not a big deal."

"He said real quick, not a big deal," Eddy said into the phone. "So be ready. I'm going to come and get you, so be outside."

Schmitt turned off the voice recorder at 2:05.

26

Red Emmerson hadn't been entirely surprised to see the mill teetering on the precipice, having read monthly statements that were mailed to him during his entire deployment. But not until he actually stepped inside the mill and saw the magnitude of the issues did he understand how close he'd come to failure. He says it took "at most a month" to get the mill running smoothly again. "I just paid attention to whatever needed my attention, made a few improvements, and ran a tighter operation than Dad had."

As soon as cash flow allowed, Emmerson installed new, more efficient equipment and began running a second shift to achieve economies of scale and lower overhead costs as a percentage of production.

"It was obvious to me that there were certain fixed expenses like property taxes and certain salaries that are the same whether you're running one or two shifts," Red says. "Your depreciation is half what it would be. Right away we were saving fifteen or twenty percent against those expenses with the second shift. I think we were making about $40,000 a month like clockwork in pretax dollars. That's about the equivalent of almost $400,000 today."

Emmerson insisted on getting more from his employees and more for his money and began searching for other men willing to work hard at what he intended to fashion into the best sawmill in Arcata, if not the county, if not the state. If they worked hard, they'd be well rewarded.

27

Seven minutes after Eddy Bauer called his son Ryan about meeting with investigators at the Cal Fire Westwood station, Ryan Bauer sat down with George Gonzales and Dieter Schmitt. Gonzales asked Bauer to spell his name and give his date of birth—which was November 11, 1986. Bauer went on to provide his phone number and address, state his height as five ten and weight as 155 pounds, and note that he had brown hair and blue eyes.

Gonzales began the interview proper by asking whether Bauer had worked the day the fire began.

"We were off that day," Bauer said. "Kelly and J. Dub [the two Howell's drivers] were skidding and water barring on Cats."

The investigators did not ask how Bauer could have known such information if he had been off that day. They asked who he worked for. He identified Bill Dietrich as the falling boss, and Eunice Howell as the owner of Howell's Forest Service.

Gonzales asked Bauer to be more specific about the names of the Cat drivers.

Bauer didn't know their last names.

"And they were working that day and you weren't," Gonzales said.

"Water barring, yeah," Bauer said. "No one else was working that day."

"Just those two?"

"Yeah."

"Okay," Gonzales said.

"Where did I get brought into all this?" Bauer asked suddenly. "Are you guys talking to all the fallers and all the loggers?"

"We're just talking to anybody who was down around that area," Gonzales said, "just trying to figure out what the fire was doing and what was happening."

"I was in town, and I called Eunice, and she already knew about it," Bauer said, answering a question that no one had asked. "I guess J. Dub called her."

Asked what time he noticed the fire, Bauer answered, "Probably like three or so." He then added a detail that his father had also gratuitously volunteered: "I guess it started like two o'clock."

And where was he when he noticed the fire? "My girlfriend's house, right here on Greenwood." They were "taking a walk," he said, "and I seen smoke, so I called Eunice."

In that phone call, Bauer claimed, Eunice Howell asked him to drive up the mountain and "try to get some equipment out . . . loaders and stuff . . . Cats and skidders."

The investigators did not ask if he had ever before driven those huge machines. Gonzales asked, "What did you end up doing after that?"

"I went over there to check it out," Bauer said. "Try and get some equipment out. We had a lot of stuff down in there."

The investigators did not ask how Bauer would know that the two drivers, Bush and Crismon, weren't still on the job, driving the machines out themselves. It was, after all, still only three o'clock, long before the usual quitting time.

Once he got to the site, Gonzales wanted to know, had Bauer ended up "tying in" with the Cat drivers.

"Yeah, I guess, well, they're the ones that spotted the fire," Bauer said.

They asked what type of truck he drove.

Ford F-150, he said.

"And that's red, your dad said?" Gonzales asked. "Red?"

Bauer may have wondered whether the investigators had already heard from Benny Wallace about seeing him speeding away from the fire in the green Toyota truck. "How did you get my name?" he asked.

Gonzales did not insist that Bauer answer the question. He explained that he and Schmitt had come in "from an outer unit" and met with other members of the team, including battalion chief Josh White. They had been given the names of several people.

"Who gave [my name] to you?" Bauer asked, his voice agitated.

Schmitt had begun another bland, noncommittal answer when Bauer interrupted: "How did they even know who I am?"

Schmitt said Bauer's name may have been dropped "by somebody you work with."

Bauer lashed out: "What's the deal with me supposedly cutting up there on Monday?"

"I don't know," Gonzales said, not explaining they'd heard that from Eddy Bauer. "I assumed you were cutting up there."

"We were off Monday," Bauer repeated.

Gonzales asked, "Then those guys on the Cats were off Monday, too?"

No, "They were water barring on Monday," Bauer insisted. "They were the only two people working."

Neither investigator asked how Bauer knew the drivers were only water barring, not skidding.

"I want to know how I was brought into the situation I was cutting on Monday," Bauer demanded. But instead of listening to the explanation, he interrupted and, unsolicited, insisted fiercely that he'd been with his "girlfriend all day."

"So you didn't cut at all that morning or period?" Schmitt asked.

"No," Bauer said, "I ain't cut since Friday."

Gonzales changed the subject. "Now, you're working on the fire—doing shift work on the fire?"

"Trying, yeah," Bauer said.

"Oh, trying to?"

"Yeah."

"Okay, you haven't got picked up yet or—"

"Well," Bauer said eagerly, "how do I get on that?"

Neither investigator pointed out that Eddy Bauer had said his son had been coming home just before dawn, filthy and soot-covered, from working salvage for Cal Fire.

Gonzales offered a few pointers about how one goes about getting picked up for that kind of work, then brought Bauer back to the issue of picking up his chainsaw off the mountain.

Bauer explained that if he'd known there was going to be a fire, he'd have taken his chainsaw with him the previous Friday.

"What is the deal with fire watch?" Gonzales asked, though what a twenty-year-old knot bumper who'd been on the job three weeks might know about state regulations was unclear.

"How does that work?" Gonzales continued. "Do you know anything about that?"

"Well, just that you had to have one, obviously," Bauer said, following up immediately with, "So do you guys think maybe it was a rock from one of those Cats?"

The investigators said they were still trying to figure out who all had been on and off the mountain, "because there's talk like of quad runners."

Quad runners? "Who said quad runners and stuff?" Bauer asked in panic. He and his parents owned at least one all-terrain vehicle, and people in town knew that. In fact, dozer driver J.W. Bush had reported seeing one as he fled the fire.

"Just somebody," Gonzales said.

"Who said there was quad runners?" Bauer repeated. "Was it someone on the crew?"

Of all the people who might have seen an ATV on the mountain, why would he suspect a crewman. That was not a question the investigators asked.

"I'm not sure," Schmitt said. "It may have been one of your dozer operators."

"It sucks that the fire happened," Bauer said, "but I don't know what to tell you."

"Uh-huh," Gonzales said.

"I was with my girlfriend all day," Bauer volunteered again. "She can verify that if I'm being blamed for the fire."

Gonzales said, "I know."

Bauer said, "I don't know."

Gonzales said, "There's people up there, in and out. I mean your dad was around there. And your mom, I guess, dad and mom together with their dog or something was in around there."

"That's what they were telling me," Bauer said.

"So we're talking to them," Gonzales said, "and talking to, you know, the first engine in there; talking to Forest Patrol. And then there's this list of names we're just going down. I don't know anybody in this town, and I'm starting to meet everybody."

Schmitt explained that the questions Bauer was being asked were more or less what they had already asked, or would soon ask, everyone else. But then he appeared to circle back, as if trying to trap Bauer into revealing how he could've seen what he claimed to know: "J.W. was on a dozer, you said, water barring?"

"A Cat," Bauer said. "It's kind of like a skidder. It's got grapples on it."

"Okay. And he was water barring on that?"

"It's for dragging trees down the road."

"He was dragging trees?"

"No," Bauer said, "they drag trees, those guys do."

"Oh. Did he drag any trees that day?"

"No. I think he was just water barring."

"Oh," Schmitt said, "did he tell you that? What about Kelly? Same thing? Water barring?"

"As far as I know, they were water barring."

"And you said that somebody told you that it was a dozer that started the fire?" Schmitt asked.

"Yeah."

"Who told you that?"

"I don't know, Kelly and J. Dub. I don't know if I should repeat it. I don't want to lose my job. So can you turn that off?"

"Do you want this off?" Gonzales asked. "Okay."

It remained off for two minutes, during which, according to the investigators' written report of the interview, Bauer claimed that Bush and Crismon each blamed the other for causing the spark that started the fire. Bauer reiterated that both had confided in him about one of the dozers being responsible. The investigators did not ask why the dozer operators had admitted their negligence to Eddy, a man J.W. Bush maintained he had never seen, and to Ryan Bauer, a young man who'd been on the job for three weeks, was not particularly liked by his colleagues, and rarely if ever worked near the dozer operators.

At 2:32 the recorded conversation continued. Gonzales asked how the front end of Bauer's truck had broken—exactly the kind of damage a truck might suffer from going too fast down a mountainside and hitting a rut.

Bauer blamed big "chips" in the road.

Then the investigators asked him to reiterate the story he'd told them about how he'd spent the day. Bauer said he'd been at his girlfriend's, saw the fire, called his boss Eunice, had driven up there to help move the equipment, stayed at Five Corners and "bullshitted for a couple hours, watched the fire, and went home. That's pretty much it."

"Okay," Gonzales said. "And J.W. and Kelly were running Cats that day."

"Yeah."

"On Labor Day, I guess it was, huh?"

"Yeah."

"You talked to Bill Dietrich, and then he gave you the number for Eunice, and then you called her up."

"Well, he's Eunice's, like, fiancé."

"Oh, okay, so they got the same number?"

"Yeah."

"So you weren't calling just necessarily to talk to Eunice. You were maybe going to get Bill or Eunice on the phone."

"Well, I asked for Bill and she told me that he's going to the fire."

"Okay," Gonzales said. "You went to check it out, help get equipment out of there if you needed to, and then you had two of your saws up there?"

"One."

"How long you been falling?" Gonzales asked.

"Three weeks."

"How many fallers you guys got?"

"Eight. Then there's knot bumpers, a loader operator, a side rod that sometimes gets on a skidder."

"What's a side rod?" Schmitt asked.

"And then there's a skidder, two Cats, a loader, a team of knot bumpers, the water truck driver, log truck drivers, fallers. That's pretty much the logging outfit."

"And the only people you saw in there," Gonzales said, "were CDF, Forest Service, Forest Patrol, and then your two operators, and didn't see anybody else.

"A guy who's in charge, like a foreman or whatever you want to call him."

Moments later, Schmitt circled back. "So," he said, "did you talk to J. Dub and to Kelly that day?"

"Uh-huh."

"Up on the fire there, or did they make it down, somewhere down here away from the fire?"

It appeared that Schmitt was zeroing in on the where, when, how, and why of Bauer's claim to have been the dozer drivers' confessor.

"Well," Bauer said, "they was where CDF and all them, where I'm sure they got my name, because we're all standing around talking."

Bauer then named some other names he said he thought the investigators were probably going to want to talk to, all of whom were "trying to get equipment out."

"Okie-doke," Gonzales said. "And you were able to get your saw out of there, but that was somebody from our outfit that went and got your saw?"

"Yeah," said Bauer, "I believe it was your outfit."

"Was your saw stashed with other company saws?"

"Yeah, it was behind a tree."

"Okay, anything else?"

"It was sitting back there for like a week," Bauer said, apparently forgetting that he'd told them that he'd worked the previous Friday, three days before the day the fire started.

The discussion then moved to bears—how they'll steal a logger's belongings, even saws, if they're not hung in trees.

Now, wrapping up, Schmitt asked if there was anything Ryan Bauer wanted to add.

"Not really," Bauer said.

"If we have any further questions, can we call?" Schmitt asked.

"I wasn't up there that day," Bauer insisted. "The only time I was up there, all I seen was smoke."

"You said you weren't up there that day, and you haven't been up there since?" Schmitt asked.

Bauer said no, he hadn't. The conversation moved to how long Bauer had been cutting wood—since the eleventh grade—and how much a cord of wood goes for now.

Gonzales asked for Bauer's cell number, in case there were any more questions or maybe the bureau chief wanted to contact him.

"What do you guys think?" Bauer asked.

"I don't know," Gonzales said. "We're just in here interviewing people, and we'll see what comes about the whole thing. I don't know. If there's equipment being used in there, so it could have been that. We need to rule out other stuff too, you know."

"Cats and rocks and metal," Bauer suggested.

"There's no doubt, you know, that could've happened," Gonzales said. "If, you know, somebody saw a quad runner in there or something, you know."

"J. Dub did tell me that he thought he heard someone cutting," Bauer said. Neither investigator asked when or where Bush might have told him that. Bauer asked if they had yet talked to Bush.

No, Gonzales said.

"We have to actually get ahold of him next," Schmitt said.

"I don't know," Bauer said. "He's probably at home, I imagine, but he might be out there at the camp."

"We may need to call you or your father for additional questions that may arise," Schmitt said, "but if you can think of anything, let us know, by all means."

He handed Bauer a business card for the CDF unit's battalion chief, Joshua White. "So if you think of anything, or you got any questions for us or something, go ahead and give him a call."

The interview ended at 2:47 P.M. on Friday, September 7.

Schmitt and Gonzales had their work cut out for them, verifying with Ryan Bauer's girlfriend that he'd spent the afternoon with her and confirming with both Bill Dietrich and Eunice Howell that Ryan Bauer had called them about three o'clock on Monday afternoon, and that one or the other of them had asked him to help get the big equipment out of fire danger. They'd probably also have to track down the two Cat drivers, Bush and Crismon, to check that they'd told Bauer what he claimed they had.

They'd then pass on their findings to Josh White. If anyone could poke holes in Ryan Bauer's apparent contradictions, White was the man. It was for precisely situations like this that he'd studied behavioral analysis at the California Conference on Arson Investigators and at the Behavioral Analysis Training Institute, where he'd learned how to identify liars through their mannerisms, their skin flushing, their body language, pupil dilation, and voice timber. As White would later explain under oath, "One of the things we learned is that everybody is different. So you want to establish a baseline. Develop a rapport with the subject, discuss things that there would be no reason for the subject to lie about. So you try to identify their truth-telling technique."

28

In October 1954 Ida Mitchell phoned Red Emmerson at his mill and invited him on a date. When she compared Red Emmerson to all the other young men she knew and had known, she realized he was the one man she could imagine building a life with, even if he never seemed more animated than when he was working or talking about work. Did she want a man with big dreams or a dreamer whose starry eyes would dim the minute the going got difficult?

"When she finally decided I was the one she wanted, she went after me," Emmerson remembers. "There was no turning back on her part. She knew her own mind, and she knew what she wanted and what she didn't want. Ida had no career aspirations. She wanted to be a wife and a mother and to make a warm home for her family. She knew that, together, we could go far. Absolutely, we were going places."

On Sunday night, June 5, 1955—at almost the same hour that a young singer named Elvis Presley was entertaining folks two thousand miles away at an Arkansas fair—Ida Mitchell walked down the aisle of Eureka's Presbyterian church and became Mrs. Ida Emmerson. The party lasted until after midnight, and appropriately the band played "Rock around the Clock."

The newlyweds took a five-day honeymoon, driving to San Francisco and Las Vegas for a bit of fun before moving into a small Eureka apartment that sometimes became an after-hours office away from the mill not just for Red Emmerson but also for key employees, supervisors, and out-of-town visitors. Emmerson says he knew he could always call Ida to say he was bringing a guest, even with less than an hour's notice before coming home around 7 p.m., and always she'd act the part of gracious hostess and prepare an excellent dinner.

Whenever the dinner guests talking shop thought of some new bright idea, the fervor might reach such a pitch that they couldn't wait even till morning. Everyone would hop into their trucks and drive back to the mill to try out the idea.

Sometimes Ida wasn't sure if Red Emmerson was married more to her or to the mill. Actually, she *was* sure, but she'd known what she was getting into when she married him and wasn't sorry. In fact, she had become endlessly curious about the work and all the thousand little decisions required at any given moment to run the business properly, and by having people over and treating them hospitably, she could eavesdrop or even participate.

One day she suggested that they should buy a house rather than continue renting an apartment, arguing that he'd then have more space to work at home.

Such was the kind of reasoning that appealed to Red Emmerson.

In late 1956, in a clapboard house on a wide leafy Eureka street, their first son, George Emmerson, was born. George's sister Carolyn followed two years later, and brother Mark a year after that.

29

On September 9, 2007, two days after his grueling interview with the Cal Fire investigators, Ryan Bauer was driving down Westwood's main drag and spotted the private forestry guard Leo Whitlock standing in front of the Cal Fire station. As it happened, Whitlock was talking with Cal Fire engineer Dan Francis about the Moonlight Fire.

Bauer screeched to a halt, jumped out of his truck, and ran over to confront Whitlock, shouting angrily. He accused Whitlock of lying about Bauer's being on the mountain that day, cutting wood. Whitlock wasn't sure whether Bauer would take a swing at him, or worse. He said only that he'd repeated to Schmitt and Gonzales what Bauer's own father had told him on the mountain, that they were looking for him because he'd been cutting up there and they were worried.

Mollified or not, Bauer drove off, and Whitlock went inside the station to find battalion chief Josh White, to whom he related a blow-by-blow of what had just happened. White said he wasn't surprised and told Whitlock that Bauer had been claiming he was out there every night working on the fire, felling scorched trees.

30

In spring 1957 the warning signs of an impending economic slow-down, such as rising unemployment (that would hit nearly 8 percent), evolved into a full-blown recession that lasted into at least the middle of 1958. But R. H. Emmerson and Son barely noticed.

"I didn't pay attention to things like that," Emmerson says. "I didn't get afraid or worried by anything I read in the papers. I just kept doing what I needed to do."

At this point in his stewardship, the only serious issue that might slow down the mill was a lack of timber. They were still having to buy logs on the open market from ranchers and landowners, and particularly in winter enough product might be hard to come by.

For years the mill was profitable every month with the sole exception of December 1958. "There weren't enough logs to keep the saws running," Emmerson says. "We had to shut down over Christmas, so that's why we came up short. It was the only reason. And I vowed that that would never again be the reason I fell short."

As it happened Emmerson had already decided to make a major investment in timber to supply the mill. An opportunity had presented itself. All he had to do was find a way to get enough money for the down payment on the exclusive cutting rights to 200 million board feet of lumber—across about 2,500 acres—on the Eel River, in an area called Camp Grant. The owner was Georgia-Pacific.

Georgia-Pacific had been founded in Georgia in 1927 by Owen Robertson Cheatham as the Georgia Hardwood Lumber Company—a wholesaler—before it began investing in its own timberlands and then, twenty years later, buying a failing West Coast mill and amending its name to Georgia-Pacific Plywood and Lumber Company.

Now, having just bought a kraft pulp (used to make paper) and containerboard (used for corrugated cardboard) mill in Oregon, Georgia-Pacific had changed its name yet again to something that would accommodate future acquisitions and expansion. From where Emmerson stood, Georgia-Pacific Corporation had gone from nothing to a colossal industry force in fewer than three decades through natural market share growth that could be credited to aggressive practices, the acquisition of other companies, and entry into new but related businesses.

Emmerson aspired to that kind of profitable growth. No one outside the company knew how much land Georgia-Pacific owned or controlled, but Emmerson suspected it was millions of acres. Maybe many millions.

For the deal to happen, the Emmersons had to come up with $200,000 just to start—more than R. H. Emmerson and Son's net worth—with the remaining three-quarters of a million to be paid in installments according to board feet taken.

"I remember thinking at the time that if we could ever pay back that much money, I'd be in hog heaven forever," Emmerson says. "It didn't seem possible, but I didn't really have a choice. One way or another, I was going to do it."

Though he was still a young man, he had already been betting on himself for twenty years. And this bet would be the biggest one yet. In Emmerson's mind, Owen Robertson Cheatham, Georgia-Pacific's founder, hadn't gotten his company to where it was three decades later by playing it safe. He'd taken chances, bought sawmills, plywood lumber mills, and the acres of forest to supply them. That's how it was done. No guts, no glory; no risk, no reward. If Emmerson ever had aspirations to someday play on Georgia-Pacific's level, he, too, would have to take chances.

He paid back the money he borrowed from his local Bank of America in less than a year, Emmerson says. "It was supposed to take several years."

31

On September 6, 2007, USFS supervisor Craig Endicott dispatched special investigative agent Diane Welton from her assignment in the Stanislaus National Forest to Susanville in order to "tie in," as she later put it, with Josh White and investigate the Moonlight Fire.

This was a somewhat tardy assignment. Dave Reynolds, the forest service investigator who'd been working with White the previous few days, had been deemed unqualified by the USFS to investigate any fire whose damages would total more than $50,000—an amount that had likely been surpassed long before Reynolds welcomed Cal Fire investigator White to the scene at 9 P.M. the first night.

Reynolds, of course, had been assigned as USFS's investigator in the early minutes of the fire, when the scene was chaotic and resources were being deployed quickly, by Larry Craggs, the district fire management officer for the Mount Hough Ranger District. And when Reynolds didn't say anything about his eligibility to work this job in the ensuing days, possibly because he enjoyed being Josh White's coequal, he stayed on.

At some point, though, someone recognized that the official report on the Moonlight Fire—which had grown hugely destructive—was going to be prepared by a USFS investigator who technically did not have the expertise to come to an unambiguous conclusion about the fire's cause; nor did he have the clearance to sign such a report for posterity. As far as USFS was concerned, Josh White's qualifications to investigate the fire competently were beside the point legally.

White worked for the state, not the feds. So Endicott sent Welton to replace Reynolds, who had already reached his own conclusion about the cause of the fire and completed his report to that effect days before Welton showed up on scene the morning of September 8.

Welton had arrived in town the night before and met with White for a briefing in which he told her that he'd already come to a conclusion about what sparked the fire and who was to blame.

The next morning White drove Welton and another USFS agent, Marion Matthews, to the area of origin. Even allowing for the site's lack of freshness and the amount it had been trampled on in the five days since the fire began, one might reasonably imagine that protocol demanded of Welton, who by her own count had investigated ninety-eight fires before Moonlight—ninety-seven of which were wildland fires—that she begin the investigation from the beginning or at least double-check Reynolds's methodology. She did neither of those.

White showed Welton around the general and specific areas of origin, then directed her to the two rocks that he had identified as points of origin. He showed her how he'd found the metal flakes through, as she put it, "the utilization of sweeping a magnet," and told her that they were consistent with the grousers of a Caterpillar. There were no flags or other markers placed anywhere, nothing to establish where they believed the fire had begun or where it had backed, advanced, or progressed laterally. She said herself that "the indicators I saw may not have been as crisp, may not have been as fresh," but insisted that she "could read them back towards the general area of origin and the specific area of origin" even if, as she admitted, she couldn't locate the area of origin herself.

"I visually observed the scene," she claimed, explaining that White "worked through his hypothesis and then what other causes he excluded."

White snapped two photos of Welton pointing a shovel at two rocks spaced about eight feet apart in a spur trail about ten feet from the rock White and Reynolds had initially identified as the specific point of origin. The two rocks, referred to in the reports as E-2 and E-3, were carried away as evidence, one of them in a green duffel bag and one in a Nomex jacket.

On September 10, 2007, Josh White called J.W. Bush and arranged a follow-up interview, which he promised would be brief. They agreed to meet at the Shell station on the main drag in Westwood. White recorded the conversation.

"Give me a rundown one more time of what transpired," he said. "Just tell me from the beginning as if I don't know anything."

Bush repeated that they'd begun work about 6:30 that morning and shut down at 1:00 before going to the yard to refuel and grease. He said he realized he'd forgotten his phone and had to drive back to "the ranch, about thirty minutes, twenty minutes, something like that, to get down there."

White asked how long it took to fuel and grease. About fifteen minutes, Bush said, putting his finishing time "probably about a quarter after or something around in there. I'm just kind of estimating because I didn't look at my watch, you know."

"Right," White said, "but an idea of whether it was one o'clock or two o'clock."

"Somewhere right in there, that area," Bush said, not understanding that that hour difference made all the difference in the world to White, who still had to reconcile how a rock strike made at about 12:45 didn't ignite into a conflagration until nearly 2:30.

"And by this time, Kelly had come down the hill?" White asked.

"He was already there," Bush said.

"He was already there?"

"Yeah, he was already there."

"So he was doing the same thing, fueling and greasing?"

"Yeah."

Bush confirmed that Crismon had driven out before him, that after driving to and from the trailer where his phone was he couldn't get back to the site for the fire walk because of the fire, and that on the way back he'd almost run over "this kid in a four-wheeler" and told him to call Cal Fire if he could. White did not ask any questions about the kid or the four-wheeler. But then Bush mentioned "this kid in the red pickup" he'd nearly run into. "I can't remember his name."

"Does he work for you?"

"No," Bush said. "I don't know who he was. I told him, 'If you can get out, call CDF.' He said he already did it."

"Really?"

Right after that encounter, Bush said, he came upon a Cal Fire firetruck with firefighters inside. "That's how quick they were." He turned around and tried to lead them back to where he believed the fire was burning.

From there he drove to the landing, he said.

"Did you guys have a rock strike back in June that caused a fire?" White asked.

"Yes," Bush said.

"I've been reading some different reports and everything," White said. "I'm a little confused, and I'm not looking for any guilt on your part, but—

"Yeah, yeah," Bush said.

"Was it the dozer that you were operating?"

"Yeah, uh-huh," Bush said.

"And were you the operator on that thing?"

"Yes."

Three months before there had been a small spot fire in an area called Moonville where Howell's had been hired by Sierra Pacific to log. The fire had started on a road after the work day and burned a few acres before being extinguished. A USFS investigator named Bridgette Foster had later gone to the scene and taken photos but hadn't interviewed witnesses or filed a report.

"Okay," White said. "So that's still the same dozer that you operate? Do you know what I mean?"

"Where Kelly was at, or where I was at?" Bush asked.

He seemed confused by the question.

"No, no," White said. "I'm talking about back in June."

"Oh," Bush said, "you mean the one then and the one now?"

"Right."

"The same one, yeah."

"You were still driving the same one?"

"Yeah."

"So the dozer that you started the fire with back in June is the dozer that was way out—that's in the area that still had the burn."

"Yeah."

"That's way out there. So this was a different dozer."

"That's a whole different unit, too, section, yeah," Bush said.

"Oh, okay," White said.

"Other job site."

"Yeah, that was on the Moon Valley or Moon—Moonville?"

"No. Might ask Damon, but I don't remember it."

It was clear the two men were having separate conversations, Bush not following along but, as he would later explain, eager to please this government employee.

"It's a natural thing, you know," he said. "It happens."

"Well, yeah," White said. "I mean, you're running steel over rock. It's just one of those things that is bound to happen."

White asked Bush about fire watches and walks, then Bush mentioned that while they were still working he could look down at where Crismon was driving on a wide road, kicking up dust that blew in the wind, and he reiterated that they already knew they'd knock off no later than 1 P.M. if the winds kicked up.

"I'm trying to figure out the time line," White said. "Because here's the thing is that—"

Bush interrupted him to say he believed he got back to his trailer in camp by 1:30. White said he'd done a time trial in his own truck, taking eighteen minutes to get from where Bush had been working to Bush's camp.

"I drive slow," Bush said, which White arbitrarily interpreted to mean he had taken twenty-five minutes to make the drive.

"So we'll estimate 1:40," he said, asking Bush how long he was in camp before heading back.

"Just a few minutes," Bush said. "I just got my phone and my drink."

"Five minutes? Ten minutes?"

"Yeah, something like that."

"Well, we'll just say ten minutes," White said.

"Okay," Bush said, estimating it took him another fifteen minutes to get back.

"So, 2:05," White said.

"Uh-huh," Bush said.

"Now, see, here's the issue," White said, "is that the lookout spotted the fire at 2:30."

Trying to accommodate him, Bush said, "It might have been a little longer, I don't know. I drive slow."

"I mean," White said, "it's really not that big of a point. It's just that I'm trying to get the time lines to match up because if the lookout called it in at 2:30, then they call the dispatch center, and the dispatch center processes it, and then they dispatch the units, and then the units have to leave—you know, get their stuff together. They have to leave the fire station."

After a few minutes of back and forth, White admitted that "there's approximately a half an hour that the two time lines don't match up," explaining that "a few extra minutes here and a few extra minutes there adds up to that half an hour."

Bush, wanting to accommodate, agreed that he could be wrong with his estimates.

"I just want you to know, just be honest with me," White said. "If there's like, you know, you went back to the camp and—"

"Yeah, I did go there."

"—and put your feet up or—"

"Oh, no, no."

"—dust your face off or—"

"No."

"—did anything like that—"

"Nope."

"I'm not here to place the blame on—"

Five days before White made that claim, an "S" had replaced "W" before Bush's name in White's official notes, as it had in front of Crismon's name, meaning that both were no longer witnesses; they were now deemed suspects.

Bush interrupted to say no, he hadn't, absolutely not, done anything like take a shower, and if White talked to the people who saw him down at Five Corners, hanging out, watching the fire, he'd know that Bush was still covered in dirt from the workday.

"Yeah, they did, as a matter of fact," White said, adding that Crismon "looked like he took a shower by the time he got back out there."

Bush more or less apologized for being stopped by the fire and not being able to get back to where he was going. "I just went back out and went to the main landing," he said. "The fire marshal or somebody, whoever he was, I can't remember his name, wanted to see me."

"Oh, Dave?" White asked.

"Yeah, Dave."

"Dave Reynolds?"

"Mm-hmm," Bush said.

White did not point out that Bush had met Reynolds twice, the second time in White's presence. Bush went on to explain that he'd left there to help move the trailer of someone named Dave Russell out of harm's way.

White asked if Dave had an ATV. Bush said no but added that George Bullard had said he'd seen one.

"Oh, and you almost hit him," White said, then asked for details on which way he was going and on what road.

Bush suggested that whoever it was on Road 3130 may have seen the smoke the same time he had and noted that when he and Crismon were driving out, a little after one, they'd smelled no smoke, even with the windows down on his truck.

"Hey," White said, "tell me about—what's the story with Bauer?"

"Bauer?"

"Ryan Bauer."

"Oh, our new knot bumper."

"Yeah."

"Yeah," Bush said, "I don't know. . . . I don't know him. He's out of here in Westwood, I guess."

"Did you see him up there at any time during the day?"

"I seen him there after I brought the firefighters in, and I came back out."

"Okay."

"He was there."

"At the landing? At the big landing?"

"Yeah, at the big landing there."

"Did you say anything to him."

"Mm-mm."

"You didn't say anything?"

"No, I was talking to that—that other guy, the fire marshal."

"Okay. Dave?"

"Dave, yeah."

"Did you talk to Leo at any time, do you remember? Whitlock?"

"I think there was two of them I talked to."

"Okay. Did you tell anybody what you thought might have started the fire?"

"I didn't—no. I didn't even know what started it or anything."

"Okay. You never told any of them that you think that it might have been a rock strike?"

"No, I didn't say nothing, no."

"Okay."

"Only thing I thought was odd is that kid coming up in that red pickup, and he already had them called and everything, and I didn't see the fire until I got there to it."

"Hmm. I wonder where he could have been."

"Yeah."

"So when you were driving back in through the meadow—you never saw any smoke?"

"Yeah, I never seen nothing. But it blew up quick, I mean."

"Yeah, it did."

In his written summary of the interview appended to his origin and cause investigation report, White said "S-1 Bush reiterated the same information he had provided to" Dave Reynolds and that White was "concerned with the sequence of events. I explained to S-1 BUSH that based on his timeline he should have been able to get back out to the meadow and call 911 from his cellular phone before the Red Rock Lookout report."

Taken together, the two statements reflected White's conclusion that the fire had been started by Crismon's dozer before 1 P.M. and smoldered for more than an hour and half before reaching critical mass. Yet White intimated that Bush had lollygagged, not that he had left the scene of a fire. This was a curious contradiction. Bush could've known that the fire's cause was a rock strike only if he had left the scene of a burning fire.

32

With his first big deal paying dividends, Red Emmerson wanted to ensure that his mill would never lack for raw product. Mere months after the Georgia-Pacific transaction, R. H. Emmerson and Son made its first major purchase—not just of logging rights but of the land on which the timber was growing.

In Cappel Creek, near Weitchpec, about fifty miles northeast of Arcata as the crow flies, on the southwestern edge of Six Rivers National Forest, there were about 2,500 acres of old-growth Douglas fir for sale. Emmerson estimated they would yield about 60 million board feet of lumber. The price was $75,000 down with the rest to be paid as the timber was harvested and the lumber cut. He didn't have to think about it long.

Red Emmerson had every right to be bullish about the lumber market, given that most serious forecasts of the American economy predicted that lumber and other forest products would grow steadily for at least two decades.

The Cappel Creek sale came with a stud mill at Weitchpec and a deck of mostly cull logs (poor or defective lumber that had been culled from the original stack) that would be prohibitively expensive to truck out. Emmerson wouldn't have minded closing down the mill and liquidating its assets; the 2,500 acres of Douglas fir were what interested him. But around that time Curly and Myrtle weren't getting along well and may even have already been separated—they were on their way to an eventual divorce—so Curly saw an opportunity to breathe free for a while. He moved into one of the small cabins located next to the

Weitchpec mill and, with a small crew and $150,000 worth of improvements by R. H. Emmerson and Son, tried to turn a profit by sawing the culls into studs.

"Dad thought he might be able to make a go of that mill, which was just sitting there with a diesel generator," Emmerson says. "We ended up rebuilding it—$150,000."

That was a lot of money to sink into a risky endeavor, but with the Arcata mill netting $80,000 a month, it didn't seem overly risky—though the venture did fail and was shut down within a year.

No matter. Under Emmerson's supervision, the Arcata mill had found new and better ways to cut that allowed the company to finish and sell higher grades of lumber, like the plank used to deck ships, at prices sometimes ten to twelve times as much as ordinary construction-grade lumber.

Most of the finished lumber, nearly 75 percent, was sent via truck and rail to wholesalers in Southern California. Only 20 percent stayed closer to home, in the San Francisco Bay Area, with about 5 percent headed for Texas.

The company's growing base of customers learned that they could count on the quality of whatever came out of an Emmerson mill, and suppliers learned that their bills would always be paid on time. This was the way to build an enduring business.

By 1961 R. H. Emmerson and Son had outgrown its own supply and was hungry for more land that might guarantee a steady supply of logs. Emmerson heard that 5,400 acres of mostly old-growth Douglas fir were for sale in the Snow Camp area south of Willow Creek. Buying it would require a down payment of half a million dollars, with the remaining several hundred thousand due as the timber was cut.

The branch manager of the local Bank of America, where Emmerson had been doing business for years, himself delivered the bad news that their loan had been turned down as being beyond that branch's loan limit.

"My father had an idea," Emmerson says. "He told me that he had a friend named George Hefter who might be able to help. George was an accountant who'd worked for another accounting firm named Lester Herrick and Herrick, which eventually sold out to Arthur Young, the big firm. Hefter lived in San Francisco but had once lived in Eureka,

which was how Dad met him. Dad knew George was pretty well connected, so he called him, told him what we wanted, and George said
he'd see what he could do. Then George called and said come to town,
so we went to San Francisco to see George. He walked us into the Bank
of America building and met a division manager named Frank Keene.
Then we walked out with the money."

33

Two people Ryan Bauer complained to about being persecuted were his boss, Eunice Howell, and longtime faller Hippie Dan Voth.

Though Bauer was the newest of Eunice Howell's employees, she was used to hearing from him more than any other. He called her often with grievances but more often just to chat, as if he considered her his confessor. He'd called her to intervene when Cat driver Kelly Crismon, who'd taken a dislike to Bauer long before he knew that the young man had implicated him in the fire, displayed his animus for Bauer the best way he knew how short of fists—by refusing even to acknowledge him. And Bauer had called Howell begging for his job when field supervisor Russell DeMarce ordered him off his landing after concluding that Bauer's presence was too toxic. Some employees would not willingly work with him.

Howell, however, felt sorry for Bauer. She remembered his previous calls about how his father repeatedly beat him and how the baby Bauer had with his girlfriend—the one for which Howell had knitted a baby blanket—was sick and had to be rushed to UC Davis hospital before dying at home. He called her crying about how the authorities were trying to pin the fire on him, and he'd called her to ask for money, explaining that he had busted his truck's front end in a ditch on the day of the fire after retrieving his chainsaws. He would later call her to say he was thinking about joining the Air Force, and afterward he called to say hello, telling her he was now in the Air Force and that he and his girlfriend had a new baby.

It was only after she'd learned that Ryan Bauer hadn't had a baby, didn't have a girlfriend anymore, and wasn't in the Air Force that Eunice Howell—who had managed to keep her husband's longtime business afloat after his untimely death fifteen years earlier, only to lose it after being blamed for four fires in the summer of 2007—realized that she had been conned by a twenty-year-old and should have listened to DeMarce, who she would later testify was "the only person alive that can call me sweetie."

Howell had decided that Ryan Bauer deserved a second chance to prove himself, and she intervened on his behalf with Bill Dietrich, one of her subcontractors who operated a logging company under her umbrella on the same parcels but with different crews. Against his better judgment, Dietrich hired Bauer as a favor to Howell, and it was on Dietrich's landing that Ryan Bauer got to know Hippie Dan Voth.

Like Howell's crew, Dietrich's guys had gone back to work in October 2007, salvaging what they could from the tract after the fire. By then the rumor around Westwood and Chester and Susanville and all the logging communities on the mountain was that a Caterpillar bulldozer from one of Howell's units working that day had accidentally sparked the fire by running over a rock and sending a small particle from its metal track, heated by friction, onto a pile of brush. But Bauer soon began telling Voth that the "authorities" were trying "to pin the fire" on him.

Voth—who wore his long brown hair parted down the middle and pulled back into a long ponytail, with a massive gray-brown beard that reached across his chest down to his sternum—looked every bit the hippie he may have once been. He did not believe that the fire had been caused by a Caterpillar rock strike. Smart and self-educated, he understood that such fires, though considered conventional wisdom, were actually more like rural myths. Everyone had heard about a fire supposedly started by a Cat, but none of these fires had been confirmed by hard science. Which made sense. For one thing, top speed of a working Caterpillar dozer is five miles an hour, and the amount of heat carried by one of the small metal flakes that are all over the mountain wherever a dozer has been—if you look carefully enough—isn't enough to burn your finger, even if it stayed warm long enough once it hit the ground. Dozens of times while working in the early-morning or late-night dark,

Voth had seen Cats passing over rocks create showers of sparks. Not once had he seen them cause a fire.

"What do you mean, pin the fire on you?" Voth asked Bauer.

"Why would I do that?" Bauer asked.

Voth hadn't asked that question, but it wouldn't be long before he wondered whether it was a projection of a guilty conscience.

Not that Voth hadn't already heard enough stories about Bauer's erratic behavior—driving through town at high speed, shouting profanities for no reason, even threatening people physically without provocation—to begin wondering about Bauer's sanity. But not until early November when Voth stopped in for gasoline at the Shell station in Westwood after being out of town for a few days did he begin to think of Ryan Bauer as capable of having started this fire, whether by accident or arson. That Bauer had claimed to see Voth bleed out on the mountain without foreseeing, or not caring, that the lie would be detected quickly and inevitably led Voth to believe that maybe Ryan Bauer was truly "mentally ill" enough to be dangerous. He approached Bill Dietrich and confided his suspicion.

In fact, the "Hippie Dan is dead" episode led Voth to think about his discovery of a few weeks earlier in a different light. Cutting timber not far from the spot that investigators Josh White and Dave Reynolds had named the fire's origin area, Voth came upon the fragments of what appeared to be a beer bottle, scorched, lying alone against the remains of a burned tree. That the bottle was by itself was the element Voth considered most unusual: loggers tend to find litter in bunches, as if those who'd left it just walked away from their picnic. And that was especially true this far from the road.

Voth watched as Greg Nunes, a private investigator hired by Howell, carefully and gingerly retrieved the bottle, placed the remains in a clean box, added a bit of surrounding soil that could have contained traces of any accelerant, and delivered the package to Dietrich, knowing that the fragments could mean absolutely nothing or that they might be an important piece of evidence.

Had the bottle been left carelessly by someone who'd paused for refreshment during a hike, it might conceivably have been turned into a magnifying glass by the sun's striking it and ignited some dry brush. But the forest canopy that existed before the fire made that scenario all but impossible, so the bottle had either been left coincidentally close to the origin or had been intended to be an incendiary device. As Voth pointed out in a deposition, the bottle was in pieces but not dust, so it hadn't been run over by a bulldozer, and the pieces were in proximity, so it hadn't been thrown from a distance.

Though not a physicist, from his thirty-five years professionally in the forest Voth knew what an empty bottle—one unaffected by changes in interior pressure—was likely to do under outdoor conditions. And what it was unlikely to do when lying on the ground, away from the hottest part of the fire, was shatter, unless it had just come from a refrigerator or freezer and been subjected to sunlight like Death Valley's. But with the ambient air temperature on September 3, 2007, above eighty degrees even in the shade, the bottle's fracturing into pieces could better be explained by something more sinister. Now, having heard about Ryan Bauer's claim that he had died in an accident on the mountain, Dan Voth began to consider two words: Molotov cocktail.

Dan Voth had come to believe Ryan Bauer was dangerous, and it seemed sensible not to antagonize a dangerous colleague whose work tool is a chainsaw. That's why Dan Voth never did confront Ryan Bauer about the bottle or lying about his death or anything else. Nor did he press Bauer about the fire. Instead, he just let the young man complain without responding.

What Voth never could understand, though, was why the state or the feds or any other investigative agency hadn't come calling to ask what he knew. In his mind, it stood to reason that the authorities were working every angle in a search for what had started the fire. So when no charges were filed against anyone for the fire, even Dan Voth began to believe that all of Bauer's grumbling about being targeted by the authorities for the fire amounted to nothing more than paranoid ravings as opposed to the psychological projections of someone with a guilty conscience.

34

By the mid-1960s Red Emmerson had essentially adopted the strategy that not moving forward was akin to going backward. So in July 1965, when he heard that Weyerhaeuser intended to divest itself of its California holdings, he pursued the opportunity to buy a plywood plant, a particleboard plant, and some timberland. The price was $2.8 million. Where could he get that kind of money?

"We were still doing our regular business with the branch in Arcata," Emmerson explains, "but there was no point even asking them for a loan this big. We just went straight to Frank Keene in San Francisco. Frank said, 'When can I take a look at it?' I said, 'When do you want to?'"

Turned out that Keene wanted to see it right away, so he flew up to Arcata the next day. Emmerson picked him up at the airport and drove him to see enough of the property, along with Weyerhaeuser's plants, for Keene to get the lay of the land. Keene liked what he saw, and he particularly liked what Emmerson had to say about his plans.

By that time, Emmerson explains, the Emmersons had begun working with an accountant named Don Riewerts, who was a genius at putting on paper exactly what a bank needed to see before agreeing to a loan.

"That was something I couldn't do at the time," Emmerson says. "I'm not sure I even knew what a pro forma was then. I could go into the bank and explain to them what the money would go for and how I was going to cut this and sell that. But all I could do was tell the story, something that made sense to me but not to them."

Bankers wanted to see a five-year forecast. "Hell," Emmerson jokes, "when they say that I ask, 'What interest rate should we use?' And they say, 'Hell, I don't know.' So how can we do a proper forecast without that? None of it means a damn thing. The only thing that counts is turning a profit."

Emmerson never doubted that he'd be able to pay off the loan, even given the incredible upheavals that American society was experiencing in the 1960s. All of society, torn by civil disturbances and sparked by civil rights protests, seemed ready to embrace a new kind of economic and social model—or so said the news media, which had begun to specialize in highlighting dissent.

No wonder a lot of businessmen without the resources of a major corporation behind them were sitting back, trying to see what developed and which way the wind was going to blow before making any serious investments in the future. Red Emmerson, though, was not a lot of businessmen. The idea that wholesale orders might, any day, begin to dry up and force him to scramble for revenue to keep current with a huge payment plan never occurred to him, he insists.

"You have to factor these things for a downturn, and you think about it so that if things do turn down, you can still live," he explains. "In my own mind, I had my own pro forma. If necessary, I always knew how to reduce costs. Anyway, I've always believed that there's always a market for lumber. Sure, sometimes it slows down a little, but then it'll eventually speed up. The world can't do without lumber. Never has been able to, and I hope it never will."

After seeing the proposal that Riewerts had prepared based on Emmerson's plans, Keene called and said, "Go ahead and deal as if you had the money."

As Emmerson recalls, "It was the biggest transaction I'd ever done in my life, so when I heard him say that, I let it sink in for a second. I didn't say, 'Are you sure?' But the whole time I was negotiating, I was always a little worried that something might happen and the bank might change its mind. Without the money actually in hand, I felt a little like I was bluffing in poker."

Particleboard, made of sawdust and shavings held together by a synthetic resin, had been introduced to the United States in the 1950s, after being developed in Europe during a postwar shortage of A-grade lumber. In the United States, particleboard became a popular material for cabinets—and a profitable product for Red Emmerson. His plant operated at a profit until 1969, when everything changed yet again.

35

Days became weeks became months became one year and then almost two, but so far Ryan Bauer's fears about being blamed for the fire were for naught. He hadn't received a call from Josh White or Diane Welton or any other government representative. No one had asked him a direct question about where he was that day. No one knocked at his door.

Nothing happened to Ryan Bauer until late summer 2009, when he was arrested, convicted, and then imprisoned for eight months for drunkenly assaulting the very sheriff's deputy who had seen him on the mountain on the day of the fire in his parents' green Toyota, not the red Ford F-150 he claimed to have driven—with chainsaws visible in the back of the truck.

Deputy Sheriff Benny Wallace, while on patrol in Westwood, noticed Bauer riding fast down Birch Street on an ATV—a four-wheel open vehicle with a single seat meant for riding off-road. It's illegal to ride them on city streets, and most of the time when Wallace encountered them, young people were behind the wheel.

Figuring that they were ignorant of the law, he'd pull them over, bawl them out, and follow them home. Slowly. Rarely, he later testified, did he have trouble with the same kid again. But this was Ryan Bauer, now almost twenty-two. Wallace prepared himself.

In the decade he'd spent as a law enforcement officer in and around Westwood, Wallace estimated, he'd had more official contact with Ryan Bauer than with any other citizen. He doubted he could even remember every run-in with Bauer going back to the kid's teenage years, and though few of the encounters ended badly, nearly every last one had been unpleasant. Or worse. Just off the top of his head, there was the time Bauer's parents contacted Wallace because they'd found Ryan crunching and snorting prescription meds. There was the time Ryan attacked Eddy, and Wallace took Ryan, who appeared to be under the influence, in on a 5150—a mental hold. There was the time Bauer was arrested for driving under the influence. There was the time Eddy called Wallace, wondering what to do about the $20,000 that Ryan had stolen out of Eddy's gun safe, which Ryan had done after planting spy cameras to secretly record Eddy's turning the combination. But when Wallace said the only thing to do was swear out a complaint, Eddy had decided to deal with it privately instead. In short, as Wallace would put it, "the contacts range[d] from him being an out-of-control juvenile to him being an adult substance abuser to him being involved in gun issues, Fish and Game issues, fights with his mom, fights with his dad. Essentially, he has been an out-of-control individual for the ten years that I've been here."

So when Wallace saw Ryan Bauer speeding on his ATV that night, he braced for the worst and hoped for the best.

Wallace pulled his cruiser behind Bauer's ATV at a safe distance. With the ATV going so fast, it wasn't easy keeping the distance both uniform and safe.

Wallace tapped on the horn lightly to get Bauer's attention. If Bauer heard the honk, he didn't respond. Wallace honked again. Bauer pulled to the shoulder. Wallace pulled his cruiser alongside and was about to say something when Bauer shouted, "So, this is another fuck with Ryan Bauer day?"

His tongue was heavy, voice slurred.

"Park your four-wheeler and get off," Wallace said.

Bauer complied.

Wallace stepped out of his cruiser and walked over to him. He smelled alcohol and asked if Bauer had been drinking.

"I had a couple beers with friends, but I'm clean," Bauer insisted.

If so, Wallace wondered, then why was his hat pulled so low over his eyes?

What was he hiding?

He told Bauer to tilt his head back and, seeing his pupils constricted to pin points, took Bauer's left wrist to check his pulse. It was weak, the heart rate all of fifty.

Bauer must've known he was failing these field sobriety tests. He doubled his fists and said, "Don't do this to me, Benny."

Wallace told him he wanted to do a Romberg's test, the standard impaired-driving test. It measures the subject's sense of balance when standing with his eyes closed and his sense of time by his estimate of thirty seconds.

Bauer said "now" after twelve seconds and failed the balance test. He stuck out his chest, balled his fists, and became defiant.

"I'm clean, you're fucking with me," he shouted. "And I'm tired of it."

He asked what Wallace thought was wrong with him. Wallace said he was sure Bauer had been drinking or taking drugs or both. "You're under arrest."

"I'm not going to jail," Bauer said. "If you arrest me, you're not putting me in your fucking car."

"I believe you've been operating your ATV under the influence. Please turn around and put your hands behind your back."

Bauer turned around but didn't put his hands behind him, forcing Wallace to grab his arms into position for the handcuffs to be placed. After struggling to get them on, Wallace frisked him, which really set Bauer off. He alternated between begging to be let go and calling Wallace an asshole.

"Ryan, get in the car," Wallace said.

"I'm not getting in your car," Bauer said. "You're just screwing with me."

"Ryan, get in the car."

"Gimme a break, goddammit, my girlfriend's got cancer," Bauer shouted, refusing to get in the car. He said he couldn't and wouldn't go to jail.

Wallace said, "It's too late to talk," and explained as calmly as he could why it was in Bauer's best interest to comply.

Bauer accused Wallace again of screwing with him and tried to headbutt him when Wallace pushed him into the backseat. Wallace leaned to avoid the blow and swung a right fist, hitting Bauer below the left ear. Stunned, Bauer fell into the backseat, then rolled onto his back and began kicking Wallace, landing blows to his hands, arms, and torso. At nearly sixty, Wallace was about forty years older than Bauer. Wallace felt the pain, but he didn't realize that one of Bauer's kicks had broken the ring finger of his right hand.

Wallace pushed Bauer back inside the car, but before he could close the door Bauer sat up, jumped onto the road, and began running. Wallace stuck out a leg and tripped him. Bauer fell on the asphalt, face down. Wallace put a knee to the back of his neck, snatched the Taser from his service belt, removed the cartridge, and held the point to Bauer's throat, threatening to tase him if he didn't comply and go quietly.

"Fuck you," Bauer said. He began struggling to get up.

For two seconds, Wallace administered something called a dry stun, which hurts like hell but doesn't leave the victim flopping like a trout on the river bank.

"Okay, okay, I give, I give," Bauer said. "I'll get in the car."

All the way to the Lassen County Adult Detention Facility in Susanville in the back of Wallace's cruiser, Bauer shouted obscenities. And he continued once they got inside the place where he would, as it turned out, spend the next eight months. He was so mouthy and obnoxious during the booking process that the deputies threatened to restrain him physically.

The date was August 25, 2009—two years and a day since Jim Hough's suicide for arson after Josh White had arrested him, and a week short of two years since the Moonlight Fire.

Four days later, the State of California, followed quickly by the United States of America, filed lawsuits. Though no state or federal investigators had contacted Ryan Bauer; though neither Joshua White nor Dave Reynolds nor anyone from Cal Fire or the U.S. Forest Service or the U.S. Department of Justice visited Bauer at home or in his jail cell to analyze his behavior, weigh his statements, assess his body language, or examine for any of the other telltale symptoms of possible guilt taught at the California Conference on Arson Investigators; though no one in any position of power or influence insisted that Bauer try to reconcile his stories that contradicted both his father's and the verifiable facts; though no one asked Andrea Terry to verify whether her ex-boyfriend Ryan Bauer had indeed "spent the day" with her— which she couldn't have, as she later testified, because he had not spent the day with her—the authorities targeted their culprits: Sierra Pacific Industries, Howell's Forest Harvesting, landowner W. M. Beaty, and dozer drivers J.W. Bush and Kelly Crismon.

In Joshua White's origin and cause investigation report, appended to the lawsuit, the only mentions of Ryan Bauer and his father were in the notes of his witness interviews with Dieter Schmitt and George Gonzales, conducted four days after the Moonlight Fire had begun:

> On September 7, 2007 at about 1:50 P.M., Investigator George Gonzalez and I interviewed Edwin Bauer at the Westwood Cal-Fire Station. Bauer said he and his wife were walking their dog near the lake in the Moonlight Road area around 12:00 noon on September 3rd, 2007. Bauer said they left to get the mail, saw smoke and stopped at the visitor center to get a better look. Bauer said they then drove down toward the fire area. Bauer said when they drove to a trailer and determined the fire was in the area his son (Ryan Bauer) worked. Bauer said Ryan Bauer works as a faller for Howell Forest Products.
>
> Bauer said he saw one engine and co-op Forest Patrolman Leo Whitlock. Bauer said Whitlock told them they didn't want to be in the area the way the fire was moving. Bauer said he took his advice and turned around and started following Whitlock out.
>
> Bauer said Whitlock had the road blocked for a while talking to someone in a green fire truck. Bauer said while he was waiting for Whitlock to move, a male driver in a silver truck drove up and stopped, and appeared to be talking on a CB radio. Bauer said he asked the driver in the silver truck how the fire started. Bauer said the driver replied that a bulldozer hit a rock.
>
> Gonzalez asked Bauer who the man was in the silver truck. Bauer said we might have to ask Ryan Bauer.
>
> Bauer said he determined Ryan Bauer wasn't in the fire area at the time. Bauer said he phoned Ryan Bauer to ask if he knew anything about the fire. Bauer said he found out Ryan Bauer was driving in to the fire area to retrieve his personal chainsaws that he left out there. Bauer said he told Ryan Bauer to stay out of the area but he hung up on him.
>
> Bauer said he could not remember the name of the company that Ryan Bauer works for because he hasn't worked there that long. Bauer said that was the crew that ended up starting the fire according to the statement of the driver of the silver pickup.

Their report about Ryan Bauer was similarly devoid of specifics and interpretation:

On September 7, 2007 at about 2:12 P.M., Investigator George Gonzalez and I interviewed Ryan Bauer at the Westwood Cal-Fire station. I asked Ryan Bauer if I could record the interview and he said yes. Ryan Bauer said he was employed by Howell's Forest Harvesting. Ryan Bauer said he was not working on September 3rd, 2007, the day of the Moonlight fire. Ryan Bauer said Bush and Crismon were operating bulldozers and constructing water bars that day. Ryan Bauer said he called Eunice Howell, the owner of the company, to let her know about the fire but she already knew about it.

Ryan Bauer said he noticed the fire about 3:00 P.M. from his girlfriend's house in Westwood. Ryan Bauer said he went to the fire to see if he could assist in getting equipment out of the fire area. Ryan Bauer said upon his arrival to the fire, fire suppression resources had already arrived.

Ryan Bauer said an employee of Medici logging company, Bush, Crismon, the Forest Service and the Forest Patrolman were in the fire area. Ryan Bauer said he had been working at the job for about three weeks. Ryan Bauer said that as a faller, they use their own chainsaws at work.

Gonzalez asked Ryan Bauer if someone had told him that a bulldozer started the fire. Ryan Bauer said Bush and Crismon told him. Ryan Bauer said he did not want it repeated because he did not want to lose his job. Ryan Bauer asked me to turn off the recorder. I turned off the recorder at approximately 2:30 P.M.

Ryan Bauer said Bush and Crismon were both operating bulldozers. Ryan Bauer said one (Operator) was in section one (1) and one was in section three (3). Ryan Bauer said he didn't know who was in which section. Ryan Bauer said Bush and Crismon told him they must have kicked up a spark and started the fire. Ryan Bauer said that Bush was blaming Crismon and Crismon was blaming Bush.

I asked Ryan Bauer if I could turn the recorder back on and he said yes. I turned the recorder back on at approximately 2:32 P.M. and concluded the interview.

36

Red Emmerson and John Crook had joint-ventured on several deals, including the Weyerhaeuser plant, since their first mill a few years before. Emmerson liked and admired Crook. Crook's college education impressed Emmerson, who hadn't had one and at the time still considered a formal education essential for business success.

In business the two had disagreed rarely. Emmerson could remember only the time in 1966 when they partnered on about 60 million feet of timber from a government sale in Inyokern and couldn't see eye to eye right away over how to build the mill. Crook wanted a simple two-by-four stud mill, maximum eight feet, and Emmerson wanted something bigger, more elaborate than just another ordinary stud mill. That dispute held up construction for a while until they agreed to erect the structure in a way that would allow for later expansion.

By 1969 social and economic forces had already begun to shrink the size of the lumber pie. Marginal mill owners and suppliers were being driven out of business, so survival required doing things better as a way of maintaining and then growing market share. For Emmerson, distribution was still primarily through the same wholesalers he'd always done business with, and his sales force—to the degree it existed—was noticeably unsophisticated. As always, most of Emmerson's lumber ended up in Southern California.

For John Crook, business as usual wasn't good enough. He had bigger, more elaborate—indeed, national—plans, and in Red Emmerson he saw someone who might help him realize them. One of Crook's visions was to found a chain of what would, in time, be called big-box stores selling do-it-yourself home-improvement items. This was a decade before Home Depot was founded in 1979.

One day Crook approached Emmerson with an idea about raising the kind of serious capital that would allow them to expand their business in any direction they might choose: merge several of the businesses they owned separately into a single entity and join it with the ventures they were already operating together, then file a public stock offering for a minority share of the resulting company.

Emmerson didn't much like the idea of people he didn't know—or even, for that matter, people he *did* know—looking over his shoulder or riffling through his drawers as he conducted business. He'd always done things his way and didn't want to have to explain to anyone what he was doing with the company that he'd built with his own two hands. On the other hand, he would also have preferred not to have to explain everything to Frank Keene at Bank of America each time he needed financing.

Emmerson talked to some underwriters and discovered that, in fact, the prospect was even better than what Crook had explained. He learned that (a) there would be underwriters willing to sign on to this deal, and (b) they could sell a mere 20 percent of the new entity to the public—thereby remaining majority shareholders and maintaining their free hand in operations—for more than Emmerson's estimate of what the entire entity would be worth.

"It seemed too good to be true," Emmerson remembers. "But it was true."

Red and Crook interviewed several underwriters before settling on White, Weld and Co. in San Francisco, who spent the next several months valuing their assets and certifying the findings. On January 31, 1969, the businesses were formally melded into a company named Sierra Pacific Industries.

The name was the winning entry in a contest open to employees of the various merged companies, with the winner selected by Emmerson and Crook. A public offering of seven hundred thousand shares at $18 a share was issued, equivalent to about 20 percent of SPI's established book value. Red and John Crook each retained exactly 40 percent, making them coequals in terms of votes. Among the company's assets touted by the underwriters in a press release were four sawmills, a board plant, a millwork plant, and SPI's standing in the top dozen lumber producers and top ten particleboard manufacturers in the United States.

Not till later would Emmerson spot the catch in the deal, and by then it was too late.

37

Though there were several codefendants, no one doubted that the real target of the federal and state lawsuits was Sierra Pacific Industries, owned by the billionaire Red Emmerson, which had far more to lose than any of the other defendants—and which, more importantly, was the only defendant with assets worth pursuing. The two dozer drivers, Bush and Crismon, could certainly not be held financially liable in a way worth pursuing, which made their naming as defendants odd. And Eunice Howell had already been bankrupted a year earlier, after she'd unquestioningly paid Cal Fire's invoices totaling more than $40,000 for two of the four fires it claimed her company had started in the summer of 2007. All of them, the agency insisted, were sparked by dozers striking rocks, though not once in her company's forty-year history, since her husband began Howell's, had a dozer ever sparked a fire. That left W. M. Beaty, the company that managed the private forest lands for a consortium of families who owned the thousand or so acres on which Howell's had been cutting, as the only other viable defendant from which enough fines could be extracted to make the prosecution worthwhile. Based on the record and the belief that the prosecutors' real target was SPI, it seems reasonable to deduce that Beaty may have been tempted many times over the ensuing years to suggest that a separate peace with the prosecutors seemed like a cheap and an attractive option. After all, Beaty's only real asset was land, not money. But a reading of the record also suggests that Beaty's attorneys, the Sacramento firm of Matheny, Sears, Linkert, and Jaime, understood that Bill Warne at Downey Brand was fighting for SPI's literal survival as a company, and they were therefore strategically wise enough to know that Warne should be lead dog on a sled that they shouldn't step off of.

Warne had, as he'd promised SPI's in-house counsel Dave Dun, assembled a team of associates and partners capable of finding every flaw in the government's case. There were, at times, eight of them working simultaneously, dividing up the work like a special forces unit, each with a critical mission, every time crates of boxes came in during the discovery process. Every word of every report was scrutinized and summarized. Every component of Joshua White's "Origin and Cause Investigative Report, Moonlight Fire" was evaluated both analytically and by experts in the field hired by Downey Brand. Every photo was studied by multiple eyes against the timeline.

Leading the case against the defendants on behalf of the state of California from her office in Sacramento was Deputy Attorney General Tracy Winsor, a graduate of the University of California at Davis, fifteen miles west of the state capital, who'd earned her bar card in 1996 after attending the UC Davis school of law. She and her federal counterparts had entered into a joint prosecution agreement, and proceeded more or less in unison, given that they would be essentially trying the same case, with the same discovery and preparation. Documents and strategies were shared freely, and lawyers from both the state and the federal government were present at almost every deposition. Winsor, though, would have to wait to try the state's case, or settle it, until after the feds.

The original assistant U.S. attorney assigned out of Sacramento in the Eastern District of California to prosecute the case against SPI in the fall of 2009 was Robert Wright. Months later, at the beginning of a conference call that had been scheduled between the two sides with the federal magistrate who'd been assigned to the case to rule on motions and other court business, Assistant U.S. Attorney Kelli Taylor came on the line instead of Wright and informed everyone that Wright was off the case. Bill Warne asked if he was all right, and Taylor snapped, "He's off the case. Why do you care?" Warne suspected that there was much more to the substitution, but asking Ben Wagner, the U.S. attorney for the Eastern District of California, was not an option. (Wright would eventually file a sworn declaration that contained all the unpleasant details, including the implication that he'd been removed for, in essence, his honesty and integrity.)

Before joining the Department of Justice, Kelli Taylor had spent the decade since graduating the University of San Diego School of Law in litigation at a large private law firm, Bullivant Houser Bailey, with offices in several Western cities, including Sacramento. Her bio listed mold, asbestos, and hydrocarbon claims as her specialties in toxic tort liability. For at least the end of her term there, she'd made partner, so her reasons for moving to the Department of Justice, where even the U.S. attorney general earns less than what she was presumably making, are open to conjecture.

In any event, Taylor had now been assigned the case that offered her the opportunity to bring home the largest civil payout for an act of negligence on federal wildlands in U.S. history. A year later, her Department of Justice superiors apparently suggested that she could benefit from an experienced second chair to help her shape the case, devise strategy, and fight Downey Brand.

That someone was Eric Overby, veteran head of the Department of Justice's Affirmative Civil Enforcement (ACE) unit in Utah. ACE's mission statement is to recover costs from people and companies who cause harm or other losses to public lands and property "or [who] seek to defraud the United States of public funds." Overby accepted the offer, which entailed relocating to Sacramento for as long as it took to finish this case, even if it lasted years—and it looked like it might if SPI and the other defendants couldn't be coerced or persuaded into settling for, say, $150 million instead of the billion or so, with interest, the government was seeking. Overby showed up ready to work in March 2011.

Overby was an aggressive choice. In the previous few years he'd sued the Boy Scouts for millions of dollars after a wildfire in northeastern Utah, sparked accidentally by some scouts, burned over fourteen thousand acres. He had joined with a whistleblower to sue a company that was making faulty flares being bought by the Department of Defense for military use. He had sued Union Pacific Railroad to recover damages incurred fighting a 3,200-acre wildfire in Price Canyon that the government alleged had been caused by a faulty turbo charger on a locomotive "emitting sparks" that ignited "dry grasses and combustible materials." And he had gone after a world-renowned paleontologist for buying rare fragmentary allosaurus remains from someone who'd claimed they'd come from private land but which Overby insisted was federal land. The paleontologist, among others, complained endlessly that he was being ruthlessly hounded for what was, at worst, an innocent mistake.

Clearly, Eric Overby was unafraid of hard, dirty work in pursuit of cost recovery and would be someone whom Kelli Taylor could count on to help her win this case and collect from SPI. But did Taylor want help? Though Overby had already appeared by himself at several depositions as the government's attorney representing federal witnesses and had corresponded directly numerous times with Bill Warne's office on scheduling matters, Taylor may not have wanted to share the glory.

On Friday, May 6, 2011, at 2:08 P.M., she sent an email to Warne responding to a request he had made to Overby, for more deposition time with some United States witnesses than had originally been allotted by the court.

"Mr. Warne," Taylor began, "I heard you just approached Eric Overby regarding a request for more depositions and to extend the expert disclosures. All discussions regarding these topics must occur only with me. Please do not approach others from my office regarding these topics and know that I am the only one who can grant authority for such changes. I do not believe any good cause for even more delays. I am available Monday, May 9 between 9 and 10 for our meet and confer on this. Thanks and have a nice weekend.—Kelli"

At the time she sent that message, Warne was in a deposition and couldn't respond for two and a half hours:

Ms. Taylor, I cannot abide by your rather strange instructions. This case is moving too rapidly and the issues are too numerous for us to direct all such communications to you. There are numerous depositions wherein you are not present, and so face to face discussions with AUSAs [Assistant U.S. Attorneys] who are present are critical. You seek input and continuance from all members of the Downey Brand team, and you are welcome to continue to do so. If there is something they cannot handle on their own or without my approval, then they seek input from me. I suggest that you do the same, as we will continue speaking with all AUSAs working on behalf of the USFS regarding this matter. Please feel free to contact me if you have any questions. Regards, Bill

Nine minutes later came Taylor's reply:

Mr. Warne—You are *on notice* that I am the only one with authority to make decisions in this case. Thus, if you choose to talk with others understand that they have no authority to make the decisions and you will still need to set a time to meet and confer directly with me. I am readily available by cell and email and always happy to set up a specific time to meet and confer on these topics. I anticipate that we will always be able to talk within 24 hours so you are welcome to send an email anytime indicating that you would like to do so. With respect to the deposition and schedule issues you raised today I already suggested we talk Monday at 9. If that time is inconvenient please suggest an alternative. I am even willing to talk on weekends and after hours so just let me know. Thanks—Kelli

Seven minutes later, at 4:50 P.M., Warne replied:

Ms. Taylor, Again, I intend to speak directly with those that attend depositions. I have no choice but to do so as issues arise when they are present and since the deadlines are rapidly approaching. I am not sure why you are sharing your thoughts on this front with me. If you wish to tell the other AUSA's working on this case that they are not to speak with any attorneys, or that they are not allowed to make any decisions without your express approval, that's your business. I think the approach that the Downey Brand team is using is much more sensible, and I would suggest you adopt it as well. Regards, Bill

It took Taylor seven minutes to compose and send a response:

Mr. Warne—I am not sure why you are resistant to this request. It will always be more efficient for you to talk directly with the decision maker than to have to have multiple conversations with people who do not have authority and then to have to have the same conversation with me. You already have my email and my cell is [redacted]. Please feel free to call me anytime including on breaks at deposition, on the way to/from depositions, on weekends, in the evening or whenever you wish to discuss the case. As you note there is a lot going on so let's be as efficient as possible. Thanks—Kelli

Ten minutes later Warne sent this:

Ms. Taylor, I find this exchange completely unnecessary. When things arise, and AUSA's are in the room, we will discuss the issues. Those who we speak to can then speak to you, if that's what you think is appropriate given the issues that arise. As to efficiency, as you know, there have been a number of requests which we have made of you which have gone unanswered for weeks, and a number of requests that remain outstanding. Moreover, as you have personally witnessed, Downey Brand's team system has provided you, Mr. Pickles [another AUSA in Taylor's office] and Mr. Overby with terrific access and quick answers to questions. Regards, Bill

At 5:13, Taylor sent the last of the emails in the thread, Warne having nothing further to say:

Mr. Warne—Your decision to go to people without decision making authority is causing some of the alleged 'delays' you are now complaining about. Again, if you direct the inquiries to me they will be responded to faster and definitively. If you continue to employ the approach you are taking you are creating unnecessary inefficiency since it will then require multiple conversations. You have my cell so feel free to call when questions arise. As for emails, it is as easy to send them to me than it is to send them to anyone else on the team. Thanks and have a safe trip back from the deposition.—Kelli

The "safe trip" referred to Taylor's knowing that the deposition Warne had been taking was at the Gaia Anderson Hotel, in Anderson, California, three hours' drive north of Warne's office in Sacramento and, coincidentally, the home of Sierra Pacific's corporate offices, a sawmill, and one of the company's cogeneration plants. The deponent was Dave Harp, Josh White's supervisor at the time of the Moonlight Fire, who had retired and now lived in Anderson. And the federal prosecutor who'd driven up to Anderson as a representative of the U.S. Department of Justice was Eric Overby.

Taylor had initiated this email exchange on a Friday afternoon when Overby was out of town, not to return to the office until Monday. On every email in the thread, she had CC'ed other lawyers in Warne's office, another assistant United States attorney from her own office, and Overby himself, knowing that he and Warne would be together, each reading the emails in real time on their smart phones or laptops.

If the intent was to humiliate an attorney whom she apparently saw as a threat to her hegemony, it worked. Overby let Warne know how disgusted he was with Taylor's behavior and said that, "by this coming Monday," he would either be in control of the case or have nothing to do with it.

Sometime the following week, after the last of Josh White's thirteen protracted and grueling days of testimony as a deponent, Overby called Bill Warne and asked to see him. Warne said sure, and Overby came by the office, where he plopped down in a chair. What Warne suspected he'd hear was what Overby soon confirmed: less than two months after arriving in California but having familiarized himself with the bulk of the evidence against SPI, he was choosing to go home to Utah.

He said, "If I thought there was anything positive that would result from staying, then I would stay," and likened his situation to a physics problem. "If I'm banging my head against a brick wall, then my head loses. In my entire career—yes, my entire career—I have never seen anything like this. Never."

By suggesting that Warne contact the deputy attorney general in Washington, Overby strongly implied that if this case had been his, he may have dropped it for lack of evidence of liability. This comported with Warne's prior impression that Robert Wright had been moved off the case for the same reason, replaced by Taylor, who, either on her own or at the direction of her boss, David Shelledy, was willing to ignore the improprieties in the investigation and do whatever it took to win this case and perhaps hundreds of millions of dollars.

A few days earlier, Overby told Warne, he'd had a screaming match with someone in his office whom he didn't identify. "It's called the Department of Justice," Overby had told him. "It's not called the Department of Revenue. And since we're the Department of Justice, we win if justice wins."

38

Even considering the $5 million that the public offering of Sierra Pacific put into his pocket, Red Emmerson insists he knew from day one that joining forces with John Crook and going public was a misbegotten enterprise. The omen, he says, could be seen in the company's share price, which briefly hit $19 before sinking back to about $17. Over the next five years, it would sometimes trade as low as $10 but never above $20.

"John wanted to go one direction and I wanted to go another," Emmerson remembers. "He was chairman and I was president, and it was kind of a dogfight on what we wanted to do. We just couldn't agree. There were certain things he wanted to do and get involved with, some crappy little businesses that I thought we should stay away from, like Rocky Mountain Stairs and Gyrotex. John wanted to get into the nursery business. He wanted to get into the big-box business. He wanted to get into the home-building business—everything but the business that we paid our bills with. He thought sawmills were bad business. He thought the grass was greener across the street."

Emmerson likens the partnership to a bad marriage that had started out as a torrid love affair. "The more we got into it, the less it worked. Nobody gets married thinking it's going to be a disaster. You only find out if it is afterward. And for a long time you keep trying to make things work."

The complicated portion can be ascribed to what Emmerson deems his "insecurities" at the time. "I was pretty naïve. John was much more worldly. He'd been to college, and I hadn't, and I gave that a lot of weight—more than I should have. Except for the marines, I'd never been out and around very much. I looked up to him. I looked up to what I thought he knew from being exposed to so much more. I didn't have the self-confidence that he had."

By the end of its first year as a public corporation, SPI employed 850, had nearly 3,000 shareholders, showed a net worth of about $12 million —and posted a net loss of $76,000, about two cents a share.

Losing money was bad enough. But for Emmerson, having to explain in the annual statement that lumber prices were down substantially from the previous year and that operating expenses were higher than anticipated was misery.

The year could be summed up, Emmerson explains, by the story of what happened to SPI's 51 percent interest in the Reeve Investment Company, founded by one Earl Reeve for the purpose of buying and leasing back industrial properties—exactly the type of thing that John Crook wanted to do more of. After a site for a shopping center was located and the property purchased, construction began on the first large structure, and before anything else could be completed, the structure burned. To the ground. End of story. Money gone.

Although he'd been trying to hide his dissatisfaction while trying to persuade himself that he and Crook and SPI had a future together, several people noticed the change in Emmerson. He no longer seemed himself.

"I always tried not to bring work home with me, not to talk about it with Ida or the kids," he remembers. "But Ida knew, and I'll bet the kids did too, in their own way. I wasn't enjoying my work."

By the fifth year, Emmerson could no longer hide from anyone how miserable he was. Worse, he knew he was letting down his shareholders. SPI's stock price closed 1973 at $9—half of its initial trading price four years earlier.

Emmerson met with Frank Keene at Bank of America in San Francisco and declared that he wanted out. Keene, knowing Emmerson as well as he did, agreed that that sounded like the only good solution.

The actual getting out would be the hard part. So far as Emmerson could see, Crook wasn't likely to agree on buying out Emmerson's shares at an agreeable price, only at the current share price. But to Emmerson, that didn't represent a fair value.

Emmerson, on the other hand, was willing to buy out Crook's shares at $18 per share—the original price of the stock the day it went public.

That plan, presented to John Crook as contingent on Emmerson's securing the financing, had a good chance of flying. But what Emmerson didn't want to end up with was 80 percent ownership of a public company and the headaches of still having to answer to shareholders.

He'd have to raise enough capital to buy out Crook and take the whole thing private. Keene agreed to back Emmerson. And so it was that Archie Aldis "Red" Emmerson was now personally on the hook to Bank of America for $20 million—and in some ways starting over.

39

Bulldozer driver J.W. Bush was fifty-five years old when he was deposed over three consecutive days at the end of April 2010, within weeks of Ryan Bauer's first three days as a deponent. Wearing wire-rimmed glasses and a brown pullover sweater over a cream polo shirt, he had graying brown hair that had receded to the top of his head, long sideburns, and a graying mustache.

Bush said he had completed the ninth grade before dropping out of school and working odd jobs, eventually finding himself in the logging business by starting as a knot bumper and later becoming a skidder operator, which he'd been for about twenty-five years at the time of the Moonlight Fire. He was able to reconstruct for the lawyers with varying degrees of detail what he did the day of the fire, beginning from the time he began work that morning. He was insistent that he did not tell anyone from the forest service that Kelly Crismon's Caterpillar had had something to do with starting the fire; he did not believe Crismon's Caterpillar had started the fire because he had seen nothing to base that opinion on.

"Is it possible," Deputy Attorney General Tracy Winsor asked him, "that you just don't recall saying that Cat tracks scraped rock to cause a fire regarding the Moonlight Fire?"

"No," Bush said.

"So you're absolutely certain that you never said that."

"No."

"That you never said Cat tracks scraped rocks to cause the Moonlight Fire?"

"No."

"Not to the Forest Service?"

"No."

"And not in front of anyone else?"

"No."

When he was shown the witness report filled out by Reynolds that bore his signature, Bush denied talking to Reynolds in the early minutes of the fire. He insisted the interview had taken place after that afternoon, though he could not recall how many days later.

"Do you remember being asked to give a statement by a Forest Service investigator on the day of the Moonlight Fire?" Winsor asked.

"Not then."

"Do you agree with me that the date of the Moonlight Fire was September 3, 2007?"

"Yeah."

"Okay. Okay. When do you think you gave a statement to the forest service?"

"He came to camp."

"So he came after?"

"Yeah."

"Okay. All right. And what do you recall telling the gentleman from the Forest Service?"

"That I just saw this fire."

"Do you recall telling the Forest Service investigator that Kelly was working in the area water barring?"

"Yeah."

"And do you recall telling that person that Kelly was operating closest to the fire area?"

"Yes."

"And do you recall telling the Forest Service investigator that you believed Cat tracks scraped rock to cause the fire?"

"No."

"Do you recall signing the statement that you made to the Forest Service?"

"Yeah."

"Can you please take a look at Exhibit 39. And can you please read for me the very last sentence, if you're able to make it out?"

"I can't see part of it."

Winsor said, "The first word, I think, is 'believes.'"

"Yeah."

Phillip Bonotto, who was the attorney for Howell's Forest Harvesting, which in effect made him Bush's attorney, asked, "Can you read that?"

"No," Bush said.

"Mr. Bush," Winsor said gingerly, "I hate to ask this statement, and I don't want to pry, but are you able to read?"

"No."

"Okay."

"Some," Bush said.

"Some?"

"Yeah."

"Okay. When you made a statement to the Forest Service, did the person that took your words down—did the person that took your statement write your words down as you were talking?"

"I can't recall. I don't think so."

"You did sign a document, though, that related to the statement that you gave to the Forest Service, right?"

"Not that day."

"So tell me," Winsor said, "to the best of your recollection what day you gave a statement to the Forest Service."

"That was the second or third day."

On his final day as a deponent, Winsor asked Bush questions about his relationship with Ryan Bauer. Bush said he hadn't really had a relationship with Bauer, had never socialized with him and couldn't remember talking to him on the job, since Bush drove equipment and Bauer worked on the ground as a knot bumper. Then Winsor asked if he'd spoken to Bauer about the fire. Bush couldn't remember if it was a "day after or three days after," but certainly not the day of the fire, that he remembered standing with Crismon on the mountain. Bauer, he said, showed up and more or less eavesdropped on their conversation about having overheard a forest service employee tell someone that the fire may have been started by equipment.

"In that conversation," Winsor asked, "did you and Kelly talk about whose equipment was closer to where the fire was?"

"No, we didn't."

"Do you remember talking to Kelly about whether or not equipment may have caused the fire?"

"No."

Near the end of the deposition, Winsor asked Bush several questions about whether he had any reason to believe Ryan Bauer had set the fire. Bush said no.

Winsor asked, "Is it fair to say that whoever may—whatever caused the fire, the fire started to become very fierce, if you will, between the time you left and the time you came back?"

"I wouldn't know," Bush said.

"Well," Winsor said, "when you left at approximately 1:10, there was no fire that you saw, right?"

"Right."

"When you came back, was that about an hour later?"

"Probably a little less. Whatever it took to get down [to his trailer] and back."

"So, forty, fifty minutes?"

"Probably, yeah."

"And between those two times, first there was no fire you could observe, and then you came back and it was very, very smoky and hot. Correct? . . . And all of that had to happen in the forty to fifty minutes that you were gone, right?"

"Yes."

"Do you have any opinion as to how that fire got so big and hot in that short of a period of time?"

Bush speculated that the winds may have driven it, and Winsor asked about George Bullard, who Bush earlier had quoted telling him he'd seen Ryan Bauer "flying out of the area." She asked, "Did you use those words, 'flying out'?"

"Yeah," he said.

Now Winsor led Bush through a series of questions intended to demonstrate that Bush's own timeline did not support the defense's possible theory that Ryan Bauer had started the fire (by accident with an illegally souped-up chainsaw missing a spark arrester) in the time Bush was away.

But it was an ironic line of questioning for a Moonlight Fire prosecutor whose case against Sierra Pacific and the other defendants was essentially built on J.W. Bush's statement to USFS investigator Dave

Reynolds, which Reynolds claimed had been made at 3:30 that afternoon, blaming Crismon's Caterpillar for sparking the fire—something Bush could have known to report only if he had seen flames.

If Winsor was stipulating that the fire had not begun before Bush left the area ("Well, when you left at approximately 1:10, there was no fire that you saw, right?"), she was tacitly confirming that White and Reynolds had no basis in fact for beginning their search for possible clues at the yard where the Caterpillars were parked, instead of around the area where the fire began. Which would necessarily imply that the fruits of their investigation were tainted by bias.

As Bill Warne would later note in a court filing, none of the lawyers on his Downey Brand team was prepared for the "pageantry of fraud," "scheme to defile our system of justice," "squall of dishonesty," and "nearly omnipresent investigative dishonesty" that they uncovered during the years of discovery. And each new revelation about the flawed investigation had raised the lawyers' expectation that both the state and the feds would be compelled by the accumulating evidence to abandon the prosecution, as is a prosecutor's legal, moral, and ethical obligation once a case has been revealed to be unjust. Not to do so, Warne wrote, twice citing Supreme Court cases establishing a prosecutor's "higher standard of behavior," would constitute a fraud on the court—and therefore on the entire system.

The case was not dropped by either the state of California or the United States of America.

40

Red Emmerson was even more relieved than he had expected to be after taking Sierra Pacific private. He slept soundly again, his enthusiasm for the business rekindled by focusing on SPI's core businesses of lumber and millwork, the same businesses John Crook had disdained.

The hours were long, and there were problems to be solved by the minute, but he calls this period "some of the happiest days of my life. I was the boss again, and I decided what would get pared down and where to pay more attention and where and how to capitalize on opportunities."

In Emmerson's mind, being able not just to service the debt but to pay back creditors early would be a good benchmark of how well the company was standing on its own feet. His immediate goal was to repay the Bank of America loan faster than even his most optimistic admirer could expect. He did. Within three years, far ahead of schedule, he'd repaid the loan in full.

41

Edwin "Eddy" Bauer and his wife Jennifer Bauer were deposed separately about their son Ryan's whereabouts on September 3, 2007. Jennifer had brown, shoulder-length hair and wire-rimmed glasses, and she wore a gray windbreaker over a cream-colored collarless sweater. She spoke in a tentative voice. Eddy's receding hairline and close-cropped brown hair made his burly shoulders appear larger. He had a brown goatee with flecks of gray on his wide face and wore a striped green and black shirt.

Their stories more or less jibed, down to both claiming to have overheard a grizzled man in a gray or silver pickup answer Eddy's question when they were stopped for a moment behind Leo Whitlock's truck in the fire's first minutes. A rock strike from a dozer, they said he'd told them, had been responsible.

They'd found themselves parked behind Whitlock's truck, both essentially said, because they had taken their short-haired pointer up the mountain to run free in a meadow. After an hour or so, near one o'clock, they drove back to town to pick up their mail from their post office box. From there, they claimed, they happened to glance up at the mountain and notice a small plume of smoke appearing to come from the approximate area where they'd been running the dog—an area several miles from Moonlight Peak, which was not visible from the post office.

They said they wondered if their own catalytic converter parked in the tall grass might have sparked the fire, though they'd been parked in the meadow long enough for the converter to cool and were there longer than necessary to note any flames that might have accidentally ignited when it was still hot.

Now, impelled by a surplus of anxiety, they drove up there to see if, in fact, they were unintentionally responsible for the fire, though they had no firefighting equipment with them and hadn't alerted anyone capable of actually extinguishing a blaze.

As they drove, they said, they were grateful they didn't have to worry about Ryan, who as far as they knew was still at home, possibly still sleeping; he didn't have to work that day and his truck was there when they'd left. And yet they worried that he really might be up there cutting firewood to sell. It was also possible that after they'd left home with the dog, someone from Howell's had called Ryan to come work.

The Bauers reached the meadow site and were relieved to see that the hot spot was not where they'd been—but nonetheless the fire further up was growing. Concerned, they claimed, about the well-being of their boy, they decided to trudge up the mountain in their truck, though they had no firm reason to believe he was actually on the mountain and hadn't yet called him to see if he would answer the phone at home. This put them in danger.

For the next fifteen or twenty minutes, they said, they ascended a steep trail known as the 3000 road, smoke from the fire close on the left side of the truck. Not until firefighting planes that had already been summoned to action began dropping the fire retardant borate too close for comfort did they abort their trek to find Ryan. Between the borate falling almost on top of the truck and the blazing fire itself, the Bauers were terrified. So after being stopped by private forestry patroller Leo Whitlock near where the 3016 and 3017 roads converge, a place not far from the yard where the Caterpillars used by Howell's dozer drivers were parked when not in use, they turned around and made their way down, following Whitlock's truck.

At some point near Five Corners, Whitlock stopped to speak to someone, and Eddy couldn't get by, they said. So while waiting he asked a grizzled man he happened to see sitting in a gray or silver pickup how the fire started. That man, who just happened to be one of two Caterpillar drivers working on a day when every other Howell's employee had the day off, happened to volunteer that he already knew a rock strike had started it. This happened to be the same man whom Ryan would later claim told him the same story, repeated by the other dozer driver, each of them blaming the other.

Rather than going home, Eddy and Jennifer testified, they parked at Five Corners, where officials from the U.S. Forest Service and Cal Fire were stopping civilian vehicles on the way up the mountain; only firefighters or authorized personnel were allowed up. They watched the fire spreading quickly in the distance, smoke thickening, and tried calling Ryan. He didn't answer, which they interpreted as confirmation of his being on the mountain and, therefore, good cause to worry for his well-being.

Both parents acknowledged that at the time of the Moonlight Fire, their son Ryan was addicted to OxyContin, Norco, and methadone. Both had seen him crush pills and snort them.

Jennifer said that the day after the fire, Ryan told her that "a guy named Bush" told him the fire had been started "by hitting a rock with a bulldozer." She said Eddy was there when Ryan said this.

Asked whether he'd told Leo Whitlock that they were looking for their son on the mountain, Eddy said, "You know, this is where it gets confusing—reading reports and this and that. I might have mentioned something, that I might have been concerned that my kid might have been up there or whatever, since he worked up there. This could have happened. It could not have happened. I don't recall."

Asked if Ryan had told him that he planned to cut firewood that day, Eddy said, "I think he might have said he was going to cut some firewood, so that's why we might have had some concern. I don't—you know, all I know is, he was at his girlfriend's house. . . . That's where he was all day."

Jennifer said she remembered asking Ryan whether he was involved somehow in the fire because, she explained, Eddy had suggested that he "may have been involved." Why did Eddy suggest that? "He thought Ryan was up there, so he was trying to find if he was, and that he didn't want Ryan to be any part of that fire. And so I asked him, just point-blank: 'Did you have anything to do with that fire? Do you know anything that you might have done?' He goes, 'I wasn't there.'"

Jennifer Bauer did not explain why either she or Eddy would wonder about their son's possible involvement in light of their claims, made separately, to have heard a grizzled man in his gray or silver pickup truck admit to Eddy in the fire's first hour that a rock strike had been responsible. Nor did Eddy explain why he told investigators Schmitt and Gonzales, four days later, that Ryan had told him he'd planned to cut trees that day, or why he told Ryan, over the phone, in a conversation that was recorded, "I thought you said you went out there that morning and cut trees."

Asked about his interview with investigators Schmitt and Gonzales, Eddy insisted that everything he'd told them on September 7 was "one hundred percent correct."

42

In Red Emmerson's memory, the years 1974 to 1988 were essentially the "good old days"—plenty of hard work but otherwise unremarkable. When he thinks of particulars, few stand out, not even SPI's first major acquisition after going private again: the 1976 purchase of three Sierra sawmills and some timberlands from the DiGiorgio Lumber Company.

What does come to mind is the purchase of two sawmills and eighty-six thousand acres of timberland at Burney, on the southeast perimeter of Shasta National Forest (northwest of Susanville). Publishers, headquartered in Oregon City, Oregon, on the Willamette River, had just joined with corporate giant Crown-Zellerbach to undertake a cleanup of the river and, in a possibly related decision, also decided to divest its Northern California holdings. That provided an opportunity for Emmerson and SPI—but determining whether the price and the property were a good match would not be easy. It would, however, be a good test of his instincts for the business.

He met with Publishers' principals both in Redding and Oregon City throughout the late summer. At issue were the previous surveys of the property, which were deemed unreliable because the syndicate that had surveyed the Big Bend–Curl Ridge areas of the property, northeast of Redding, had been convicted of falsifying the reports as a way to defraud the government by investigating only a small portion of certain townships. But when Emmerson pulled the trigger, he more than doubled SPI's timberlands acreage—to 130,000 total acres.

Even so, Red Emmerson insists he was no Nostradamus when it came to predicting how thoroughly the environmental movement would eventually impact the lumber business. At the time, timber sales put up by the USFS were still the primary way companies like SPI bought the logs they turned into lumber. And, he explains, if you had asked him on the first Earth Day, in 1970, whether this would become a serious political movement with clout to match, he would have laughed. "There was," he says, "no way to know that one day finding trees to cut would be a problem for lumbermen."

In retrospect, Emmerson believes the movement began in earnest in 1973, with President Nixon's signature on the Endangered Species Act that Congress had just passed, "endangered species" being defined as any species "in danger of extinction throughout all or a significant portion of its range." The law gave the government power to impose limitations on activities that might affect those species.

One of the species on that first list of those considered endangered was the northern spotted owl, which resides in the old-growth forests of the Northwest and whose native importance to the ecology, as distinct from any other kind of owl, didn't have to be established in order for it to deserve protection. Its de facto status automatically conferred its de jure status.

Three years later, under President Ford, came the National Forest Management Act, which required the forest service to "maintain viable populations of existing native and desired non-native vertebrate species in the planning area," with "viable population" defined as "one which has the estimated numbers and distribution of reproductive individuals to insure its continued existence is well distributed in the planning area."

With this law the noose appeared to be tightening for the logging industry; and indeed, a year later, the USFS and the Bureau of Land Management began trying to preserve old-growth forests around spotted owls. Not yet, however, did there appear to be any decrease in the number of timber sales or the amount of public lands declared off-limits to loggers.

Then in 1978 President Carter added some fifty thousand acres to Redwood National Park, effectively doubling overnight the size of the park, which had been created a decade before by President Johnson.

Though that change under Carter didn't directly affect SPI because the company wasn't involved in redwood milling, there were some serious companies, including Louisiana-Pacific (whose dealings with SPI back then were in part triggered by the park expansion) and Arcata Redwood, that lost access to those raw materials and were none too happy about the change. Several logging companies had to lobby the federal government to make sure that the loss of timber created by the park's expansion was offset by access to other areas in Six Rivers National Forest and portions of Trinity and Klamath National Forests. The industry's lobbying arms had to work to strip out of Carter's bill a provision that would have allowed the Interior Department to regulate timber harvesting on remaining *private* lands in the Redwood Creek basin.

Maybe most telling of all was Secretary of the Interior Cecil Andrus's provisional plan, in conjunction with the bill, to replace lost logging jobs "and help diversify the local economy." This suggested that the government itself recognized that its cumulative policies so far, even before implementing future plans, would have a profound impact on the logging industry and the municipalities that were supported by it. It was therefore not paranoid to worry that if redwood was off-limits today, tomorrow might bring edicts against fir and pine.

"It was going to be harder to come by timber," Emmerson notes. "I'd begun to think of having land as security. If you owned land, you knew what your costs would be. If you were always going out and having to bid on other people's lands, whether they belonged to the government or a private owner, you'd never know and you'd always be at their mercy."

43

Ryan Bauer was serving the remainder of his eight-month sentence for attacking Deputy Sheriff Benny Wallace at the Lassen County Adult Detention Facility, a 156-bed, level-two prison in the California Department of Corrections, in Susanville, when he was deposed on March 29 and 30 and April 16, 2010, dressed in an orange California Department of Corrections prisoner's uniform while sitting in a room set aside for legal visits.

The government lawyers present at the deposition were California Deputy Attorney General Tracy Winsor and Assistant U.S. Attorney Todd Pickles. For the defendants: Richard Linkert on behalf of W. M. Beaty, Phillip Bonotto for Howell's Forest, and Bill Warne and Annie Amaral for Sierra Pacific Industries.

Also present to observe was Josh White, Cal Fire battalion chief.

As Bauer had been called as a plaintiff's witness, Winsor was the first questioner. Bauer explained that in late spring or early summer 2007, two years after graduating Westwood High School, he had driven out to a logging site run by Bill Dietrich and Eunice Howell, where he spoke to supervisor Damon Baker about employment. That site was on Moonlight Road in the vicinity of Cooks Creek. Bauer told Baker about his experience cutting firewood and claimed he would "fall timber, buck logs, limb them"—that is, cut down trees, cut them into length, get rid of extraneous limbs.

Bauer was not hired, though, until he spoke with Eunice Howell on the phone. The jobs were divided into logging, which was Howell's side of the operation, and falling, which fell under Bill Dietrich's purview. After the fire was out, the whole team went back to work salvaging the lumber that was still good. Bauer hurt himself in January 2008 and stopped work.

In his time on the mountain, he said, "There was always people going up Moonlight Road, up into those mountains, riding quads and dirt bikes." There were also hunters, and in the week before the fire he'd seen hunters on quads and wearing camouflage in the logging area.

"And do you recall how far from Moonlight Road they were when you saw them?" Winsor asked.

"They were right by it," Bauer said.

"Right by it?"

"Yeah. One time, they were right on the road. The other time, they were entering that 3131 Road."

"I'm going to leave that for now," Winsor said.

That the area where the fire had broken out was teeming with activity not noted in White's report may have seemed like a rabbit hole friendly to the defense.

But then Winsor asked Bauer whether he knew before that Labor Day which landing Bush and Crismon would have been working out of on that day, a day he acknowledged he hadn't been assigned to work.

"I wasn't there," he said. "I wouldn't know."

"Did you hear anything after the fire about what landing those skidder operators were working from on the Monday that the fire started?"

"What I heard was that they were making water bars."

"Let's just focus on the landing for now. Do you know what landing they were working out of?"

He said that he assumed that it had been the landing he'd helped move equipment to the previous week, "about a mile or two" away.

"Okay," Winsor said. "So you're not sure, but your guess is that the skidder operators on Monday were working out of the old landing where you put a circle on the map?"

"Yes."

"And what are you basing that on, that statement?"

"Hearsay," Bauer said.

"Okay. Do you recall anybody in particular telling you that those skidder operators were working out of the old landing?"

"Yes."

"Who would have told you that, if you recall?"

"After the fire, it was the talk of the town, so everybody was saying something about it, you know."

Some minutes later, Winsor asked him if he typically left his chainsaw or chainsaws up on the hillside overnight.

"Not that I recall," Bauer said. "I never did leave a saw up there."

Winsor asked if he had worked the Friday before Labor Day. He said he had. She asked if he knew that "there would be skidder operators doing some water barring on Monday."

"No, I didn't," he said.

"At some point, did you learn that people were doing water barring on Monday?"

"Yes."

"And how did you learn that?"

"After the fire."

"How close in time after the fire did you learn that there were some operators doing some water barring on Monday?"

"A couple of days."

Winsor asked Bauer how he had spent that Labor Day. He said he'd awakened at seven in his apartment on Cedar Street and spent most of the day with his girlfriend, Andrea Terry, at her parents' house, getting there around one—and calling her ahead of time to say he was coming. They went for a walk and watched movies and were in her front yard, "messing with her dogs or something," when he saw the smoke and called Eunice Howell. He said he then drove up there to try to help move out the equipment but was stopped by Cal Fire.

"So you were near the vicinity of the trailer when you got stopped?" Winsor asked.

"The trailer wasn't there at the time, but, yes," Bauer said. It had been "moved because of the fire" about "thirty minutes before I got there."

How did he know that?

"They told me that. J. Dub moved it."

"Who told you?"

"Kelly or J. Dub."

"Okay. So at some point, when you went out here to where the trailer used to be, did you run into Kelly?"

"Yeah, right where the fire crew was." He said he didn't remember anything specific that they talked about. "We were just conversating [*sic*]."

Before wrapping up her questions, Winsor marked an exhibit (no. 5) of excerpts from the investigation report, and Bill Warne interjected: "Can you ask if there's any other reason he went up to see the fire other than what he said, which was to help them out, before we try to refresh on this, because it's hearsay?"

Winsor did ask that. Bauer said no, then added, "I do recall why I went up there." Asked to clarify, he said, "I initially went up there to see what was going on. You know, I was a little worried about it. And once I got up there, I wanted to help pull out some equipment, if I could. I mean, they got a lot of money up there, loaders and whatnot."

"Would there have been any chainsaws up there, to your knowledge?" Winsor asked.

"Not to my knowledge," he said, "there wouldn't have been."

Winsor asked if he knew back then that he was obliged to tell the investigators the truth and whether he indeed did tell the truth. He said he did and had, apparently not remembering he had claimed more than two years before that he'd gone up there to rescue his chainsaws.

"Given that the events of the fire were pretty fresh in your mind at the time that you gave the statement, and that you were giving an interview to Cal Fire people and felt you should tell the truth," Winsor said, "do you believe that, to the best of your ability at that time, you truthfully and accurately related what you knew at the time?"

"Yes," Bauer said.

"So if, for example, you read something in your statement here, would you have any reason to believe that you were, for some reason, untruthful when you gave it?"

"Not to my knowledge."

When Bill Warne's turn came to question Ryan Bauer, he reminded the witness that he was under oath, an oath as binding as it would be in a court of law, and if he were found to be lying under oath, there could very well be legal consequences carrying a jail sentence for perjury. Bauer said he understood.

Warne asked Bauer from whom he'd heard, on the day of the fire, that there were already rumors going around Westwood to the effect that he'd been responsible for starting the fire.

Zack Hart, Bauer said, a longtime friend, had passed that onto him.

"Do you recall talking to Bill Dietrich on the day of the fire?" Warne asked.

"Yes."

"Do you recall meeting up with him after the fire started and talking to him about the fire?"

"Yes."

"Do you recall telling Bill Dietrich that you thought that people were trying to blame you for the fire?"

"On that day?"

"Yes."

"No."

"Do you recall ever telling Mr. Dietrich that you thought people were trying to blame you for the fire?"

"Yes."

"And when do you think you said that to Mr. Dietrich?"

"It was about a week after the fire, when he pulled me off the falling crew because people on the crew were, I guess, talking."

Warne then spent a long time leading Bauer through the "Hippie Dan is dead" rumor, which Bauer admitted hearing but denied having originated. Warne asked if it was possible that, maybe over beers, he'd made it up as a lark. "Is it possible that you did it?"

"No," Bauer said.

Winsor objected. "Calls for speculation," she said.

"I don't want you to speculate," Warne said. "Speculating is just pulling stuff out of your hat. I want you to tell me if you have any recollection whatsoever of saying anything to anybody about Dan hurting himself on the mountain."

"Quite honestly," Bauer said, "I've gone through enough with this situation about this story, and I'm not going to answer any more questions about it."

"Well, yeah, you are," Warne said. "And if I have to get a court order, you're going to answer every question I've got about it, sir, because that's the way this process works. I want you to understand that. And if I have to stop this deposition and go to court and get an order that forces you to come back and talk to me while you're here in this facility, that's exactly what I'm going to do. Do you understand that?"

"Yes," Bauer said.

Warne reminded him that he was obliged to answer, but Bauer continued to evade answering whether he'd started the lie about Hippie Dan.

"Not that I recall," Bauer said.

"And when you say 'not that I recall,' are you saying you could have and you just don't remember, or are you saying that you absolutely never did?"

"Quite honestly, I don't know how to answer that question," Bauer said.

"Tell me why."

"Because it seems like you're coming at me where I could get in trouble either way for saying—answering this question, and I might need a lawyer present for it."

"You can't get in trouble for telling the truth. I'm only asking you—"

"I may need a lawyer present for it, sir."

"You want a lawyer present?" Warne asked.

"I may. Let me speak to a lawyer about it."

"About this particular question?"

"Yes."

Warne then asked about the stories Bauer had told others, including Eunice Howell, about his personal life. Yes, he said, in 2008 he impregnated a young woman from Medford, Oregon, whom he'd met on the internet, but "I can't tell you" her name because "I just can't." He did not know the name of the hospital where she had the baby. He was not there when she gave birth, did not see either mother or child after the baby was born and then died from "a bad heart" at three months old, and had no idea where the baby boy was buried.

Warne then led him through his work history cutting firewood on the side and as an employee, first of Dietrich's, then of Howell's, his first day being two weeks before the fire. Bauer said he preferred to drive up to the job site in his own vehicle, a truck, rather than ride up from town in a service vehicle with other crew members. At the time of the fire, he said, he was driving a Ford F-150 pickup, maroon color—"like the chair."

He got rid of it, he said, "about a month or two after the fire" because "the front end went out on it."

"And when you say the front end went out, what do you mean by that?"

"The axle."

"What happened to the axle?

"It came apart."

When?

"Actually, it happened on that very day" of the fire.

"Did you hit anything?" Warne asked. "Did you run into a ditch? Did you run into a car? Was it just decided to break down that day?"

"A couple weeks before then, I hit a pothole on Moonlight coming from work," which "could have been the start of it. I'm not sure."

"And then did something that you can recall actually happen on September 3, 2007?"

"Not that I recall."

It broke down, he answered, on Moonlight after the fire.

Warne reminded Bauer he'd told Tracy Winsor that he'd used Moonlight to go look at the fire after seeing the smoke. "And you get to the intersection of—what was it—3100 and Moonlight, is that right?"

"Yes."

"And that's as far as you got?"

"Yes."

"And by the time you got up there, Mr. Bauer, had your truck already broken down or was it on the way back?"

"I'm not sure when it happened."

"Was it drivable after it happened?"

"Yeah. Barely."

"Do you recall it being barely drivable as you were making your way up to the fire before you got stopped?"

"No, it seemed fine at the time."

"So if it seemed fine up until that point in time, it must have been on your way back that it broke down?"

"Yeah, I think so."

"And the intersection of 3100 and Moonlight is as far as you got up the mountain that day, right?"

"Yes."

"And you were never on the mountain before that on that day, right?"

"Correct."

"And so, on the way back down, the tie rod goes out and all hell breaks loose on the truck, right?"

"Yes."

Who did he talk to up there at the clearing for the hour he said he was there? Warne asked.

A Cal Fire employee named Jim Rust, the guard Leo Whitlock, and the two dozer drivers, Bush and Crismon, Bauer said.

"What do you recall talking to J.W. Bush about?"

"I really don't know."

"Do you recall him saying anything to you at all about the fire at that point in time?"

"Yeah, just about that they were up there."

"Other than telling you that he was water barring, did J.W. say anything else to you during this one-hour period?"

"Yes."

"What else did he say?"

"That they struck up a spark."

"Now J.W.—your testimony here today, under oath, is that J.W. told you that they struck up a spark up there?"

"Yeah, that they must have hit a rock."

"Now, do you remember J.W. saying this to you, sir?"

"Yes."

"And do you remember J.W. saying anything else other than they must have struck up a spark?"

"Yes."

"What else?"

"They were blaming each other, who did it."

"You recall Kelly and J.W. pointing fingers at each other?"

"Yes."

"In front of you."

"Yes."

"And what were they saying to each other about? What do you recall the words that were used?"

"It was something about someone leaving early, to my—to what I recall."

"You recall J.W. or Kelly mentioning something about somebody leaving early?"

"Yeah, something about Kelly leaving."

"And what did Kelly say in response to that?"

"I don't remember."

"You have no recollection?"

"No."

"Do you recall Kelly, Mr. Bauer, saying anything about hitting a rock and setting off a spark?"

"No, I don't."

"You just recall J.W. saying that?"

"Yes."

"Did J.W. or Kelly ever pull you aside and say anything like, 'Hey, we think we started the fire'?"

"Pull me aside? No."

"Was anybody else with you when you heard J.W. say something about, 'I must have hit a spark' or 'I must have struck out a spark'?"

"Everybody that was mentioned was around there."

That day's deposition soon ended, with 9 A.M. set as the scheduled start the next morning. Warne began by asking if Bauer had lived in the area all his life and therefore was intimately familiar with the terrain—"as well as anybody you know, correct?"

"Yes," Bauer said.

Warne asked what kind of hunting he did.

"Actually," Bauer said, "I was told yesterday that I will not answer personal questions. I'm a witness, not a suspect."

"This is not—" Warne said before Bauer interrupted. "Quite frankly, I felt like I was being interrogated yesterday, and I was told that I'd have to get an attorney, and to tell you to take me to court if you want to ask me personal business."

"You think me asking you what you hunt—that's a personal question?"

"Just the questions you asked yesterday, I spoke to someone about them."

"Did you talk to an attorney?"

"No, my father."

"You called him here, from the prison?"

"I do have an attorney."

"No, but you talked to your father last night?"

"Yes."

"Okay," Warne said. "I'm going to put in front of you a map. And the reason I asked you a question as to where you were born and how much time you've spent in the woods is because I'd like to get a sense of where things are in the context of this map. And what I've got in front of you, Mr. Bauer, is a map which I think shows Westwood in the lower right-hand corner for you. Do you see that?"

"Yes."

Warne asked Bauer to indicate on it where his house was, which Bauer did, then to indicate where his girlfriend Andrea's house was, which he did.

"Now," Warne said, "there was a lot of talk yesterday about where people were, where forest rangers were, and where Leo Whitlock was, and I really don't want to get into that right now. What I'd like to do is find out how it is that you got from your house up to Cooks Creek for purposes of working. You and—well, if you're in Westwood, what road would you take up on a sort of a regular basis to get up to that work site?"

Bauer had difficulty, saying he was unfamiliar with that particular map. Then another, larger map was offered, but to little avail. At that point the lawyers agreed to take a break and try to find a map he could work with.

Just when they were ready to resume with an overhead map, Warne was handed a fax that had just arrived from the law office of Eugene Chittock. It said that Ryan Bauer was his client and would refuse to answer any more questions without counsel present.

Warne asked Bauer if he'd spoken to Chittock, whose offices were in Susanville. Bauer said his father must have hired him that morning. Warne left to call Chittock and came back to say the rest of the deposition would have to be rescheduled.

But when the attorneys arrived for the deposition seventeen days later, and Warne placed a map in front of him, Bauer refused to mark the route he would've taken from Westwood up to Moonlight. He explained that he was not, in fact, represented by an attorney because he couldn't afford one but that he had talked to his father and had decided that he was going to assert his Fifth Amendment right to not answer questions. Warne explained that California law is clear: "We are entitled to have you mark maps if that's part of our question."

Over the next three hours, Ryan Bauer refused to answer over one hundred of Warne's questions. They ranged from questions about Bauer's own reputation, to his use of chainsaws, to his being on the mountain that day, to what he'd reported the dozer drivers had told him, to what he was wearing the day of the Moonlight Fire.

At a break, Tracy Winsor tried to persuade Bauer that Warne had the right to ask those questions. When Warne found out about it, he asked Bauer whether the deputy attorney general had suggested to Bauer that he get an attorney. "Yes," Bauer said, and Warne immediately terminated the deposition on the grounds that that was inappropriate conduct, and he said he would seek a court order compelling Ryan Bauer to answer questions.

44

The most momentous land purchase SPI made—the one that guaranteed the company's future—seemed to share something in common with Red Emmerson's heritage as a descendant of pioneers.

In 1984 Santa Fe Industries merged with the Southern Pacific Company. It was a merger that encompassed much of the American West's history. Santa Fe Industries owned the Atchison, Topeka and Santa Fe Railway, which had played such a huge role in the population growth and infrastructure development of Northern California. The Southern Pacific had done the same in Southern California by opening up Los Angeles and its environs to millions of midwesterners and easterners intent on changing their lives by moving to what was then considered the promised land.

The business goal of the merger was to create the Santa Fe Southern Pacific Railroad. But the Interstate Commerce Commission and Department of Justice feared the monopolistic effects on freight transport prices and nixed the grand scheme. That led to jockeying among competing railroads for these suddenly available rail lines and assets, with several sales resulting in both consolidation and fragmentation— as well as not a little uncertainty and chaos. Santa Fe South Pacific would have to sell the Southern Pacific, so it went looking for a buyer, but in the meantime the company had to merge several of its directly or indirectly wholly owned subsidiaries into a single holding company to monetize the real estate and natural resources. When the dust settled, there were underperforming assets to liquidate in order to make the corporation less vulnerable to a corporate raider—and a core business to concentrate on. The company's vast landholdings in Northern California would have to go.

Crony capitalism and outright corruption had accompanied every aspect of the transcontinental railroad's construction during the nineteenth century, from routes to materials suppliers to locales where the trains would stop (and therefore bring almost instant prosperity) to the land granted to the railroad owners—millions of acres—for the rights-of-way. It's no coincidence that some of California's richest men 150 years ago—Leland Stanford, Mark Hopkins, and Charles Crocker—got rich and stayed that way through railway construction and ownership.

Much of the land granted to the railroads came in checkerboard patterns along the rail corridor, up to forty miles on each side, with every other parcel owned by the railroad and by the government, with the public lands gaining value by their proximity to the rail lines. Or so went the reasoning. In reality, the lands didn't increase in value at all because settlers moving west had little money; besides, who would build anywhere right next to and among railroad lands unless the trains actually stopped there?

As the decades passed, the parcels changed hands and often the railroads picked up some unwanted government parcels for pennies on the dollar. In any event, their vast holdings had to be managed and monetized, sometimes by selling smaller parcels to developers and often by selling temporary timber rights—in competition with the forest service—to the highest bidder. One of those frequent bidders, and usually a winner, was Sierra Pacific.

"We had been buying a lot of the timber from Southern Pacific for years," Emmerson remembers, "so we knew the land well. And when it came up for sale, I knew I wanted it. The railroad was nervous about being stretched too thin and becoming a target for a hostile takeover. They needed to get rid of assets."

The corporate entity that controlled the rights to the properties in the Northwest had been named Santa Fe Pacific Timber, and its president was Bill Herbert.

"I had heard from Bill," Emmerson says, "that they wanted to get rid of this parcel—522,000 acres. I really didn't even think about it. I decided that I wanted it, so I went to Bank of America and met with Tony Zanze"—the man who'd become SPI's point man at the bank since the retirement of Frank Keene.

Zanze didn't have to be persuaded that buying the land was a good idea. This gigantic swath of timberlands in the Sierra was, he foresaw, a path to the future for SPI, the company simply buying now the raw materials that would feed its mills for years to come.

Nor did he try to talk Red Emmerson out of borrowing what was likely to be hundreds of millions of dollars at a time when SPI's worth wasn't a third of that. He arranged to get Emmerson in to see Robert Krebs, president of Santa Fe Pacific, at company headquarters in Chicago. The meeting was held the first of May, 1987, a beautiful mid-spring day. Zanze accompanied Emmerson. Krebs asked one of his associates, Fred Schulte, to join them; it would be Schulte handling the sale details for the railroad regardless of who bought the land.

In Emmerson's recollection, Krebs did not ask how a family-owned company that at present owned "only" 130,000 acres of timberlands planned to pull this off. Krebs had agreed to the meeting, Emmerson says, based on the recommendation of Tony Zanze, whose presence two thousand miles from home represented a tacit guarantee that if they could strike a deal, the funds would be there.

But they did not strike a deal. In fact, Krebs didn't even hint at a price.

Despite a three-hour meeting, with Krebs taking the measure of Red Emmerson and Zanze advocating well for him, followed by a cordial social lunch, Emmerson and Zanze flew home without quite knowing what to think.

45

By the time she was deposed in December 2011, Andrea Terry was no longer Ryan Bauer's girlfriend. In fact, she was no longer Andrea Terry. She'd since married and was now Andrea Jackson.

Jackson had grown up in Westwood but attended high school in Susanville, where Bauer accompanied her to the junior prom soon after they met in the fall of 2006. She was fifteen at the time, a sophomore. He was nearly twenty. They dated, she testified, for only about a year.

"He could never sit still," she said. "He had to always be doing something. If something would happen that made him mad, it was just—instead of just calmly talking about it, he would just freak out. It wasn't a buildup or anything. It was just, boom, he was done."

Under oath, Jackson remembered that she'd awakened around nine or so on the morning that the Moonlight Fire broke out. She'd then eaten breakfast and by ten was out in front of her house in Westwood, helping her dad wash their three cars—his, her mother's, and her own.

At some point, she said, Ryan suddenly showed up, unannounced and unscheduled. Grimy, dirty, covered in sawdust, he looked the same as she'd seen him other times after a day of cutting, including when she'd helped him offload the rounds out of his truck bed and stack them in his parents' yard. That was his job on the side, cutting and selling firewood. And that was why, she explained, she'd decided without asking that he must have come straight from the mountain after cutting or doing something else that required physical labor. His Stihl chainsaw, she said, lay in the truck's bed next to at least one other chainsaw.

Minutes after he got there, she said, while helping her wash her car, he glanced up over the top of the house and said something like, "Oh my gosh, there's smoke where we're working."

Preoccupied as she was, it did not occur to her, she explained, that Bauer's noticing the smoke in the first place or identifying the exact location of the fire from the plume that only he seemed to notice over the house was odd. Nor did she realize then that the geography and architecture of the house, as well as the adjacent trees that obscured the view in the mountain's direction, made it difficult, if not impossible, to recognize that "there's smoke where we're working" probably wasn't something that could be determined.

At that point, Jackson said, Ryan Bauer ran to his truck—the green Toyota owned by his parents—retrieved his cell phone, and made a call. Meanwhile, she continued washing her own car, an old Corolla, the last of the three to be washed. She was alone. Her father had gone inside or into the backyard when Bauer arrived.

No, she answered, she had not heard any of Bauer's phone conversation that she estimated lasted ten minutes before he returned and announced he'd been speaking to his boss, who "wanted him to check out the area where they were working."

How long total was he with her that day? she was asked.

"He could have been there maybe twenty, thirty minutes. And he was on the phone for a little while, and then he came over and talked to me for little bit before he left. So it could have total all been maybe about an hour."

Jackson had no compelling reason until much later to suspect anything unusual. That her boyfriend's boss might want someone who'd been working for the company all of a few weeks to "check out" a fire and risk his life to try saving some equipment that he didn't know how to drive anyway—when there were already borate bombers dropping retardant on the flames, dozens of trained fire personnel on the scene, and officials preventing visitors from passing a checkpoint—did not, at the time, strike her as being out of the ordinary. She was sixteen years old. As far as she knew, the fire had begun only seconds before.

At school the next day, talk of the fire usurped all other conversations, even though the semester had just begun. No wonder. The smoke made breathing difficult, soot was dropping like snow, the main drag had become a staging area with fire trucks parked tail to nose, and hundreds of strange faces were rushing to and fro, many of them showing signs of exhaustion. No one was unaware that a fire this big—and growing—was bound to impact, directly or indirectly, almost every family in the area. Jobs would be lost, and if the wind shifted, maybe homes and even lives. It was scary.

Late that afternoon, Jackson texted her boyfriend: "What's going on?" He wrote that some of his coworkers had accidentally started the fire. She did not think to ask how he knew that already.

As for the week after the Moonlight Fire began, when he'd told her he was out fighting a wildfire in Graeagle, she said Bauer's mother Jennifer later told her Ryan was actually home the whole time. "It turns out that he was drinking."

Graeagle, she learned, had been left untouched by fire. Ryan Bauer had again lied about something for which the truth was easily and inevitably discovered.

The last time she saw her former boyfriend, Jackson said, was at a high school reunion he attended while she was still a student. He told her he had liver cancer. She didn't know whether to believe him. Before the barbecue, he'd told her via MySpace that it was his girlfriend who had cancer. And also, "she could be pregnant."

Did she ever have any sense that Ryan Bauer had started the Moonlight Fire?

"Anything," she said, "is possible with Ryan."

46

Days after flying home from Chicago without having been offered a chance to buy the half-million acres Santa Fe Pacific wanted to sell, a disappointed Red Emmerson learned that the company had hired the investment banking firm Salomon Brothers to find a buyer for the property. SPI would be competing against potential buyers from around the world, the sale to be conducted through blind bids.

SPI was no stranger to the blind-bidding process. For years the company had been bidding for timber on both government lands and private lands, with the bids sometimes open, as in a live auction, and sometimes sealed. The difference here was the magnitude of the information-gathering process that would help Emmerson decide how much he was willing to pay for the 522,000 acres he wanted as much as he'd ever wanted anything. Fortunately, he and SPI had something of a head start on the data, having already harvested millions of feet of timber from this parcel over the years.

SPI's team, led by chief forester Bud Tomascheski, had less than four months to cruise and assess the Santa Fe lands in terms of potential yield and degree of harvesting difficulty. He later memorialized what he and his crew found on the half-million acres under review: "The timber was located in streamside zones, in recreation areas, alongside mountain lakes, and on mountaintops. There were acres and acres of granite ridges with small patches of trees scattered among the crags, especially north of Donner Summit. The volume of merchantable timber was almost four billion board feet."

More important than the existing amount of timber, Tomascheski insisted, was the land's capacity to continue providing timber over the years and decades. What would guarantee such an outcome, he said, was proper stewardship of this 815-square-mile property—the exact size of the Great Smoky Mountains National Park that sprawls across the Tennessee–North Carolina border. (All of Rhode Island is only twice as big.)

Emmerson and his CFO, Dick Smith, began working on the bid from the numbers side, calculating the expected yield projections against the projected price of lumber minus all costs, including debt servicing, which was going to be enormous. And when they agreed on a ballpark figure, Emmerson added a few million extra, just in case. The exact figure wouldn't be decided until just before he turned in the bid.

What gnawed at him was not knowing who the other bidders might be or whether there might be foreign investors eyeing the property too; this was the era when Japanese moneymen and corporations were buying everything from Rockefeller Center to Columbia Pictures. Some people had begun calling the trend "an economic Pearl Harbor."

"I wanted it, and I don't know what would have happened to the company if we didn't get it," Emmerson says. "Without it, the price of timber contracts would have gone up a lot because this parcel was going to be off-limits, and finding other tracts to make up for it would've been hard. All the pressure from environmental groups was really making the feds nervous."

Just a year before, a draft supplement to the Final Environmental Impact Statement for an Amendment to the Pacific Northwest Regional Guide had been published. Called the SEIS—Shared Environmental Information System—it resulted from the agriculture secretary's ruling that the plan had to consider additional biological information on spotted owl habitats. Any proposed plan of action was obliged to be built on the established theory that the greatest risk to the owl population was a reduction in old-growth habitat, which would lead to a reduction in reproduction.

The railroad had not provided a preformatted bid form, so the bids were essentially slips of paper with the amount and whatever conditions the bidder insisted on inside envelopes. They could even be written out by hand, if that's what the bidders wanted. That was what Emmerson did.

He says he didn't decide on the amount until just before he and Dick Smith arrived at O'Hare Airport in Chicago on that October evening in 1987. At the last minute, he added in an extra $40 million above the amount he'd believed would be not only a profitable bid but also a winning one. So the final figure that Emmerson wrote down was $465 million.

"I had to make sure I got it," Emmerson says, explaining that his sons, George and Mark, were just beginning to come into SPI as autonomous executives, George in operations and Mark in finance. "If I hadn't, I would've regretted it forever. Overpaying and getting it was much better than bidding just enough and not getting it. If someone else had gotten this timber, we'd have had to curtail a lot of things. We'd have lost the timber that we were buying from the Santa Fe lands. Then, with the government cutting back their sales, that would've hurt us in both directions. So that's what I was thinking. One thing's for sure: we'd have been a smaller company."

Emmerson handed Santa Fe Pacific's Fred Schulte the sealed envelope and was told they could wait a while as the offers were weighed, however many there were (Emmerson never found out).

"We just hung around the office for a few hours, Dick and I," Emmerson remembers, "and then just before noon Schulte came out and said, 'You guys might as well go home.' I guess the look on my face looked like he shot me, so he said, 'Looks like you got it.'"

To this day, Emmerson says, he doesn't remember how he reacted. "I think I just went numb. I really don't remember how we celebrated. Or if we did. Maybe we celebrated the whole way home on the plane. That might be why I don't remember."

47

Three months after his former girlfriend Andrea Terry Jackson was deposed—and eight months after he'd refused to answer Bill Warne's questions in order to avoid self-incrimination—Ryan Bauer was again deposed, this time not in confinement but in a room at the Best Western Trailside Inn on Main Street in Susanville. The deposition lasted three days. He answered all questions. Present for the State of California was Tracy Winsor and for the United States, Assistant U.S. Attorney Glen Dorgan.

In the weeks before the fire, Bauer said, he often cut firewood after hours and on weekends in order to earn money to support his drug habit.

"You didn't," Warne said, confirming what Bauer had previously claimed, "do any woodcutting Friday, Saturday, or Sunday—true? Labor Day?

"I may have," Bauer said.

Warne asked if he knew why using chainsaws is prohibited on red flag days. Bauer said "a chain could hit a rock, spark arrester could get hot, if you have a bad enough or souped-up saw. If your saw is not in good condition, then you could start a fire."

As for his whereabouts the day of the fire, he said he showed up at Andrea Terry's house "around ten or eleven" that morning. He said her parents were having a barbecue and yard sale in the front yard. He said that before showing up, he called her. He said he helped out at the yard sale by helping to carry items from the yard to the buyers' cars. He said his clothes were clean, not covered in sawdust and dirt. He said he did not have his chainsaw on the job site that Monday and did not recall telling anyone that he needed to get to the fire in order to save his chainsaw.

He said he and Andrea took a walk, and "that's how we seen the smoke."

He said he immediately recognized that the smoke "was up in Moonlight Road."

He credited his "sense of direction" for knowing that the smoke ten miles away, at least one mountain range over, was, on this windy day, coming from the area where his crew had been working.

Richard Linkert, attorney for the landowners, asked, "Is it your testimony that from where you were standing on Third Street, you could actually see a ridge line, and see smoke coming up from a ridge line?"

"I don't know if I seen it over trees or houses or a ridge line. I can't remember."

"You felt confident enough that whatever you saw, you felt you need to call Eunice Howell, correct?"

"Yes."

Bauer said he regretted calling Howell and trying to drive up there to help out with the equipment because if he hadn't, he wouldn't now have to go through being deposed.

He said that when he saw J.W. Bush and Kelly Crismon at Five Corners, they told him they were making water bars in "the old logging site" that was "the last place they cut," and they were arguing over who'd kicked up the spark.

He said he had not read the joint origin and cause report filed in the case, though his parents obtained a copy. He said he had not read the transcription of his interview with Cal Fire investigators Schmitt and Gonzales but had read the summary of that interview appended to the report.

He said he did not remember being interviewed that week.

He said he was under the influence of four scheduled substances on the day of the Moonlight Fire.

48

After winning the Santa Fe Pacific bidding process, Red Emmerson and Dick Smith spent a week at a law firm in San Francisco, meeting with railroad executives and lawyers from that side. Meanwhile, Bank of America began putting together a syndicate of banks for the loan that no single bank could or would take on alone.

Bank of America was one of the largest banks in the country, but its position in the American economic firmament was anything but solid at the time. It had recently suffered enormous losses through overaggressive loans made in Latin America, resulting in the forced sell-off of several operations as a guard against a hostile takeover. Only recently it had implemented more prudent and stringent lending practices. So the fact that this bank at that time was willing to lead a syndicate of nearly a dozen banking institutions with the goal of lending a colossal amount of money to a small, family-owned business in Northern California—the amount being nearly four times as much as the actual value of the small company—was noteworthy. If SPI had defaulted and the lenders had seized every last SPI asset, the syndicate would still be owed the majority of its loan. What this banking syndicate was betting on as a solid, worthy, remunerative investment was, in essence, a single man: Red Emmerson.

As Zanze later told *Forbes*, he had banks lined up to loan the money. Or, as Emmerson put it in 2017, "The loan was oversubscribed."

Two weeks later, on October 19, 1987, the stock market crashed, falling more than five hundred points, a drop of about 22 percent—and this after a two-week period in which the market had already fallen 15 percent, eerily echoing the famous conditions of the crash in October 1929.

Not one bank, all of which took huge hits during the crash, pulled out of the deal.

49

In early 2011 Bill Warne's office filed a motion in front of Edmund Brennan, the federal magistrate assigned to adjudicate the pleadings, interrogatories (lists of formal written questions one side in a civil action submits to the other), and assorted other legal arguments. There had already been thousands of pages worth of documentation, an amount not unusual in a case with so much at stake (which is why a magistrate adjudicates instead of the trial judge, who, if he or she had to rule on every pretrial filing, would have little time to preside over trials).

So far Brennan had generally decided favorably for the prosecution. In fact, one of his rulings—the one this new motion was asking the judge to reconsider—seemed on its face to violate both the U.S. Constitution and the federal rules of civil procedure.

An outside lawyer that Warne's firm had sent to a public meeting in Westwood about the Moonlight Fire had stood up and asked a question of the local authority presiding, believing that the public forum was open to everyone. When she learned about it, Kelli Taylor protested. Brennan agreed and issued a contempt order. From now on, he'd ruled, anyone connected with SPI or its attorneys could not contact any federal employee for the purpose of seeking information about the Moonlight Fire without first identifying himself as connected to the case.

To Warne, that seemed self-evidently to be an overbroad ruling deserving of an appeal, but it was otherwise in line with what he'd come to believe about Brennan: the magistrate would scan Downey Brand's motions before reading, with greater concentration and credulousness, the responses filed by Kelli Taylor or her department, then grant unwarranted weight to the government's arguments. He did not, it appeared to Warne, believe that U.S. attorneys could be less than scrupulous.

One part of Warne's reply motion accused the government's lawyers of covering up misconduct by the USFS. The specific accusation pertained to what had happened or might have happened at the Red Rock lookout just before the fire was spotted. The government, Warne contended, was hiding something and preventing SPI from discovering it.

Long before the United States and California filed their suits against SPI, a USFS employee had told Sierra Pacific's John Forno—the forester who on September 6, 2007, had been promised by Josh White that all allegations and rumors of arson would be diligently investigated—that from what she had heard, there may have been a problem with the fire lookout's behavior. "I better not say any more than that," the woman had told Forno.

Downey Brand filed several discovery requests, but as Warne's motion to compel made clear, "the United States' responses were not only false, but a brazen continuation of a long-running effort to hide what really happened on September 3, 2007. . . . [T]he U.S. Forest Service's scheme to cover up critical information harmful to its claims began immediately and, with the assistance of its counsel, that scheme has extended through discovery in this matter, as well as through its oppositions to Sierra Pacific's present and past motions to compel."

The motions to compel concerned the government's obligation to produce all personnel records for Karen Juska, the fire prevention technician who had visited the Red Rock lookout station the afternoon of the fire, and Caleb Lief, the lookout. What Warne's team hadn't yet learned was precisely what happened during Juska's visit.

Warne had earlier sent an interrogatory to Taylor: "Describe in detail the activities of all USFS employees who were present at Red Rock lookout on September 3, 2007, including (without limitation) the identity of all persons present and all conduct and action taken by those persons."

Responses to interrogatories are signed under penalty of perjury, and this one, signed by Kelli Taylor and also by Larry Craggs, USFS Plumas division chief, stated "that the term 'all activity' is vague and ambiguous and potentially calls for information that is not relevant to any party's claims or defenses."

In a long paragraph, their response went on to declare that Caleb Lief had "conducted lookout activities throughout the day" and was visited a bit after 2:00 by Juska, who "performed a 360-degree scan of the horizon from the lookout." Neither employee, it said, saw signs of fire until they went downstairs to Juska's truck. Juska phoned it in and drove away, while Lief ran back upstairs to determine the exact location using the Osborne fire finder (a device used by fire lookouts to determine a directional bearing). "The United States," it concluded, "will supplement this response as appropriate."

To Warne this sounded suspicious. He couldn't imagine that the government was trying, on principle, to protect Caleb Lief's privacy. No, there had to be something else. The more the government stonewalled, the more determined he became. And as he would later explain, the government's reluctance told him two things: First, the government lawyers were less interested in doing justice than they were in winning. Second, whatever had happened at the Red Rock lookout was serious enough to lie about in order to support their case, or at least not undermine it.

Warne sent another interrogatory requesting an admission that Lief had "engaged in conduct prohibited by USFS, while he was on duty at Red Rock lookout" and that Juska had witnessed his conduct.

The response, bearing Taylor's signature, said, "the United States in no way concedes that Caleb Lief engaged in any misconduct at the Red Rock lookout" . . . or that there was any delay in reporting the Moonlight Fire.

Brennan, to Warne's surprise but delight, ruled against the government, forcing Taylor to turn over all pertinent documents.

Taylor's team delivered what's known in the trade as a "document dump"—some thirty thousand documents' worth—a common technique that sometimes succeeds in obscuring any damaging information the way a haystack hides a needle. In order to not miss anything, Warne assigned six people to go through each of the hundred-plus boxes and methodically inspect every document. Working at least twelve hours a day, seven days a week, they not only uncovered evidence that Caleb Lief was stoned the afternoon of the fire but also evidence that in the weeks after the Moonlight Fire, his supervisor had been forced to (a) overlook Juska's allegations of Lief's misconduct, (b) give Lief a satisfactory employment review, and (c) rehire him as a lookout for the following year. There had been no investigation into Juska's accusations that she'd seen and smelled pot in the lookout. Which suggests that long before Kelli Taylor had ever heard of Red Rock, the USFS had engaged in a cover-up of its own. (By signing that interrogatory denying that Lief had engaged in inappropriate conduct, Taylor had exposed herself to an accusation, if not a charge, of perjury.)

At issue was whether the Moonlight Fire could have been put out quickly, cheaply, and with a minimum of damage if only Caleb Lief had been more attentive instead of high enough to be unaware of Juska's noisy arrival at the lookout station. If the jury believed that the fire could have been knocked down quickly had the lookout spotted it in time, any possible damages assessed against the defendants would be reduced as a matter of statute and case law.

From Warne's perspective the cover-up was something the jury would find sexy and disturbing. Instead of an abstract discussion about whether fire lookouts are critically important and how every second counts, the jurors would be able to see that the U.S. Forest Service and the Department of Justice were willing to lie, cheat, and deceive in order to win. Once he brought that sequence of events to light, he believed, the jury might then be inclined to question the entirety of the government's case.

50

Just after the deal for the half-million Santa Fe Pacific acres was consummated, restrictions on logging in national forests due to the presence of the northern spotted owl began to reach critical mass and quickly took their toll on the amount of timber harvested. The impact was immediate and brutal. If you owned a sawmill that relied on timber sales from national forests for product to harvest and mill, you were in worse shape every day, as nearly every week more land was placed off-limits by the Department of the Interior. As a result, the quantity of lumber from the Northwest declined. And the price of what remained went up.

Sierra Pacific, with its new Santa Fe lands compensating (and then some) for what the company could no longer cut on government lands, began earning more per board foot.

Even Red Emmerson's most hopeful projections when he bid on the tract included the need to cut more timber in order to keep current on the loan. If that had meant running all of SPI's ten mills on double shifts to produce enough, Emmerson was prepared to do so. But now, because of the spotted owl, that wasn't necessary. Sierra Pacific had, for the first time, become a dominant force in the retail lumber industry.

"I had thought that we'd suffer to make the interest payments on the big loan," Emmerson says. "I really worried about that. But I guess you'd have to say that we got healthy on the spotted owl."

SPI, he says, paid back the loan years early.

51

Among the thirty thousand documents that Kelli Taylor's office dumped on Downey Brand after the court order were two versions of the same report, both filed by Karen Juska. One, a business-as-usual summary of her visit to the Red Rock station that day, was appended to the origin and cause report filed by Diane Welton. It indicated that nothing untoward had occurred while she was there.

The second report was a longer version of that report, more detailed—and not helpful to the government's case. What Warne and his team concluded was that the USFS believed Caleb Lief's misbehavior as a fire lookout was potentially damaging to the agency and to the Moonlight Fire case—damaging enough to make sure that no one inside the agency let anyone outside know the details. That Lief's behavior hadn't been disclosed earlier, let alone investigated, and that there were both a real report and a sanitized one implied that the prosecutors considered the Red Rock issue to be anything but moot or irrelevant.

In the first document, intended for the official report, Juska said she arrived at the lookout tower at either 2:05 or 2:10 and talked with Caleb Lief before making "a 360 scan from inside the tower of the country/ landscape." She said Lief asked her to "take down a bag of trash" to her truck that was parked in front. He carried it down and was about to leave when she looked over his left shoulder, pointed, and said, "You got a smoke right there I think it's Moonlight Valley." She jumped in her truck and called it in, unsure "if the fire was in section 3, 10 or 16," before driving toward the fire on Lights Creek Road. "I decided this route to be the best way of travel in order to access each section depending on the true location of the fire."

The rest mentions running across J.W. Bush in his pickup before connecting him to USFS investigator Dave Reynolds, "who said that he was right out at the staging area just about 1/4 mile behind me."

Juska's longer report suggests that the short version may have been filed under orders from her supervisor, Diane Welton, trying to protect the USFS. Bill Warne suspected that Juska had written the longer report to protect herself. In it, she noted that as she drove to the station, "Any person at the lookout would be able to see my rout [sic] of travel form [sic] the dust on the road and know that a vehicle would be arriving within 10–15 minutes." She said she pulled to a stop in front, as always, walked up the steps, "and when I got to the landing Caleb was standing right out the door facing me urinating down the catwalk slats onto his bare feet. Caleb was stunned/surprised by my arrival and presence. Caleb turned around away form [sic] me and finished urinating on his feet while saying 'don't think I am weird or gorse [sic], it's an old Hot-shot trick to cure athlete's foot.'" (Hotshots are crews specially trained in fighting wildland fires.) Lief, she said, "walked right in the lookout with his bare feet."

Now Juska admitted to feeling "uneasy because of what I witnessed," mentioned a crack in one of the windows that would need replacing if it grew larger, and described a "blue/green in color marijuana pipe on the counter, by the sink." She said Lief grabbed the pipe and hid it behind him, admitting that she shouldn't have seen it. "We both were aware that I did witness this and at that time I did not verbally address the situation. I did make a disapproving facial expression."

That was when Lief "handed me a radio" and she noticed that it "had a heavy odor of marijuana." She said nothing to him but "am documenting this and passing it to the employee's first line supervisor, Ron Heinbockel."

Juska reiterated the 360-degree scan claim, bolstering it with a parenthetical—"Whenever I visit the lookout I make a habit of scanning the landscape/country completely"—that, to Bill Warne, insinuated the opposite effect from what she presumably intended: why had she needed to explain something that otherwise needed no explanation?

The rest of the report more or less proceeds as the shorter one did, to the point where she notices "a thin line of top smoke" and calls it in, except for the last paragraph: "I do not want to imply in anyway [sic] that because of the events documented above that Caleb did not call

178 Joel Engel

this smoke in within a timely manner. As soon as I/we saw the smoke I called the Plumas ECC [Emergency Command Center] and Red Rock followed up with the further report. Caleb gave a full size up, with location with frequent updates of fire status."

Juska seemed to understand that her report had put the forest service in a precarious position. And her report was contradicted by Lief when he was deposed in January 2011, by which time he was working as a custodian at Feather River College. He said that Juska's claims of his pot use were fabrications and that he thought she was incompetent and not a "good worker." He said they didn't get along because she knew he thought she wasn't good at her job. He said it was actually he who had spotted the smoke when they were down at the truck. He said he'd heard rumors she was intimate with their supervisor, Ron Heinbockel.

52

By early 1990 most Americans had heard of the northern spotted owl. And thanks to television and newspapers, they considered the little feathered animal to be as critical to the health of the biosphere as oxygen, nitrogen, and carbon. According to the Interagency Scientific Committee report published that year, though not peer-reviewed, the spotted owl was "imperiled over significant portions of its range because of continuing losses of habitat from logging and natural disturbances. Current management strategies are inadequate to ensure its viability. Delay in implementing a conservation strategy cannot be justified on the basis of inadequate knowledge."

A few months later the U.S. Fish and Wildlife Service officially listed the northern spotted owl as endangered, and the U.S. Forest Service implemented an internal forum for employees who were unhappy over the agency's reluctance to revoke *all* logging permits.

Meanwhile, several federal agencies published the findings of a research team that had been looking into the likely impact of reduced logging. It estimated losses of more than twenty-five thousand jobs in the Pacific Northwest. The inevitable blow to communities large and small could hardly be overstated, given the multiplier effect of those millions of dollars removed from the economy. Yet environmental groups continued to file lawsuits and donate substantial funds to congressional candidates believed to be either sympathetic to the cause or willing to have their voting sympathies bought.

Several subsequent court rulings either halted or permitted timber sales, with logging companies appealing the former and environmental groups appealing the latter. Sometimes there were appeals upon appeals. Each side won just enough victories to make clear that the fight would be long, ugly, and costly. The difference was that the environmentalists were being funded by outsiders, and the loggers' side was funded by companies for which a day not logging was a day closer to insolvency. Dozens of companies did go out of business.

In March 1991 federal judge William L. Dwyer issued his ruling on a lawsuit that had been filed by the Seattle Audubon Society against the USFS. He ruled that the forest service had not complied with the National Forest Management Act of 1974, which required that the agency maintain "viable populations of existing native and desired non-native vertebrate species in the planning area." A corollary ruling forced the forest service to abide by the Endangered Species Act. That meant more than preventing extinction. It meant maintaining a "viable" species—which at that point had yet to be defined or quantified.

Unmoved by arguments about the economic impact on human beings, Dwyer later wrote: "The timber industry no longer drives the Pacific Northwest's economy. Job losses in the wood-products industry will continue regardless of whether the northern spotted owl is protected. The argument that the mightiest economy on Earth cannot afford to preserve old-growth forests for a short time, while it reaches an overdue decision on how to manage them, is not convincing today."

Dwyer rejected as inadequate the USFS's revised plan to set aside 5.9 million acres in three states. Not until late 1994 would he approve the Northwest Forest Plan as in compliance with the National Forest Management Act. The new plan permitted the harvest of 1 billion board feet of timber on public land in Washington, Oregon, and California.

That amount represented less than a quarter of what had been cut in the 1980s. To Red Emmerson, it was obvious that the force SPI would have to surmount in order to succeed going forward was this alliance between the federal judiciary, environmental groups, progressive legislators, and a public that accepted as received wisdom claims made by environmentalists.

The result, Emmerson explains, was a kind of bizarre public-interest corruption. Citizens donated money to environmental groups, environmental groups funneled much of that money in the form of donations to friendly politicians, and the politicians voted for further environmental regulations that allowed environmentalists to prevail in court against logging companies.

From the time SPI bought the Santa Fe lands in 1987 until 2012, timber harvesting on national forest lands fell by nearly 80 percent, from 11 billion board feet to 2.5 billion board feet.

"I don't blame the average guy for not knowing what really happens in the forest," Emmerson says. "He's been told that what we do is evil. He thinks leaving the forests untouched means that they're healthier than they would be if cutting were allowed at the level we cut even twenty years ago."

The truth is the opposite, he says. "We harvest, replant, and care for our forests according to best practices. Our forests are healthier and more hospitable to native life, and less susceptible to the bark beetle, than USFS forests. Ours are a lot less likely to have catastrophic wildfires."

The reason is that fires are more prone to become devastating conflagrations when trees are weakened by insect infestations, or fires are more likely to "crown"—or both. If overgrowth isn't mechanically removed, Nature will eventually have its say.

Of course, U.S. forests are not subject to clear cutting, a practice that the average person considers a crime against nature. Though "clear cutting" is an accurate term, it's become a loaded one. On SPI lands in California, twenty-acre parcels (on average) are subject to a clear cut, but then are replanted and tended to so that the lands can be harvested again in decades to come.

"Most people aren't really interested in what's true if it contradicts what they already believe," Emmerson says. "They hear the words 'clear cut' and automatically think that that area is denuded forever. They don't understand, and many don't want to understand, that trees grow back quickly. Someone has shown them a picture of a clear cut just after it's done, but not a year or two or three later. Some of the things I've heard people say at public meetings when they stand up and tell why they don't want us to get a permit to do this or that is so far from the truth, so far from science, that there's no point in trying to explain it to them. They believe what they believe, and nothing is going to change that. They're told we cut down the forest and turn it into a desert, and they believe it."

At the turn of the millennium, SPI compiled a document whose name suggests a view of the future that an environmentalist would approve on principle alone: the 100-Year Sustained Management Plan.

Here are a few of its year 2100 minimum-target outcomes that SPI aims to guarantee: (1) average diameter of SPI trees will triple, from today's eighteen to twenty inches (about 50 percent greater than the worldwide average in industrial forests) to thirty-four inches; (2) SPI lands will continually provide habitat suitable for all 246 species already known to use those forests for breeding, feeding, and shelter, and several species, like the northern spotted owl, Pacific fishers, and northern goshawks, will increase in real numbers; (3) cold, clean water habitats for all native residents and anadromous salmonids will allow the company's reintroduction program to add new species, both common and rare; (4) sustainable harvest yields will increase from 500 million board feet to more than 1.2 billion, thus providing sustainable work at far-above-average wages to many more families.

Emmerson wonders why environmentalists don't credit SPI for being one of the first mill companies to invest in cogeneration plants that simultaneously generate both usable heat and power. SPI's move to investigate this environmentally friendly technology began in the technology's early days and required tens of millions of dollars, Emmerson says, as well as on-the-job learning with such retrofitted parts as 1950s turbines.

The way Emmerson remembers it, SPI's first cogen plant at Quincy, California was built almost entirely in-house and produced only about three megawatts of power—just enough to power the sawmill. Then came a cogen station at Hayfork, which cranked out eleven megawatts; followed by Susanville, capable of twelve megawatts.

By then, Emmerson says, SPI had gotten the hang of these things and was happy enough with the economies of scale that were realized by it to push forward with a twenty megawatt cogen plant at the Burney mill, followed by a retrofit of the Quincy plant to bring it in line with the others. Eventually, the Anderson mill adjacent to company headquarters would produce thirty-two megawatts.

"Why environmentalists still don't give us credit for doing this, I don't know," Emmerson says. "The cogen plants are run with waste products like sawdust and bark and chips, and we actually resell power back to the utility. But they don't like anything we do. Sometimes I think the only way they'd like us is if we went out of business."

53

Ron Heinbockel was a reluctant witness for the government at his deposition in mid-May 2011. He did not, it was clear, like being asked questions about Caleb Lief or Karen Juska or Red Rock lookout or even the Moonlight Fire, and he did everything he could—until he was left with no alternative—to avoid answering them.

Wearing his khaki short-sleeved USFS shirt with a white tee visible underneath, the balding pale-haired man with the graying brush mustache squirmed like he was trying to scratch an itch. In response to dozens of questions, he squinted, widened, rolled, and shifted his eyes side to side, then grabbed his silver travel mug for strategic sips, hemming and hawing before finally responding. He tried as best he could without an actor's formal training to make it appear as if he were really searching his memory instead of trying to think two steps down the line and avoid the corner Warne was pushing him into. He did not, it was clear, want to disappoint or displease the deputy attorney general, Tracy Winsor, and certainly not the assistant U.S. attorney Kelli Taylor. Both he and Taylor, after all, received their paychecks from the same treasury, and she was significantly higher on the food chain than he was, even if they worked for different agencies.

Heinbockel, Warne could see, had been prepped and was terrified of answering in a way that might cause trouble for the prosecution. Warne asked if Heinbockel had ever been deposed. Heinbockel said he had, not that long before, on the Storrie fire and had not enjoyed the experience.

"I would say," Warne began, "there is nothing too horrible about sitting here and telling the truth when people are accused of starting a fire and the government is seeking over a billion dollars."

"Speaking as a human being," Heinbockel answered, "I would say this is not a comfortable place to be."

Heinbockel's answer was an example of why lawyers instruct their clients to answer only the question that's being asked. The federal magistrate had granted Warne a single day with this witness, so Warne now knew that if Heinbockel proved to be overly recalcitrant, he could probably get the witness to open up by threatening to call the judge for more days and force him to sit longer in "not a comfortable place."

"I'm going to try to make it not too horrible for you, sir," Warne said. "And one of the ways we'll do that is just, I'm going to be asking questions and if you tell me the truth, then there is nothing horrible about that. That's your obligation as a U.S. citizen. You understand that, right?"

"Yes."

But Heinbockel knew where the questions were heading because he knew that Warne knew Heinbockel had given Caleb Lief a satisfactory performance review after the Moonlight Fire. Warne was going to ask why, and he was going to inquire why an investigation into Juska's allegations about Lief's pot possession and misbehavior hadn't been conducted. Why had Heinbockel hired Lief back again for the following fire season?

"Do you know a gentleman named Nick Beecham?" Warne asked.

Heinbockel rolled his eyes and fidgeted and pretended to be thinking about the question. But the question should have needed little thinking. Nick was the grown son of Rick Beecham, Heinbockel's longtime neighbor in Meadow Valley, about fifty miles south of Westwood.

"Yes," he said at long last.

Warne asked if Heinbockel had spoken with Rick Beecham about what happened at the Red Rock lookout on the day of the fire. Beecham had already talked to Warne's team, so Warne knew that the two had spoken and about what. Heinbockel's pausing farcically between the end of the question and the beginning of his answer struck Warne as sadly funny.

"I don't recall," Heinbockel said.

"You have no memory of that?"

"Not a hundred percent, no."

Warne explained that whether he had a 2 percent or a 95 percent recollection of an event, he was obliged to testify truthfully or risk perjury charges.

"I still cannot answer that," Heinbockel said.

Now Warne rephrased his explanation and implicit warning, concluding with, "And is it your testimony here under oath that you have no sense whatsoever of any topics that you may have raised with your friend Rick Beecham relating to what could have occurred in the Red Rock lookout tower on September 3, 2007? Is that your testimony today here, sir?"

Heinbockel rolled his eyes, shifted his posture, squinted, tried his best to look like he was thinking, then said, "I'll make a general statement that we talked about the first day of the fire and my part in it, and I'm in charge of detection, which is lookouts. And may have talked— and I want to emphasize *may*—"

"Don't guess," Kelli Taylor interjected.

"Please," Warne said to Taylor.

"Do not guess," Taylor instructed Heinbockel. This was just days after the departure of Assistant U.S. Attorney Eric Overby from the case.

"Ms. Taylor," Warne said as Heinbockel looked down at the table in front of him, "your actions in this case from the start have been to suppress information. We all know that. Eventually your supervisors are going to know that, too. But I have already told the witness what I'm entitled to, and your constant efforts to try to keep us from the truth are nauseating."

"Mr. Warne," Taylor said, "don't speak to me like that. And when the witness . . . indicates that he may be guessing, he is entitled to know he is not supposed to guess."

"He didn't say he may be guessing," Warne said. "I spent five minutes with the witness telling this witness that I'm entitled to his memory regardless of how vague it is. And when the witness starts to say, 'I may have discussed,' and you interrupt with, 'Don't guess,' it's kind of like writing interrogatory responses that aren't true either."

Taylor said nothing. There was nothing to say. Warne reiterated for Heinbockel's sake that if he had any recollection of talking with his friend Rick Beecham, he was legally obliged to come clean.

"We have a fire and I had a lookout and," Heinbockel said, pausing for seventeen seconds of eye rolling and squinting and chewing his cud and looking up and down and everywhere except at Bill Warne, before spitting out, "leave it at that."

No, Warne said. "I don't want you to leave it at that. Because your job is to tell everything that you remember, regardless of how vague. If you talked to him about the fire and you talked to him about the lookout, what do you think you may have told Mr. Beecham about the lookout as it relates to the fire?"

After another five seconds in which he was apparently searching his own mind for a way to answer that wouldn't reveal anything he feared would be revealing or incriminating, Heinbockel said, "I'm going to hold firm on, I don't want to state anything that I'm thinking could have happened."

Warne reminded him that not telling what he knew meant that he was not being truthful.

Then Taylor instructed Heinbockel not to guess, by pointing out that he couldn't be held responsible for not remembering. He said, "May have, and I, I'm going back, I hate to even use 'may have.'"

Why?

Because, he said, if he used that term it would be documented, and Warne would therefore be able to pull it out of his hat the rest of the day. "I'm not trying to stall," he said. "I'm trying to think up an answer, and I don't like having to think up an answer."

Warne said he wanted him only to be truthful and that, by the way, he'd soon be taking Beecham's deposition. And if the stories didn't jibe—well, "then we all start getting into trouble."

Nearly fifteen minutes had passed since Warne's first question about whether Heinbockel knew a Rick Beecham. Heinbockel finally said, "I may have talked about possibly Caleb Lief."

And what did he think he'd actually said to Beecham about Lief?

"Inappropriate behavior."

That needed a bit more explication, Warne said.

"Oh, you know, peeing on his feet and possibly an alleged assumption that he might have been—he might have had alleged marijuana."

Warne asked if Heinbockel had spoken with his "good friend" Beecham about how he'd reacted professionally to the allegations. Had he regretted being unable to leave anything other than a satisfactory review of Lief, since that review opened the door to Lief's rehiring the following season?

Heinbockel thought a while and asked Warne to repeat the question but break it down. Warne said there was no way to break it down further. He repeated it nearly verbatim.

"Not that I recall," Heinbockel said tentatively.

Did Heinbockel ever admit to Beecham that he felt as though he'd been "forced" to write a review for Lief that Lief hadn't earned?

"No."

"Do you believe that you were forced by the U.S. Forest Service to give Mr. Lief a review that you did not believe was consistent with the facts?"

"We're jumping tracks a little bit here," Heinbockel said.

"Not really," Warne said. "We are on the same issue. I'm asking you if you believed that you were forced by the U.S. Forest Service to give Mr. Lief a review that was inconsistent with the facts, yes or no?"

"Define forced."

Define forest?

That's what Warne thought Heinbockel had said, so he sarcastically explained that the U.S. Forest Service was the outfit for which Heinbockel had worked for thirty-five years.

Until now in the deposition, Heinbockel had listened to Warne's questions with a combination of squirming, facial gymnastics, and tics. This time, knowing that he could answer well and truly and truthfully, Heinbockel sat still and looked straight at Warne until he could make his point:

"You used the word was I forced."

"Oh, 'forced,'" Warne said. "I don't know how to say that other than how I said it. Do you believe that you were forced to give Mr. Lief a review that you thought was inconsistent with the facts as you understood them?"

"No," Heinbockel said, leaning back and taking a sip from his silver travel mug.

"Do you believe that the review you gave Mr. Lief was something that you thought was consistent with the facts?"

It was really the same question that had just gotten a no. This time Heinbockel answered, "Which review are you talking about?"

The review, Warne said, that Heinbockel had written on September 14, 2007—less than two weeks after the Red Rock incident.

Heinbockel asked him to repeat the question. Warne repeated it.

Heinbockel, after ten thoughtful seconds, asked whether he could see a copy of the review. Warne said that they'd be looking at it later, but for right now he was only interested in Heinbockel's recollection of whether Lief deserved the satisfactory review he'd given him. Yet again he repeated the question.

Now Kelli Taylor interjected with her opinion that the witness is "entitled" to refresh his recollection, which Heinbockel seconded. "You're asking me," he said, "to say yes or no on a document I can't see."

Warne explained that for right now the proper answer did not require seeing the document; it had to do with state of mind. Heinbockel therefore had no right to review the report at this moment. Warne repeated the question for either the fourth or fifth time over what had become three minutes and reminded Heinbockel that he was bound by a duty to testify truthfully. "Do you believe that in the fall of 2007 that the review you gave Mr. Lief was consistent with the facts associated with his employment during that year?"

"Vague, overbroad," Kelli Taylor said, followed several seconds later by Heinbockel: "Define the word facts," he said, "since I can't see it. What facts am I agreeing to?"

"The facts as you understood them as his boss."

"I really don't know how to answer that."

They had now been going at this one question for five minutes. Whether Heinbockel thought he was successfully evading answering was irrelevant to Warne's certainty that, sooner or later, he would get the truth from his witness. He asked why Heinbockel couldn't answer. Heinbockel said he was confused. And they went at it for another full minute before Warne asked the direct question yet again.

Heinbockel asked him to repeat.

Warne had reached his limit.

"Ms. Taylor," he said, "I just want to let you know I will be moving for a continuation of this deposition. It's clear that we are not going to finish within seven hours. I have had to repeat on a number of occasions very clear questions to this witness. He is clearly being evasive and he has been coached in a way that has caused him to seize up in this deposition in a way that is completely inappropriate."

"You know what," Taylor said, "I disagree with your characterization and your comments and your constant attacks. That's what's inappropriate."

"Well, I'm just putting it on the record what everybody in this room can see"—and after laying it out Warne said that he would be asking for another seven hours of time from Judge Brennan. "We have been experiencing these kinds of issues in this case from the day it started. And my patience with respect to what has happened on this case has been—apparently as witnessed by everybody but you—extreme. So I don't really care if you see it that way or not. I'm just telling you that this is absurd and I should be able to ask this witness questions and get answers pretty quickly, truthful answers. And that's not what's happening here today."

Rick Linkert, the landowners' lawyer, jumped in with his agreement and a suggestion that they break for a few minutes so that Kelli Taylor could advise her witness in private to start coming clean. Warne asked if she'd like to take a break and do just that.

"No," Taylor said without a pause—or checking visually with Heinbockel, who looked disappointed.

Warne agreed to continue, but if the "charade" didn't stop, he'd call Judge Brennan "because this is just ludicrous."

"Can I defend myself?" Heinbockel asked.

"Sir," Warne said, "all you need to do is tell me the truth. Okay?"

Heinbockel said he wasn't trying to evade anything, that he'd taken an oath and wanted to answer clearly. The look on his face suggested that he'd suddenly found religion.

Warne pointed out that the questions had been nothing if not clear and reminded Heinbockel that his job today was simply to tell the truth. He again asked, "As you sit here right now, sir, do you have any memory of what you understood the facts were when you gave Mr. Lief the review that you gave him on September 14, 2007?"

Nearly twenty minutes after he'd first broached the subject, Bill Warne got the answer he already knew.

"Yes," said Heinbockel.

"And what is your memory of those facts when you gave him the review?"

"That part of the rating was based on allegations."

"And what did you understand the allegations were, sir?"

"Possession possibly in the lookout."

"Possession possibly of what in a lookout?"

"Marijuana."

"Which would be a violation of policy, correct?"

"Yes."

"And you understood those allegations at the time you gave him a review on September 14, 2007, correct?"

Heinbockel looked up at the ceiling for several seconds and shifted his eyes in thought before answering, "Yes."

"And you gave him a fully successful review, correct?"

"Yes."

"And you did that against your will, didn't you?"

Heinbockel squinted his eyes and thought. Then: "Yes."

He was still somewhat reluctant, but the truth was out now, so there was little point in resisting further. Whatever bad might happen from this was going to happen anyway, so over the next several minutes he confirmed that it was the acting ranger Dave Loomis who'd "forced" him to write Lief's satisfactory review even after all concerned knew through Karen Juska's report that she had allegedly seen Lief in June with some pot and on the day of the fire saw and smelled his pot pipe.

"You didn't like the fact that you were being forced to [write the report], correct?" Warne asked.

"Yes," Heinbockel said.

"And you did it anyway, correct?"

"Yes."

"And you didn't like the fact that you were being forced to do it, correct?"

"I was disappointed."

A few minutes later Warne asked Heinbockel why he didn't try to go around Loomis and fill out the review properly and honestly. Heinbockel said he didn't know why. He'd wanted to give Lief an unsatisfactory review. He just hadn't done it.

Warne pressed. "I signed it but the ranger has to also sign it," Heinbockel answered. "So I just figured at the time maybe there was something they knew that I didn't."

Over the next several hours Heinbockel, who on September 3, 2007 was the strike team leader, revealed a number of other things that would prove helpful to the defense, including his having had two dozers and a hand crew working in the area where the fire began, which would mean that any metal found in and on the ground could have come from a government Caterpillar as easily as any other tractor.

These facts and others were important pieces of the puzzle but in most ways were superfluous to the primary point that Warne believed had already been made. It was a point that Heinbockel's own supervisor, Larry Craggs, would confirm in his own deposition when he noted that Diane Welton had claimed that a mere allegation of marijuana use or possession wasn't enough legally to trigger a full investigation. And it was a point Craggs underlined when he acknowledged with clear regret having signed, along with Kelli Taylor, the interrogatory that was supposed to have been a complete description of Caleb Lief's activities on the day of the fire but was in reality a sanitized version.

54

It had become clear to Red Emmerson that SPI's survival and continued success depended on never having to endure a shortage of logs for its mills. So with the success of the Santa Fe tract behind him, there was every incentive to keep investing in additional lands when they became available, paying whatever price seemed remotely plausible in terms of cost to yield.

More often than not, SPI was the highest bidder for lands that it wanted—and the reason is that Red Emmerson knew better than other lumbermen how to get the highest yield out of a single log. So when it came time to bid on lands for sale, he and SPI could pay more for the properties and, if he and his staff had calculated properly, still turn a useful profit—plus get the additional advantage of having more acreage on which to make up for the present and anticipated future loss of U.S. forest lands.

Before the Santa Fe purchase, more than 80 percent of SPI's timber was harvested on public lands. Even among some of the larger landowning companies, that was a common percentage. So as other companies had less and less access to timber and therefore fewer logs to sell and mill, SPI's market share rose even if its output stayed essentially the same. (In 2017 SPI's share of the lumber market, Emmerson says, was about 6 percent, up more than 50 percent from the days when the northern spotted owl saga began.)

Emmerson agrees that the history of SPI after the Santa Fe purchase can be accurately described as a series of further acquisitions, both of mills and of timberlands.

"I had some and wanted more," he says. "It wasn't all that complicated."

In the decade or so after Santa Fe, SPI went on a serial buying spree, gobbling up smaller parcels from the likes of Georgia-Pacific, Louisiana-Pacific, Fibreboard, and Roseburg Lumber.

The price tag was about half a billion dollars for more than half a million additional acres. By the mid-1990s, SPI was cutting its own Ponderosa pine, sugar pine, white fir, Douglas fir, and cedar on about 1.3 million acres that stretched from the Oregon border on the coast to central California as far south as Yosemite.

"Once we got on the radar, we were besieged by people pitching deals, wanting to get in business with us," Emmerson says. "We were approached all the time by people wanting us to buy. We paid the highest price, so it made sense that they'd come to us."

Six years after Fibreboard sold SPI forty-nine thousand acres, the company decided to go back to the well with an even better parcel. SPI wanted it.

The *New York Times* described the sale on June 22, 1995: "The Fibreboard Corporation said yesterday that it planned to sell 76,000 acres of its remaining California forest land to Sierra Pacific Industries for more than $240 million, as the company moves out of the wood services business and expands into the building products industry. It will also sell four lumber mills. Fibreboard, of Walnut Creek, Calif., asked a high price—more than $3,000 an acre—because the land is one of the few remaining tracts of nongovernment-owned forest in the state located near lumber mills."

Two years later, Georgia-Pacific sold SPI a sawmill and a particleboard plant in Martell, on the western edge of the Eldorado National Forest, and 127,000 acres of timberland in Amador County—all for $320 million. That same year, Louisiana-Pacific sold SPI 38,000 acres of white fir and pine near Oroville for $50 million.

Clearly, anyone selling timberlands wanted SPI as a suitor.

"We did our homework better than anyone else did," Emmerson says. "We assessed the potential yield better than anyone else, and we knew that we'd get more salable lumber out of each log. Our recovery was higher than our competitors."

A bid price that made sense for SPI didn't necessarily make sense for anyone else. Case in point: the 1989 Fibreboard purchase—almost fifty thousand acres near Truckee, along with cutting rights to another twenty thousand acres that would still be owned by Fibreboard.

Other timber companies, whose yield per log was less than SPI's, would lose money if they had paid SPI's overbid price.

"Over the years after the Santa Fe purchase," Emmerson remembers, "I heard some grumbling from others about how we were buying up all the good lands. No one likes hearing that kind of thing, but it was true because we did a better job. I don't get any thrill over someone else's failure. We were expanding and the competition was shrinking. Some of the deals we made, if I'd had the figures that some of the other guys had to look at after doing their homework, I wouldn't have bought the parcel either. But I had different estimates to work from. They were usually higher, and we made them work."

55

Special investigative agent Diane Welton of the USFS, who'd replaced Dave Reynolds days after the fire had begun, believed the
findings of Josh White (and, by extension, Dave Reynolds). At the site,
she had (a) posed for photos holding a shovel pointed at the two rocks
determined to be the specific point of origin; (b) drawn her own diagram of the fire's path, which in the report bears her signature; and
(c) specifically excluded the possibility that an incendiary device or other
cause was responsible for the fire.

"Active timber sale area," the report says. "Dozer operator observed
no one else in the area just prior to the fire other than himself. Nothing
to indicate this was a deliberate act. No device recovered at the Point
of Origin."

She did not recall, however, whether those were her words or the
words of Dave Reynolds. And when Bill Warne asked whether she'd
personally participated in "any form of investigation which might con-
tribute to the conclusion that this fire could not have been caused by
an arsonist," she replied, "I guess what I'm getting tripped up on, sir, is
'investigation.' What do you mean by that?"

56

Bohemia, Inc., was an Oregon company in search of a buyer for its California properties, which included two mills, a medium density fiberboard plant, and about thirty-five thousand acres of timberlands. (Willamette Industries, Inc., headquartered in Eugene, Oregon, had agreed in principle to buy Bohemia's Oregon properties.)

For years Bohemia had been flailing and at last put itself on the auction block about six months before the announced sale in September 1991. SPI was among the many companies that took a hard look at the books, as well as the mills and, of course, timberlands, and it was Emmerson who outbid the other companies based on SPI's capabilities in operations and utilization.

But the Department of Justice's antitrust division objected. Its lawyers were concerned with SPI's buying power in relation to sales of timber by the U.S. Forest Service. The word they used to block the sale was *monopsony*.

A monopsony is a situation in which there is a single buyer and many sellers, giving that buyer as much of a theoretically unfair advantage as a monopolist would have as a sole seller (see: logging rights to U.S. forests). SPI was far from the only buyer for USFS trees. But the fact that the government was ruling on a market condition that affected the government itself entitled it to initiate an investigation and to hold up, or even cancel, the sale.

The irony, of course, was that the logging industry's consolidation over the previous few decades resulted directly from policies that closed U.S. forests to chainsaws and drove companies like SPI that had the means to buy as many private timber tracts as made sense financially. Hundreds, maybe thousands, of smaller mills had been driven out of business or would be soon. In essence, the government had seeded a sort of Darwinian approach that forced Sierra Pacific to compete single-mindedly, then decided to punish SPI for withstanding the onslaught and prospering.

One of the first questions from the Department of Justice was why SPI wanted to buy two mills, the land, and the medium density fiberboard (MDF) plant. The short answer would have been, "Because we think we can make money." But that would've ended the matter on the wrong side of yes. So Emmerson and his team wrote a series of memos to explain their reasoning:

> The MDF plant is a new business for the Emmerson family. It will provide an additional source of income and smooth out some of the peaks and valleys of the timber business.
>
> The timber supply is decreasing. There's only so far one can go west; ocean blocks the way. To the east is a desert and there are no logs there. To the north is Oregon, where there are more and larger companies with mills that are facing log shortages as well. The south presents the best opportunity to find logs (e.g., the Eldorado forest).
>
> The 33,000 acres of fee land are at the south end of the Tahoe. The land will add approximately 5–7 million board feet of logs on a sustained yield basis for SPI's mills. This timber is second growth and will supply small logs.

Et cetera, for several pages.

Given that the sale was eventually approved, one might reasonably suspect that someone at the Department of Justice, reading such memos, felt embarrassed at requiring a forty-year-old company that had survived both brutal competition and terrible economic conditions to explain Business 101 to a bureaucracy that never has to turn a profit, meet a payroll, or justify its own decisions.

But then came Sierra Pacific's attempted purchase of the California timberlands and sawmill owned by the Michigan-California Lumber Company.

Mich-Cal operated a mill in the town of Camino in the Eldorado National Forest just east of Placerville. Thanks to the government's tightening of timber sales, its supply of logs for the mill had been harshly impacted, and its company-owned lands were not enough to feed the saws. Mich-Cal needed a buyer willing to keep the mill operating, one with its own timberlands located inside, say, a sixty-mile radius of the mill. Anything farther out would make the purchase impractical because of the costs to transport logs.

Several larger companies came calling, including Georgia-Pacific. But after inspecting the mill and its books, none could figure out how to make a profitable go of the enterprise.

Then Sierra Pacific assessed the situation, estimated the amount of board feet it would take to keep the large mill running gainfully, calculated how much timber from its own lands within a given radius it could divert to the Mich-Cal mill, added that to the amount currently being taken from Mich-Cal lands, and concluded that a deal was worth doing.

It bears noting that science has yet to develop a scanner capable of determining the optimal number of cuts and where those cuts should be made across a sixty-inch log in order to maximize the amount of board feet it yields. And even if the complicated algorithm could be written and implemented, the radiation from the scanner would require that everything be done inside an industrial-strength lead-lined building. So cutting remains, as it ever was, a mostly unscientific process. All of that makes SPI's ability to assess a log through look and touch that much more remarkable and accounts for SPI's ability to pay prices others would shy from. It could also explain why others would be suspicious of SPI.

The deal between Mich-Cal and SPI was this: SPI would acquire the Mich-Cal mill and its timberlands through an exchange of sorts, with SPI transferring some of its own lands to Mich-Cal as payment, and the jobs of three hundred millworkers would be saved. This was critical, because in that area of the Sierra there were few operating mills. The chance that the laid-off workers would be able to find gainful work was near zero.

But the U.S. Department of Justice's antitrust division issued an objection. Government lawyers did not accuse Sierra Pacific of operating a monopoly. They again accused SPI of being a monopsonist.

The government noted that of the few remaining sawmills in the immediate area around the Mich-Cal mill, SPI already owned one, plus two additional mills in the broader geographic area. Essentially, the feds had challenged SPI for winning a game whose rules they'd written. This in turn punished the employees of Mich-Cal's mill, who would soon lose their jobs because their mill couldn't survive on the amount of timber it was allowed to harvest.

A reasonable person might conclude that explaining this situation to the Department of Justice would have remedied the situation. But the government's fear was not that people would lose their jobs and economic activity would be curtailed. It was that a reduction in the number of potential purchasers of government timber through SPI's purchase of an independent mill would result in fewer bidders, and therefore lower prices, for timber sales on government lands—sales that at this point were only theoretical anyway, given how little land was opened to cutting.

SPI pressed forward and was informed that something called a *second request* would be required in order for the Department of Justice to determine the pertinent facts and reevaluate its decision. A second request is not unlike an appeal, except that the process is designed to dissuade the appellant from refiling. This particular second request would have required an enormous amount of paperwork by attorneys for both Mich-Cal and SPI, followed by equally extensive and detailed answers to hundreds, even thousands, of questions from government lawyers. Just answering the questions, SPI's lawyers decided, could take months. And for its part, the Department of Justice said that it would offer no promises or assurances about whether there was even a reasonable chance the second request might result in a reversal.

In the meantime the mill was scheduled to close down. All those jobs would be lost, and even if the mill someday reopened under SPI's ownership, many of its workers would have already left the area in search of other work, most of them possibly unable to go more than a few weeks without a paycheck of some sort. So the stakes were high— several hundred direct jobs and an incalculable number of indirect jobs that could have reduced Camino to a ghost town.

Nonetheless, the Justice Department steadfastly declined to revisit its decision without SPI's second request. The merger, it seemed, was destined to die on the vine.

Then SPI contacted California senator Dianne Feinstein and asked if she would be willing to intercede, less on behalf of SPI than on behalf of the workers whose jobs were at stake. After her staff confirmed the facts, California's senior U.S. senator wrote a detailed letter urging the

Department of Justice to abandon its insistence on a second request and forthwith approve the sale.

Emmerson says he was surprised when the DOJ signed off on the deal without comment. And he gives an interesting footnote to the saga: SPI had agreed to buy the California assets of Bohemia, but before the deal closed, Willamette bought Bohemia, so the eventual transaction was between SPI and Willamette. "We negotiated the deal with certain people at Bohemia," he says, "and closed it with completely different people at Willamette. They had to abide by the contract."

57

In August 2011 Alan Carlson was deposed over a two-day period in a
suite at the Bonanza Inn in Yuba City, California, fifty miles north
of Sacramento. The previous December he had left his job as deputy
chief for fire prevention and law enforcement for the northern region of
Cal Fire and had opened Alan Carlson Associates, LLC, a wildland fire
investigation consulting firm. He referred to himself as a retired peace
officer. At nearly fifty-nine, Carlson had close-cropped brown hair and
a bushy brown mustache, and though he was not a particularly large
man, he had the air of a bouncer outside an Irish pub on Saint Paddy's
Day—pleasant enough but focused and businesslike.

Back when he was still a Cal Fire deputy chief, Carlson had attended
dozens of depositions related to the Moonlight Fire. When Bill Warne
asked which depositions Carlson could recall attending, Josh White's
was the only one he mentioned by name.

Warne had learned that Josh White was, in most ways, Alan Carlson's protégé and star pupil. "White," Carlson testified, was someone
"who can ask the right questions to get clarification from me so that
they can carry out their job assignments. Someone who comes back
and asks the right questions to clarify anything that I need to give
them. Accomplishes their work assignments. Learns from their mistakes. Is consistent. Comes to work on time. Willing to work long, hard
hours."

At the time of the Moonlight Fire, though White technically reported to Dave Harp, he really reported to Carlson, head of the so-
called Goon Squad, the unit that collected and disbursed funds from
the WiFITER (Wildland Fire Training and Equipment Fund) unit.

Warne hoped to find out whether Carlson had called Harp on the day the fire broke out to insist that he assign White to the fire, suspecting that Carlson would already have learned that Sierra Pacific was harvesting timber in the area near where the fire began.

Eight years earlier, in 1999, a fire that would come to be known as Gunn Fire 1 broke out in the Plumas National Forest. Only a few hundred acres burned before the blaze was brought under control by Cal Fire units. Some weeks later, a large pile of slash (woody debris left on the forest floor in piles after logging) that had apparently been smoldering ignited when the wind came up. What would come to be called Gunn Fire 2 eventually burned sixty thousand acres of national forest—about the same swath as the Moonlight Fire.

In the weeks between the fires, timber fallers working for Sierra Pacific near that area had noted that the slash pile, at the bottom of a steep hill, was smoking. Both Cal Fire and USFS people at the site saw the smoldering heap, but it was Cal Fire, under Carlson's command, that had the responsibility for extinguishing it. No action was taken, though, and when fire spread, Cal Fire refused to accept blame for the conflagration. The agency filed a preliminary report naming Sierra Pacific's subcontractor and blaming logging operations that it claimed had begun too soon after the first fire, suggesting that the logs they were hauling out were still hot. Unfortunately for Carlson, Sierra Pacific tracked down the forest service personnel who'd been there the day the smoldering slash pile was identified.

Cal Fire took the hit, and Carlson felt it personally. As battalion chief of the unit deemed responsible for the fire, it was his crews that hadn't done their job. Either he hadn't given the order or hadn't ensured his order was followed.

The hit to him personally didn't seem to affect his rise in the organization. He continued to enjoy promotions until he became deputy chief of the Cal Fire northern region, the position he held on the day of the Moonlight Fire.

Still, by 2007 there were Sierra Pacific foresters who believed that Alan Carlson reserved a special place in his craw for SPI, and after the Moonlight Fire, many people at Sierra Pacific who knew enough to have an opinion on the matter suspected it was no coincidence that Carlson's protégé had been assigned to lead the investigation.

Carlson testified that the first conversation he had with Josh White about the Moonlight Fire was on September 6, when he said White requested "additional resources"—that is, investigators Dieter Schmitt and George Gonzales.

"At that point in time, sir," Warne asked, "did he give you any sense as to the status of his investigation of what may have caused the Moonlight Fire?"

"I'm sure," Carlson said, "we would have had some kind of conversation about what it was encompassed with. The only thing I'm sure of is that he made a request for resources."

No, Carlson said, he didn't second-guess Josh White when he read the report, even though the scene had been released barely thirty-six hours after the fire started.

No, he didn't have any concerns about the document that identified SPI as the defendant dated that day.

"Okay," Warne said. "And you knew at the time that you saw that report that Sierra Pacific Industries had been identified as a defendant before a number of interviews had been taken by the investigators, correct?"

"I knew," Carlson said, "that one of the investigators had written a document that identified SPI on the document as a defendant. That's what I knew."

58

In 1992 SPI spent $350 million on 320,000 acres of prime California timberlands (most of the Paul Bunyan and Diamond Match tracts) that had belonged for many years to Roseburg Forest Products, one of the country's largest family lumber concerns.

But before the deal's consummation, there were several twists and turns that led to significant changes at SPI.

Roseburg had been founded in the 1930s by Kenneth Ford, who was still at the helm more than five decades later at eighty-three. It was with Ford that Emmerson believed he'd reached an agreement in principle to buy the assets that were on the market after Roseburg had suffered a couple of down years, resulting in the closure of some mills and several hundred job losses.

Emmerson, his son Mark, and SPI's general counsel David Dun flew up to Oregon to meet with Ford and a slew of Roseburg lawyers, accountants, executives, and others. They gathered in a conference room in the airport's executive terminal to hammer out the deal. But then Ford said he wanted to think about it. The next day he announced that he'd changed his mind about the sale.

"Ken," Emmerson remembers, "said that it had been his life, and he couldn't see parting with it."

So that was that, Emmerson concluded. There was no point trying to talk someone out of such a determination.

But several months later, Emmerson received another call from Kenneth Ford, who wanted to know if they still had the same deal. Emmerson said they did. He and Dave Dun flew up there.

This time, though, Emmerson took his wife along. Ida wanted to do some shopping in Portland, and Emmerson figured that the amount of time she'd be busy doing that would be more or less the amount of time he and Dun would be busy at Roseburg with the paperwork.

Around ten in the morning Emmerson walked into the office of Frank Spears, Kenneth Ford's attorney.

"Frank wasn't there," Red says, "so I used his phone and made a bunch of calls while I was waiting. Around ten-thirty or so Frank came walking down the hall. I said, 'Good morning, Frank, how are you today?' He said, 'Not very well.' And I knew what that meant. Sure enough, he said, 'Kenneth can't decide whether he wants to sell this thing or not. I've got the contract. It's all signed. But he won't let me release it.' We talked a little, but obviously there wasn't much to say. Anyway, I didn't say much. He promised to get me a decision one way or another within a couple of days. So we left."

But because it was still early in the morning, and Ida wasn't expected back from shopping for at least another couple of hours—believing that the paperwork would've taken that long—there was nothing for Emmerson and Dun to do but wait for her at the airport. That's where he was an hour later when Kenneth Ford himself strolled in, wearing a big smile, and said to Red, "We have to talk a little bit."

"What he told me," Red says, "was that parting with that land was like parting with his wife Bonnie. That was pretty much the gist of the conversation."

As annoyed as Emmerson might have been, there were few men in the world who could better appreciate Ford's reluctance to sell that land.

Kenneth Ford was born in 1908 and grew up in eastern Washington, where he worked for his father's small lumber business and became known for his uncanny mechanical aptitude. He was always tinkering with salvage equipment to turn out something new.

In 1936, at the height of the Depression, he struck out on his own and bought a sawmill near Roseburg, Oregon, which he fittingly called the Roseburg Lumber Company.

Ford kept it going and managed to turn a profit with refitted salvaged equipment from other mills. Though he supervised a crew of twenty-five, he also made himself head salesman and sometimes filled in as cook at the logging camp. There was nothing he wouldn't do, and no one who could outwork him. With his revenue from the mill, he bought up timberlands in the area that otherwise would have gone bank-owned after foreclosures.

By 1944 his balance sheet was attractive enough to secure a loan that allowed him to build a new and larger mill near Dillard, Oregon. Revenue from that one was used to buy thousands of acres of prime forest. Before long Ford owned 160,000 acres in Douglas County alone. But he didn't even log his own lands.

Instead, he bought cutting rights on state and federal parcels for the logs that supplied his mills. When World War II ended, Roseburg was well positioned to take advantage of the postwar building boom.

As the company's sole shareholder, Ford didn't have to answer to anyone when he kept reinvesting profits into the company. And as one of the first to spot the potential of plywood, veneer, and particleboard, he invested heavily and was rewarded lavishly. By the end of the 1970s, Roseburg was one of the country's largest plywood producers, the largest period in sanded plywood. Annual revenue was about $400 million, and some industry observers estimated Kenneth Ford's personal net worth at $500 million (multiple billions in 2017 dollars).

In 1979 Roseburg outbid several other companies—some of them, like Weyerhaeuser, much bigger than Roseburg—for 323,000 acres of Northern California timberlands owned by Kimberly-Clark. The cost was a quarter billion dollars, and it brought Roseburg's total landholdings to half a million acres.

Now, a dozen years later, the price for that same parcel that SPI wanted to buy had risen by a hundred million dollars. SPI wasn't haggling over price, but Kenneth Ford got cold feet for sentimental reasons.

Emmerson and Dave Dun went home not knowing whether the deal would ever be completed.

"Then," says Emmerson, "about a week later they FedExed the signed contracts to us. We wanted to sign them but sat on them as long as we could, because the meter would start the moment we drew the money down"—that is, moved the funds from the bank syndicate to Roseburg. "I think it was weeks before we mailed the contracts back and they got their money." (Ever since the successful Santa Fe purchase, Emmerson says, banks have stood in line to loan SPI money.)

To this day, Emmerson says, he's as sympathetic to Kenneth Ford's reluctance to sell as he was then—and not just because of the striking biographical similarities between them or because Emmerson himself says he'd never agree to sell a parcel without a compelling reason (which in Roseburg's case was Ford's desire to fund a private, charitable foundation that did indeed come into existence with the SPI funds).

The reason is that Emmerson could see what work itself—that is, getting up every morning and doing something useful and gainful with the hours—meant to Kenneth Ford. Work, having little to do with the money it brought in, was Kenneth Ford's reason for living. Just like it was for Red Emmerson.

"You could tell that if he ever sold Roseburg or retired, he'd be dead in a month or so," Emmerson remembers. "The man worked harder than anyone right up to the day he died" in 1997, at age eighty-nine.

Yet even that emotional parallel isn't why Emmerson recalls the Roseburg deal in such detail. It's because, he says, he learned a lesson from Kenneth Ford, one that Ford surely didn't intend to send or even know he was sending.

"I saw that Kenneth had his son Allyn working with him," Emmerson says. "Allyn was supposed to be his heir, but he never gave him any significant responsibility—not really. Allyn was smart, too. A very capable young man."

Indeed. Allyn Ford had graduated with an undergraduate degree from Yale in 1968, and a couple of years later earned an MBA from Stanford. "But Kenneth wouldn't turn over the reins on anything," Emmerson says. "Allyn worked for him, and what Kenneth said was the way he did it. Ken couldn't give up control."

In fact, during the 1980s Roseburg Lumber experienced some executive turmoil, in part because Ford wouldn't relinquish power.

"Allyn stuck around in that environment," Emmerson says. "Good for him. I salute him. To his dying day, Kenneth couldn't give his son any real authority to speak of. He just refused to let go. If I had treated my boys that way, I doubt they would've stuck around. They'd have left the company."

And that, most of all, is what Emmerson took from the protracted Roseburg Lumber Company purchase.

"I always had a lot of respect for Kenneth Ford. I looked up to him," he says. "But I learned that I didn't want to be like Kenneth Ford in that one way. It was a wake-up call for me. I made a conscious decision that I didn't want to treat my sons the way he treated his son."

59

Over thirteen days in late 2010 and early 2011, Josh White was deposed for nearly seventy hours in a Downey Brand conference room on the Capitol Mall in Sacramento. For most of those days his boss, Alan Carlson, was present as a professional observer. Kelli Taylor for the United States and Tracy Winsor for California were always present.

Federal law allows a magistrate to limit the number of hours a government witness like White can be deposed, and magistrate Edmund Brennan had limited Sierra Pacific's access to a mere three days. But the State of California, according to the rules of civil procedure, cannot limit "reasonable" access to such an important witness as White was in the Moonlight case. As long as the questioning is considered productive and not punitive—and with White there were about four thousand pages of productive information—the deposition can proceed.

White was, as Bill Warne argued successfully, a linchpin of the case, so Warne and his team completed the final ten days of Josh White's deposition under the aegis of the State of California. Anything he said in the state depositions would be admissible at the federal trial, and vice versa, if what he testified to on the stand at trial contradicted previous sworn testimony. The defendant—and, for that matter, the plaintiffs—would be entitled to read back for the judge and jury the testimony transcripts or play the videotape.

The investigator with blue eyes and looks to burn walked into the first deposition with a swagger and a smirk, but over the course of days he visibly became a timid, tentative witness who sometimes exhibited the kind of reactive behavior that his own training in law enforcement might have identified as suspicious.

Halfway through the sixth day, Warne asked White why he hadn't mentioned Caleb Lief in his joint origin and cause report, cosigned with the USFS's Diane Welton.

"I just didn't put it in," he said.

"Well," Warne said, "you're interested in turning over every lead, correct?"

"Leads, yes. Relevant information, yes."

"Right. But it would be relevant to you as one of the investigators if it turned out that Mr. Lief, who was in the tower that called in the fire, was under the influence of marijuana at the time, correct?"

"Yes."

"And since Ms. Welton conveyed to you in 2008 that there had been some allegations regarding potential marijuana use, why didn't you follow up to find out if in fact that marijuana use took place on September 3rd, 2007?"

"I don't know."

Warne asked for a short break to make a phone call. It was 1:55 P.M. White never returned from the break and didn't answer calls from Tracy Winsor's staff. Only later did Warne learn that Josh White had collapsed on Sacramento's Capitol Mall, having suffered what appeared to be a heart attack. When he returned months later, he appeared to be about twenty pounds lighter and admitted only to a "stress-related event," for which he had been prescribed medication that he refused to identify, though he claimed it would not impair his ability to answer.

The roasting continued. But White would not have the moral support in the room of Alan Carlson, who in the three-month hiatus had retired as battalion chief of the Cal Fire cost-recovery unit.

Answering one of Warne's questions, White said he was unaware of a supplementary report compiled by Cal Fire investigator George Gonzales, who with Dieter Schmitt had interviewed a number of witnesses. Warne asked why it hadn't been included with his origin and cause report.

"I wasn't aware of this document existing," White said.

Warne asked why it was different from the investigative interview summaries Gonzales had written that White had included in the report.

"I don't know," White said.

Warne asked him whether he had heard anything about Ryan Bauer from Gonzales "at any point in time during his work for you on the investigation relating to the Moonlight Fire?"

"Just generally I remember them telling me that they found Ryan Bauer and that they interviewed him," he said.

Warne asked if the two investigators had ever mentioned to him Leo Whitlock's suggestion that they talk to Bauer, "a known wood thief," which had been recounted in the supplementary report

"Not that I recall," White said.

Warne asked if, before Moonlight, he'd worked with Gonzales.

He had. On the Jim Hough case. The man who'd committed suicide.

Warne asked White why he insisted on claiming that Ivan Houser, the Cal Fire forester who'd brought the GPS unit to the area of origin, was there with him in the morning when the photos of the metal fragments were taken. "He indicates that he didn't arrive at the scene until 11:30 in the morning—an hour and a half later [than the photos were taken]."

White, Warne believed, had not appended Houser's report (which had been discovered by Warne's team in Kelli Taylor's thirty thousand-document dump) to his origin and cause report because if Houser had indeed arrived at 11:30, White's official narrative would have been revealed as fiction.

"I believe [Houser] was there earlier," White said.

Warne had anticipated White would contend that Houser's arrival time stated in the report was wrong, and he knew White could not have anticipated that he had enough data points to discredit White's revision: Houser had said it took him from five to ten minutes to reach White and Reynolds after parking his truck on the landing. That meant it would have taken White and Reynolds, walking downhill instead of uphill, about five minutes to reach their truck from the area of origin. But since the first photo of the metal fragments was taken on the hood of White's truck at 10:02, the latest White and Reynolds could have left the area of origin was 9:57. By everyone's account, though, Houser was on the hill with them for at least twenty minutes. That would have made his arrival, according to White's story, no later than 9:35. Subtracting from 9:35 the walk up the hill meant that, to be early instead of late, Houser would have arrived a full thirty-five minutes early. Had that been true, Josh White would've had no reason to put the note on his windshield directing Houser to the area of origin.

Warne asked, "Did Mr. Houser follow you down to your pickup truck for purposes of taking the photographs that we just mentioned?"

"No," White said, before adding that Houser was present at his pickup when the photos were snapped.

"He doesn't mention that in [his] report," Warne said. "Correct?"

"I don't believe so, no."

Question from Warne: "Why didn't Ivan Houser's information get included in the report that you submitted to Chief Carlson?"

"I don't recall," White said.

"At some point in time did you conclude where the point of origin was?" "Again, we identified two locations it could have been," White said.

"And why did you identify those two locations?"

"Because of the evidence that was found at the scene."

"And what was the evidence found at the scene?"

"The competent ignition source."

"And what was that?"

"The metal flakes."

"And that is something you found on the 5th?"

"Yes."

"Did you look for any competent ignition sources on the 4th?"

"We ran out of time."

"On the 4th you did?"

"On the 4th," White said.

"And then you came back on the morning of the 5th?"

"Yes."

"Okay. So you didn't conduct a search for competent ignition sources on the 4th. You did that on the 5th, right?"

"No."

"You did *not* look for competent ignition sources on the 4th, correct?"

"In the realm of looking through the specific origin area on the 4th, no, we did not."

Question from Warne: "Your testimony is that you found that metal on September 5, 2007, right?"

"Yes," White said.

"And that you found that metal dragging a magnet when you were working with Mr. Reynolds in the morning of September 5th, correct?"

"That's correct."

"Do you have a sense as to what time of day it was when you found that metal?"

"On September 5th it would have been prior to 10 o'clock in the morning," White said, looking at the photos.

"And why do you say it was prior to 10 o'clock in the morning?"

"Because I have two photos here indicated at 10:02 A.M."

"And do those photos indicate a location where the metal was taken from?"

"No, these photos do not."

"Is there anything in that log you're looking at that would indicate where the metal was taken from?"

"No."

"Why not?"

"I don't know."

Question from Warne: "I take your testimony to state specifically that you never placed a flag or an indicator of any kind next to the two points of origin when you processed this scene, correct?"

"Yes. I did not place a white evidence flag where I had located the metal fragments."

"And in fact you didn't place an evidence flag where you believed the fire started, correct?"

"That's correct."

"And you believe the fire either started at one place or two places, correct?"

"That's correct."

"And with respect to each of those places, you never placed a flag next to either of those places, correct?"

"I did not place a white flag next to either of those locations."

"You say white flag. Did you place any kind of indicator, whether it's a flag or an indicator plate or an evidence tent, next to either of those rocks where you believe the fire started?"

"No, I did not."

"And tell me why you didn't do that."

"It wasn't a matter of having a reason not to do it."

"I just don't understand what that means," Warne said. "You just said, 'It wasn't a matter of having a reason not to do it.' I'm just asking you as the investigator in the Moonlight Fire, can you tell me why you never placed any flags or indicators next to the points that you believe are the points of origin?"

"At that time is when Ivan Houser had arrived."

Question from Warne about the night of September 6, when Cal Fire investigators Dieter Schmitt and George Gonzales arrived in Westwood and were given a list of names to contact for interviews: "And when you say you briefed both investigators of the status of the investigation, do you recall what you had told them at that point in time?"

"I don't remember the particulars. . . . I just know that I would have provided them an overview of the entire investigation up to that date."

"Did you tell them at that point in time that you suspected that the fire was caused by a dozer striking a rock?"

"I don't believe that I would have said it. I'm not sure if I would have said it that way or what the phraseology, but I would have given them the status of the case. And the evidence that we had found and the individuals that were involved."

"And was the status of the case at that point in time your belief that the fire may have been caused by a dozer striking a rock?"

"It was a hypothesis at that time."

"Okay, and you told them of that hypothesis?"

"I would have shared that information, yes."

Question from Warne: "Is there a reason you didn't include Mr. Houser's report in your origin and cause report?"

"No," said White.

"Did you decide not to put it in for some reason?"

"No."

"Is it typical for you to select certain supplementary investigation reports and include some and not include others?"

"No."

"Can you tell me, is it typically your practice to include in your cause and origin investigative reports all of the supplementary investigation reports?"

"As necessary," White said. "I mean, I hadn't requested Houser to write the report. I don't remember when I received the report."

"My question is," Warne said, "is it your practice to include supplementary investigation reports in the final origin and cause report with respect to your investigation?"

"Yes."

"And your testimony right now with respect to why this report is not in your final joint origin and cause investigative report is because you are not sure if Mr. Houser gave it to you?"

"Well, I'm not sure when I received it," White said.

"And had you received it before completing the report, would you have included it in the report?"

"I would assume so, yes."

"And you can see that the date of the report here on this particular document [Houser's report] is dated 9/21/07, correct?"

"That's correct."

"And you don't know why Mr. Houser wrote this report?"

"I hadn't asked him to."

Question from Warne: "Did you include anywhere in your report the fact that you met with Mr. Houser on September 5, 2007?"

"No, I don't believe so."

"And is there a reason you didn't include those events in your report?"

"I met with Mr. Houser when we were meeting with the SPI representatives [forester John Forno, who had told White that he'd heard rumors of arson as the cause and received assurances from White that all avenues of investigation would be pursued] for purposes of the 5th. There was no intent to exclude him from the report."

"Well," Warne said, "my question is based on the fact that we know that Mr. Houser spent some time with you on the 5th, correct?"

"Correct."

"And we know that you had discussions with him about the applicable legal codes that you put in the front of the report, correct?"

"Correct."

"And we know that you actually went back and you looked at identification marks on some of the equipment that was stashed on the backside of 3130, correct?"

"Yes."

"And based on his assessment at the time, he believed that he spent approximately an hour with you that day, correct?"

"Based on his assessment," White said.

"Is that consistent with your memory as well?"

"It may have been longer."

"All right," Warne said. "Whether it was an hour or longer, my question is still in light of the fact that you met with him in the context of your investigation. Why didn't you reference that fact in your narrative?"

"It just wasn't something that I obviously identified in the narrative."

"No, I understand that," Warne said. "That's self-evident. But my question is, Why? I'm looking for a reason why you didn't do that."

"There was no specific reason."

"Well, are you trained to include what you did in the context of a particular investigation all the way through?"

"Define 'all the way through,'" White said.

"The fact that you met with Mr. Houser and actually called him up to the scene and met with him on 9/5/2007, you didn't find that relevant to your narrative in terms of what occurred on the 5th?"

"There was no intention. If it was relevant, then the level of relevancy —I just didn't include him in the report."

"Do you think your training would indicate that you should have included him in the report?"

"I cited him as one of the witnesses."

"Right."

"I referenced Mr. Houser when we had our meeting with SPI representatives."

"You just said on the record that you cited him as one of the witnesses. Did you do that?"

"I don't believe I did."

"Can you tell me why?"

"No reason."

"You just forgot?"

"I wouldn't say that I forgot. For the purposes of the origin and cause he was able to assist me in the information related to Forest Practice Rules and Regulations."

"And in light of the fact that he assisted you with those regulations, why didn't you include him in the report?"

"Again," White said, "there was no specific reason."

"When do you recall first seeing this supplemental investigation report that was apparently completed and signed by Mr. Houser on 9/21/2007?"

"Probably sometime in 2007."

"And when did you submit this to region? I think you said January of 2008?"

"When you say, When did I submit 'this,' the report?"

"Yes."

"Yes," White said.

"And in light of the fact that you believe you found this supplemental report, or you had this supplemental report, from Mr. Houser in 2007 and you hadn't submitted your draft join origin and cause investigative report until January of 2008, you still don't know why you didn't include this, correct?"

"There was no specific reason to exclude him," White said.

"Do you believe it was a mistake not to include this in the report?" Warne asked.

"I would have added it in hindsight.

"And why would you have added it?"

"So we wouldn't have had to go through the last 30 minutes in discussion about it!"

Question from Warne: "How would you go about developing the intent for arson?"

"Well, with no physical evidence of arson at the scene, it would be largely dependent on witness interviews."

Question from Warne: "You also know as a part of your training that most arson fires are hot set, correct? Do you understand what 'hot set' means?"

"I do understand what 'hot set' means."

"What does 'hot set' mean?"

"Where somebody may start with an open flame device and take that device with them."

Question from Warne: "And in light of the fact that a significant percentage of arson fires are hot set, what's relevant about your statement that there was no evidence of any incendiary devices found in the origin? I'm reading from your report. What is relevant about that?"

"That it didn't appear to be any time delay or any other devices for me to be able to justify or specifically identify this cause of the fire as arson."

Question from Warne: "And did you and Mr. Carlson ever find a motive in terms of what Mr. Hough [the arsonist who had hanged himself with a jail bedsheet shortly before the Moonlight Fire] was doing?"

"No."

"Was that surprising to you?"

"Not necessarily."

"Are you taught in your training that sometimes arsonists just don't have a motive?"

"I don't believe that that is taught anywhere."

"Had you been involved in an arson case where you couldn't figure out what the motive might have been?"

"Of all the arson cases that I have ever been involved in?"

"Yes."

"Yes," White said.

"So this wasn't something new to you?"

"That's correct."

Question from Warne: "Do you have any recollection as to what your arson training tells you in terms of what the primary motive might be for arson?"

"The FBI has six classifications for motives for arsonists. . . . It identifies revenge/retaliation, excitement, profit, vandalism, crime concealment, and extremism or terrorism."

Question from Warne: "We have established that by the time you met with Schmitt and Gonzales you were keeping open the possibility that it was an equipment fire, correct?"

"Correct."

"And the question I've got is, at that same point in time when you met with Schmitt and Gonzales on September 6th, were you keeping open the possibility of any other possible causes for the Moonlight Fire?"

"We would be keeping open other causes if there were any additional information that would have been provided to us."

"And at the point in time you discussed with Mr. Schmitt and Gonzales their role, did you discuss with them any other potential causes that you thought might be something to investigate?"

"I didn't ask them about any specific cause. I wanted them to go out and get as much information regarding the witnesses or anybody that had tangible information regarding the start or cause."

"When you spoke with them, did you think there was a possibility the fire could have been started by arson?"

"When I spoke with them?"

"On September 6, 2007, when you spoke with Mr. Gonzales and Mr. Schmitt, did you believe that the Moonlight Fire could have been started by arson?"

"Based on our examination of the scene, based on the information that we had at that time, there was nothing to indicate arson at that time," White said. "But again, witness interviewing can sometimes bring in new information. So I would say that we hadn't completely excluded arson as a cause."

Question from Warne: "Tell me when you took this [photo], sir."

"That was taken on September 5th, 2007, at 8:18 A.M."

"Is that your first photo on that particular day?"

"Yes, it is."

"Do you recall what you and Mr. Reynolds did prior to taking this photo?"

"I do not."

"And what are those blue flags indicating to you?"

"Blue flags to me would indicate a backing indicator."

"And what are those red flags indicating to you?"

"Advancing."

"Do you see any other flags there?"

"I see at least two blue flags, and what appears to be four red flags."

"And what about the white flag, what does that indicate?"

"I'm sorry?"

"What about the white flag there?"

"There is no white flag in there."

"Can I have a blowup on the laptop here? If I can have the record show that I'm giving the witness a laptop that has got a picture of this blown up so you've got high resolution. Do you see that, sir?"

"I do."

"Do you see the white flag?"

"I do."

"And you can take that down and I'll show you that that is a white flag right there."

"Okay."

Question from Warne: "Do you now see the white flag in the photograph?"

"I do," White said.

"And do you see where this photograph is being taken from? Is that from one of the rocks you marked?"

"Yes?"

"And why is that white flag there?"

"I do not know."

"You testified earlier that you hadn't placed any white flags prior to finding that metal, right?"

"I had not."

"And you don't have any understanding as to why that white flag is there?"

"I have no recall of that, no."

"And do you know what a white flag typically designates?"

"Typically evidence."

"Evidence or point of origin?"

"It could."

"Well, what do you use it for?"

"Evidence."

"And what does the training manual say with respect to the placement of a white flag?"

"If there is evidence to indicate the point of origin, then it can be used as such."

"Right. It's used to designate the point of origin, correct?"

"That's one of the functions of a white flag."

"And do you have an understanding, sir, as to whether or not this white flag is placed in the same area that Mr. Reynolds was photographed by you on four separate occasions at about 6:32 at night on September 4th?"

"No, I do not."

Near the end of the ninth day of depositions, with the final four days of depositions scheduled for three months later, Bill Warne briefly turned over the questioning to Richard Linkert, an eponymous partner in the law firm representing the landowners.

Linkert got White to concede that Ivan Houser had informed White and Reynolds on the morning of September 5 that the dozer opera-

tors could have violated section 938.8 of the California Forest Practice
Rules of the state's code of regulation—one of the sections on which the
state was basing its lawsuit—only if they'd performed activities that required a fire walk.

"What," Linkert asked, "did Mr. Houser tell you about whether or
not water barring required a fire watch of any sort?"

"I don't remember the specific," White said, "but I know that water
barring is not identified in 938.8." He went on to correctly identify falling, yarding, and skidding as activities that would require a fire walk.

"Okay," Linkert said. "So in terms of your state of mind, when you
approached this investigation you knew that if you concluded that the
fire was caused by timber operations, then the timber operators and
anybody else who was responsible for their conduct was going to be the
subject of a cost-recovery effort following the fire?"

"I was familiar," White said, "with the [California] Health and Safety
Code [Section] 13009 requiring either negligence or violation of law." *

* (a) Any person (1) who negligently, or in violation of the law, sets a fire, allows a
fire to be set, or allows a fire kindled or attended by him or her to escape onto any
public or private property, (2) other than a mortgagee, who, being in actual possession of a structure, fails or refuses to correct, within the time allotted for correction,
despite having the right to do so, a fire hazard prohibited by law, for which a public
agency properly has issued a notice of violation respecting the hazard, or (3) including a mortgagee, who, having an obligation under other provisions of law to correct
a fire hazard prohibited by law, for which a public agency has properly issued a notice of violation respecting the hazard, fails or refuses to correct the hazard within
the time allotted for correction, despite having the right to do so, is liable for the fire
suppression costs incurred in fighting the fire and for the cost of providing rescue or
emergency medical services, and those costs shall be a charge against that person.
The charge shall constitute a debt of that person, and is collectible by the person, or
by the federal, state, county, public, or private agency, incurring those costs in the
same manner as in the case of an obligation under a contract, expressed or implied.
  (b) Public agencies participating in fire suppression, rescue, or emergency medical
services as set forth in subdivision (a), may designate one or more of the participating agencies to bring an action to recover costs incurred by all of the participating
agencies. An agency designated by the other participating agencies to bring an action pursuant to this section shall declare that authorization and its basis in the
complaint, and shall itemize in the complaint the total amounts claimed under this
section by each represented agency.
  (c) Any costs incurred by the Department of Forestry and Fire Protection in sup-
pressing any wildland fire originating or spreading from a prescribed burning operation conducted by the department pursuant to a contract entered into pursuant
to Article 2 (commencing with Section 4475) of Chapter 7 of Part 2 of Division 4 of
the Public Resources Code shall not be collectible from any party to the contract,
including any private consultant or contractor who entered into an agreement with

"And if your report established negligence or violation of law on the part of, in this case, SPI and Howell, then you had reason to believe that they were going to be the subject of a civil cost-recovery section, did you not?"

"That would be my general understanding," White said.

"Was it your state of mind at the time," Linkert asked, "that if the fire was caused by arson that there could be a civil cost-recovery effort made against SPI or Howell?"

"Well, no, it would depend on the context," White said.

"Did you do anything to take into account potential bias on your part that if you found Howell and SPI and perhaps landowners responsible, there was going to be a civil cost-recovery effort being made? But if you found the cause of the fire to be undetermined or third-party arson, there would be no cost recovery? Do you see what I'm getting at?"

"Well," White said, "it started off with my potential bias on my part."

"Right. So if you find that SPI's responsible, big company, can potentially pay a lot in damages. If you find that somebody else is responsible who doesn't have assets, then there is no cost recovery. How do you deal with any potential bias you might have?"

"There is no bias going into that," White said. "If there were to be any bias to look at it one way or another, I think that it would start the investigation flawed from the very beginning. To set your sights on one specific—undetermined would be easy. You label it undetermined, you file it away, and you wouldn't have to worry about any litigation."

---

that party pursuant to subdivision (d) of Section 4475.5 of the Public Resources Code, as provided in subdivision (a), to the extent that those costs were not incurred as a result of a violation of any provision of the contract.

(d) This section applies to all areas of the state, regardless of whether primarily wildlands, sparsely developed, or urban.

60

In a monarchy, the order of ascension to the throne is predetermined by precedent, law, and custom. Few monarchs ever step down voluntarily as opposed to going out feet first. Charles V of Spain stepped down in the sixteenth century for political and territorial reasons (and also due to poor health; he died soon thereafter), and England's Edward VIII famously did it for love in 1936. Otherwise, the passing of the monarch's scepter has occurred in history only at the king's death.

But in a family-owned business, the transition is seat of the pants, with no rule book, no infallible precedent, no hard-and-fast policy about the best and surest way to assimilate or incorporate adult children who wish to make that family business their careers. Couple this with the unavoidable fact that, throughout the history of business, companies frequently fail or are damaged after that leadership transition from the founder to his or her heirs. Red Emmerson had occasionally worried that his children's relatively cushy upbringing—even considering the hard labor they'd been forced to do as kids at various mills—would hobble their drive to succeed.

But after graduating college in 1979, Red's oldest son, George, began working for Sierra Pacific at the bottom and was expected to prove his way up. Carolyn, Red and Ida Emmerson's middle child, would eventually choose to go into business with her husband, Bob, but youngest son, Mark, studied business in college and got his CPA license before going to work for Sierra Pacific in finance. In 2017 he was the company's chief financial officer and chairman of the board of directors, and George the president.

While Red Emmerson long ago reached the age where men typically slow down or retire outright, he says he stopped working for money much longer ago than that. Since then, he says, he's worked for the joy and pleasure of working and building something and furthering the enterprise. He says he'd prefer to remain SPI's chief executive far into the future, but has agreed that it's better for everyone else and therefore the company if he leaves the strategic and operational decisions to George and Mark.

"If I hadn't agreed," he says, "I think George would've gone out on his own, to see what he can do without anyone looking over his shoulder. Mark, too, for the same reason. They might've even gone out together. And that was the last thing I wanted to happen. There've been some tough times here about who does what and about what should be done, but we have never had a meeting that ended with someone mad at somebody else."

61

After thirty years as an employee, Dave Reynolds left the U.S. Forest Service in September 2008. He took his pension and went full-time into the carpet-cleaning business, which he had been in and out of on the side for more than a decade. Two years later, Cal Fire hired him as a part-time consultant on the state's case against Sierra Pacific. He was paid $60 per hour to read the transcripts of Josh White's depositions, pore over several expert reports commissioned by SPI—all of which concluded, independently of the others, that the fire had likely started atop the hill, some 250 feet southwest of where Reynolds and White had concluded it had—and consult with White about the diagram that Reynolds had drawn of the origin site.

What there was to consult about, given that their reports had long ago been filed, with Reynolds's work appended to Diane Welton's official origin and cause report, was a good question. That's why the judge had granted Bill Warne access to Reynolds for another day, though he'd already been deposed for three days.

There is nothing unusual or inappropriate about having a former employee who was essential to an incident called back to consult if he or she retired in the interim and is willing to accept an hourly paycheck at a negotiable rate; and, of course, even if he hadn't been hired on an interim basis he would be expected to testify in court, presumably as a plaintiff's witness.

But in this situation there was reason to wonder what, exactly, the state of California—and, by proxy, the United States of America— expected of Dave Reynolds. Primary among his duties, it appeared, was reviewing the transcripts of Josh White's depositions, all four thousand pages, the most of any witness in this case.

It was reasonable for the defense to wonder what, exactly, the government expected Reynolds to learn and then do by reading the transcripts, reviewing the diagram, and meeting in January 2011 with White in the presence of Kelli Taylor and Tracy Winsor, who as officers of the court were obliged to ensure that nothing outside the realm of the factual was discussed.

Warne wondered whether they'd brought in Reynolds, a former federal employee who was now, like White, a state employee, to coordinate their stories and try retroactively to devise credible explanations for many of the holes now left uncovered by White's testimony.

Reynolds had originally been deposed in March 2011, after Josh White's first nine days of depositions in November 2010 but before his final four days, which came in May 2011. During his March depositions, Reynolds had insisted that on the evening of September 4, he and White had planted colored flags indicating the spots where they believed the fire had advanced, moved laterally, or backed. He had denied, however, that they had planted any white flags beside or in front of what white flags are intended to indicate: the point of ignition.

"Do you recall placing any white flags at any point in time when you were processing the scene, either on the night of the 4th or on the 5th?" Warne had asked him on his second day as a deponent in March.

"No, no white flags?" Reynolds had said.

"No white flags whatsoever?"

"No."

At that point Warne had turned a laptop toward Reynolds on which some photos taken by Josh White from the site were on display and enlarged. Warne had directed Reynolds to look at the center of the first photograph. "Tell me," he'd said, "if you recognize a white flag with a post on it."

"I see what looks like a chipped rock," Reynolds had said, echoing what Josh White had said in his own testimony.

"And do you see the flag?"

"No."

"You don't see any white flag?"

"It looks like a chipped rock right there," he'd said, pointing. "It looks like a chip and a chip and a chip."

"There is a white flag right there," Warne said, pointing.

"Okay."

"Do you see it?"

"Well, I don't really see a flag. It almost looks like a wire here."

"That's right," Warne had said. "And do you see the flag on top of it, sir?"

"I guess if that's what that is."

Two months before that, Bill Warne's office had sent to Kelli Taylor's office photos taken by Josh White on the morning of September 5, photos that had been processed to increase their resolution. Now there could no longer be any serious disagreement about there being a white flag affixed to a thin metal stem planted in front of a rock.

Reynolds had been shown those photos in Taylor's office. He'd seen them with White and Taylor and Winsor and, as he would soon reveal, Diane Welton. And all agreed that it was a white flag. Yet when he was questioned in March, Reynolds hadn't admitted to seeing the flag.

Now, in November 2011, something had changed. What? Warne would have one day to try to find out but would have to limit the scope of his questions only to what transpired at that meeting.

If, at that meeting, Reynolds and White had wanted to brainstorm a fictional explanation—that is, assuming a plausible one could be imagined—they would have been prevented from doing so by the presence of the government lawyers who would have then been suborning perjury by knowingly allowing either or both men to testify to something that they themselves knew to be untrue. Or, possibly, the two lawyers had gone to the restroom or to answer calls and emails, leaving the men alone. Or maybe the men had taken lunch together or met for a beer afterward. As long as Taylor and Winsor didn't overhear them, as long as they met outside the presence of the government attorneys, Reynolds and White might have been able to fill the holes in their story.

Bill Warne explained that he was entitled to know what they said to each other when they were together, regardless of whether the topic was baseball or fire. Reynolds denied that they'd met alone.

So Warne moved on to the flag. And Reynolds, as White had during his four days of testimony in May, agreed at last that the photos he'd previously insisted were of a chipped rock were actually of a white flag atop a stem planted beside a rock and that the photo had been snapped before 10 A.M. on September 5.

What remained to be agreed upon, at least under oath, was how the flag got there and perhaps also how it happened to be planted beside a rock located precisely at the coordinates where Reynolds had recorded his investigation's one and only GPS reading. That, by the way, was a moment captured by Josh White in a photograph of Reynolds poised with the unit over the rock, whose whereabouts were now unknown.

Then there was the question of the handwritten diagram Reynolds had made that morning. On it was a depiction of the rock beside the written GPS coordinates and the acronym that meant ignition source.

Dave Reynolds was a large man with thinning brown hair, possibly colored, a brown mustache, possibly colored, prominent mottling from the sun across his high forehead and cheeks, dark bags under tired eyes, and a classic Roman nose. He had broad shoulders, meaty hands—one of which bore a wedding ring—and a deep, baritone voice. Until his first day as a deponent in the Moonlight case, he had been deposed only once before, as a board member of a condo complex that was involved in a lawsuit. He did not appear comfortable answering questions, but neither did he appear intimidated. At least not at first. That may have been because he was no longer an employee of the U.S. government or because he had been well prepared. Either way, Reynolds repeatedly insisted that, no, he had not discussed the Moonlight Fire with anyone since leaving the USFS until he was hired by Cal Fire. And since then, he said, all communications had been appropriate and legal.

Reynolds acknowledged not believing until viewing the photos in January that the image was of a white flag.

Warne asked about his reaction to seeing the metal stem and white flag in the high-res photos taken by Josh White.

"I was surprised," Reynolds said. "Because there's no recollection of there being a white flag for Josh or myself."

"Did the two of you discuss how that white flag got there during this meeting?"

"I don't recall there being any discussion about it, because we just have no recollection that there was a white flag."

Warne asked if he and White had reached any conclusion during that meeting as to why the white flag was placed in the ground.

Reynolds, like a lawyer, said that Warne was assuming facts.

"You acknowledged together that it was placed in the ground," Warne said. "Correct?"

"No," said Reynolds."

"What do you mean, sir?"

"We—that's exactly it," Reynolds said. "We don't acknowledge that it was placed in the ground. You can see it in the high-resolution photo, which would suggest that there's one there. But neither of us have any recollection of putting a white flag out there. That's what we're saying."

Based on the photo, Warne asked, could Reynolds identify where in the area of origin the white flag was planted?

"It was," Reynolds said, "within the main skid trail."

"The main skid trail, which would be south of the V that's formed by the spur trail and the skid trail, correct?"

"Correct."

Now Warne got to the GPS reading and the sketch Reynolds had drawn. At the meeting, Warne wanted to know, was the subject of the distance and bearing measurements from two reference points discussed?

"Oh, no, not at all," Reynolds said.

Warne was incredulous. "You didn't ask any questions about that?"

"No."

"Based on all that you saw during that meeting," Warne said, "did you consider, in the context of that meeting, with others or with yourself, whether or not the distance and bearing measurements that were taken by you from two separate reference points lined up so that they met in the area where the white flag was placed on the skid trail, as depicted in the high-resolution photography?"

"No," Reynolds said. "These have nothing to do with any kind of a white flag." And he repeated that neither he nor White recalled the flag being there; the photo was inexplicable. "Neither one of us remember putting out a white flag. We don't know where that came from."

Bill Warne did not expect Dave Reynolds to blurt out that, yes, one of them had planted a white flag in front of the rock that they'd originally identified as the specific point of origin but then had moved it after realizing that there were problems with that story. Even just saying yes to having planted a flag would have implied the rest and made retroactive perjurers of both men. Still, Warne found something useful in Reynolds's couched suggestion that the white flag had been immaculately planted. If the best they could come up with was to admit the flag was there but claim not to have planted it, the jury would need little convincing to infer that the investigation had been fatally flawed, if not also corrupt.

After the lunch break, during which Reynolds and the attorneys had presumably conferred about certain issues and details, Warne asked what had caused Reynolds and White at the January meeting to conclude that the white flag was alongside the rock where White snapped Reynolds taking the GPS reading.

"The photos of me there," Reynolds said.

"And you were able to look at those photos and conclude that the white flag was alongside the same rock, correct?"

"Approximately."

Warne soon moved back to wondering if Reynolds and White, at that January meeting—which was after White's November 2010 deposition dates but before the rest of their dates—had attempted to resolve how they were going to reconcile the presence of the white flag under oath.

"We discussed that that was something that was going to come up, that neither of us remember there being a white flag, and that was the end of that."

When asked, Reynolds then said he didn't talk about his GPS reading either, or the fact that he'd apparently written down the coordinates.

Did they discuss the impact of the photos showing him with the GPS unit atop the rock, near the white flag?

"There was no impact," Reynolds said. "That rock and the supposed flag have no impact on anything. You apparently believe so, but I sit here today and I don't know why we are spending the time we are on it myself. But you apparently have a reason."

"Well," Warne said, "did you discuss the fact that you're taking the photographs for a reason, in the context of your investigation, when you met in January of 2011?"

"Are you saying, was there a reason we took the photograph?" Reynolds asked.

Glen Dorgan, the assistant U.S. attorney present, clarified for Reynolds that Warne was inquiring whether he and White discussed the issue.

Warne asked, "Did you discuss in January of 2011 the fact that the photographs that were taken in the area of origin had a significance as they related to your investigation?"

"They had no significance," Reynolds said. "That's what we discussed."

"Are you saying," Warne said, "that all the photographs had no significance?"

"No, those photos had none."

"Which photos?"

"Any of that rock and the supposed flag."

Warne went on to ask whether Reynolds, as an investigator at the time with the USFS, had looked into the allegations about Caleb Lief's misbehavior in the lookout. "It wasn't a concern of mine," Reynolds said, reiterating what he'd said at his earlier depositions.

Why didn't he have concerns?

"I don't have an answer for that," Reynolds said.

Now Warne asked about Ryan Bauer. Not till reading White's transcripts as a Cal Fire consultant, Reynolds said, had he heard the name or its possible importance to the story of this fire. And, he insisted, at the January meeting Bauer's name had not come up.

Would he have conducted the investigation differently if he'd known about Bauer earlier?

"No."

Even if he'd learned that Ryan Bauer's story about having been with his girlfriend "all day" was a fiction? Would that have changed his approach?

"No."

At that meeting had he asked anyone whether Bauer had been properly investigated?

"No."

Suddenly, and apparently out of nowhere, Warne asked Reynolds whether during the lunch break he had spoken to anyone "about the substantive testimony that you gave this morning."

The question took Reynolds by surprise. "Only that we—I already forgot whatever it was," he said. "It was something that I think we misinterpreted between us, and we have already cleared it up. I can't remember back what it was."

Well, what was it, Warne wanted to know. Reynolds still couldn't remember.

Take your time, Warne said.

"I think," Reynolds said, "it was a point of clarification, and I was going to bring it up, but you brought it up, and you cleared it up. What was it? It was right in the beginning."

About the timing of the meetings?

No.

Warne said fine, you can dredge it up later.

He asked whether Reynolds had read Diane Welton's transcript before being deposed.

No.

Had he ever read it?

No.

Had he read all of Josh White's depositions?

As far as he knew.

Had he taken any notes while reading?

No.

Had he sent anyone an email about what he'd read?

No.

Did he understand why he'd been asked to read the transcripts, for which he was, after all, being paid by the state?

"To see if there was anything that might have been—that I didn't agree with, I guess."

"Okay," Warne said, "and who told you to review the transcripts to see if there was anything you might not agree with?"

After Tracy Winsor objected on the grounds that Warne had assumed facts not in evidence, Reynolds said he wasn't sure who'd asked him to read the transcripts to see if he disagreed with anything—then suggested that the transcripts might have been sent to him by the feds, not the state. Warne pointed out, though, that it was the state that had hired him.

In quick order he got Reynolds to reveal a number of details he'd previously not disclosed, including a meeting with Kelli Taylor before Josh White's first set of deposition dates; the existence of notes relating to the Moonlight Fire that hadn't been appended to the materials given to Diane Welton; the admission that a DVD Sierra Pacific had discovered of aerial footage shot in the early minutes of the fire that he was supposed to have viewed in the previous year was taken back from him by Kelli Taylor when he said he had technical trouble trying to view it; and that he had determined that the distance and bearing points on the sketch he'd made corresponded to a place closest to the skid trail a few feet from the white flag.

Warne asked Reynolds where and when he'd created the hand-drawn diagram. Between September 3rd and 5th, Reynolds said, claiming that he'd done it both on scene and after getting back to his desk.

"You actually created the sketch at two different places—on the scene and at your desk?" Warne said.

"Correct."

"Well, which part of this did you create on the scene?"

Dorgan objected. This was, he insisted, beyond the scope of the deposition.

So Warne agreed to move on, not yet revealing that while staring at the two photos of the fragments lying on the white paper atop the hood of White's truck, he had discovered one of those damning pieces of evidence that are the lifeblood of television detective dramas but happen rarely in real court cases. Barely visible lines at the photos' perimeter suggested that another sheet of paper had been placed under the ones with the fragments. On the bottom sheet are faint scribbles that are undeniably the sketch that Dave Reynolds had already drawn before 10:02 that morning. If necessary, Warne would save this dramatic moment for court, at which point it would undermine not just Reynold's timeline claim but also White's testimony that he never saw this sketch until years later.

Where Warne moved on to was an invoice Reynolds had sent to the Department of Justice for two hours of travel time and seven hours of field work in conjunction with the Moonlight Fire investigation. Reynolds had previously testified that Kelli Taylor told him he wouldn't be compensated by the feds for his work.

"This was never paid," Reynolds said; he didn't know how it "got sent out."

"Well," Warne said, "it's not just sent out." It was paid: $546. Did he recall receiving that?

"I do not," Reynolds said.

Warne produced additional documentation suggesting that Reynolds had been less than candid, then came a break, then several more questions about conversations with others, including whether Diane Welton, in whose name the federal origin and cause report was submitted and whose signature appears at the bottom, had asked any questions about the sudden appearance of the white flag in the high-res photos. No, she hadn't, Reynolds said.

Beyond that, Reynolds's memory for other conversations was hazy or nonexistent. No one that he recalled had asked about the other two rocks or the water bar or the photos and raft of evidence that appeared to contradict their assertions.

The deposition soon ended. The four hours had been brutal to the government's case. One of its main witnesses, a man whose findings were foundational to the proceedings, was not going to look good in front of the jury. Glen Dorgan would have to report that to Kelli Taylor.

By the time Taylor heard later that afternoon from Dorgan that the day had not gone well, she had already received an encouraging ruling from Judge Brennan on Sierra Pacific's motion to have the contempt order clarified.

In his motion on behalf of SPI, Bill Warne had expressed confidence that Brennan had merely misworded his prior ruling. Surely he couldn't have meant it as broadly as it appeared. Surely it was wrong to instruct SPI's lawyers or investigators not to talk to anyone in the federal government at any level without first identifying themselves as connected to this case; that would be a peculiar interpretation of the established rules of civil conduct, which apply only to contacting principals of an entity on the opposing side—that is, those with decision-making power. It had never been interpreted to apply to drones.

Warne was right: Brennan had not meant it as he'd written. What he'd meant, as he clarified in a new written order, was that anyone connected with SPI was now prevented from talking about this case or anything having to do with this case to anyone in the federal government— whether at the U.S. Forest Service or, for that matter, the White House— without the express consent of Assistant U.S. Attorney Kelli L. Taylor.

62

Nearly three years after Ryan Bauer's final deposition, Bill Warne received a phone call from Edwin Bauer, Ryan's father, who wanted Downey Brand to return to him some documents that had been copied from his computer's hard drive pursuant to a court order issued in the state lawsuit. Offhandedly, Bauer mentioned "the bribe."

What bribe? Warne asked.

Bauer apparently believed, with good reason, this would not have been news to Warne. But since it was, he related how Eugene Chittock, the lawyer he'd briefly hired to represent Ryan at his deposition, had told him that Sierra Pacific's attorneys, on behalf of the company, offered Ryan $2 million to claim he'd started the Moonlight Fire. Bauer said he'd conveyed the bribe offer directly to Assistant U.S. Attorneys Kelli Taylor and Richard Elias.

Startled, Warne contacted Chittock, who denied having made such a representation to Bauer. But Chittock, too, was surprised by Warne's ignorance of the alleged incident, given that the FBI had separately interviewed both him and Bauer at length in spring 2012. Whatever Bauer had told the investigators, Chittock didn't know, not being either Eddy's attorney or Ryan's. But, he said, he had assured the two federal investigators there was no truth to the claim, and though not under subpoena volunteered to open his phone records for them to peruse. The records proved that his sole contact with Downey Brand or SPI was one call from Bill Warne the morning of Ryan Bauer's second deposition, after Chittock's fax arrived at the prison. (Had they checked Eddy Bauer's records, they would have found a call he'd made to Red Emmerson's son George, president of Sierra Pacific.)

Offering to bribe witnesses in order to effect any outcome, but particularly when the intended outcome would have undermined the government's case, is a serious crime—a violation of U.S. Code § 18, punishable by up to fifteen years imprisonment and/or a fine three times the bribe amount. Further, any lawyer caught purveying a bribe would face disbarment, and discussion of the crime would likely be admissible in court and interpreted by the jury as suggestive of guilt.

One can safely assume the Department of Justice thoroughly investigated the claim and dismissed it as false. Had there been a hint of credibility, Downey Brand would have been contacted, its records subpoenaed, its personnel questioned; had there been any reason to suspect wrongdoing, either a federal grand jury would have been impaneled or charges would've been filed by the U.S. attorney for the Eastern District of California.

But Downey Brand had not been contacted. Warne learned of this episode from Edwin Bauer. Whoever had originated this falsehood could have been indicted under U.S. Code § 1001, which is a felony (making "any false, fictitious, or fraudulent statement or representation") punishable by up to five years in prison. Martha Stewart, for example, was convicted under this statute.

From Bill Warne and Downey Brand's perspective, described in a subsequent brief, Edwin Bauer wasn't indicted for the same reason the prosecution willfully failed to inform them of the false allegation: the government's case had not been a good-faith effort to do justice in assigning liability for a fire. Rather, it had acted in bad faith, willing to ignore or cover up inconvenient facts in order to achieve a preordained result.

> The Moonlight Prosecutors knowingly and willfully failed to reveal the existence of a federal investigation into the matter concerning the Bauers, even after the investigation revealed the falsity of the charges.
>
> Revealing such information to Defendants or to the Court would have been damaging to the government's case, as it would have tended to prove that Edwin Bauer made a false assertion to strengthen the government's claims against Sierra Pacific while diverting attention from his son. Obviously, had it been true, it would have been more serious than the charges set forth in the federal ac-

tion. Since it is not true, the false report of such a crime is also serious, demonstrating, among other things, a willingness on the part of the Bauers to manufacture evidence harmful to an innocent party and an effort to deflect attention away from someone who may have actually started the fire. Bauer's false claim raised numerous questions, including whether the Bauers had engaged in similar conduct when Edwin Bauer told investigators that a man in a silver pickup had told him that 'a bulldozer hit a rock,' and when Ryan Bauer claimed that he too had overheard a different statement by one of Howell's bulldozer operators supposedly admitting to having started the fire by striking a rock with his dozer.

Edwin Bauer's false allegation of a multi-million dollar bribe by Downey Brand or Sierra Pacific can only have been made in an effort to falsely inculpate Sierra Pacific, and thus it actually has the opposite effect, tending instead to incriminate Mr. Bauer and his son Ryan as a failed attempt to deflect focused attention from themselves and whatever role they had in starting the Moonlight Fire. But instead of receiving this information, which is harmful to the government's case, the Court and Defendants heard and received nothing in just one of many instances of the government purposefully withholding harmful evidence.

In a criminal case, prosecutors are legally bound to provide the defense with any exculpatory evidence uncovered in its investigation—unhelpful evidence that the prosecution would not otherwise have introduced unless the prosecutors had become convinced that the defendant was not, in fact, guilty of the crime, in which case the prosecutors are legally, ethically, and morally bound to drop the charges. Failure, willful or not, to provide the defense with exculpatory evidence violates a citizen's constitutional right to due process. It's called a Brady violation, after the landmark 1963 Supreme Court decision *Brady v. Maryland*.

In civil cases between two private parties, Brady does not apply; neither side is under an obligation to help the other. But when the suit is being prosecuted by a government entity based on a government investigation paid for by the public, the responsibility is at least implied, if not compelled. In this instance, Warne argued, the damage that the government inflicted on Sierra Pacific by failing to reveal the false bribe claim was egregious and irreparable.

Shortly before the federal trial was to begin, Kelli Taylor filed several motions to prevent the jury from hearing evidence pertaining to Ryan Bauer.

By then, Warne's team had spent millions of dollars amassing evidence that included eyewitness and expert testimony, scientific demonstrations, and real-time video to debunk the prosecution's theory and facts. These puzzle pieces would be presented to the jury as complements to Warne's cross-examination of the government's own witnesses, whose inconsistent and contradictory statements in depositions had already led one assistant U.S. attorney to quit the case, and would compel another to file a sworn declaration. Warne believed that all the pieces would form a picture of both a fatally flawed investigation and a prosecution blind and deaf to its flaws. In one of their periodic update meetings, he told Red Emmerson, George Emmerson, Mark Emmerson, and David Dun that he and his litigation team at Downey Brand were confident they had discredited the government's case. He said he believed the jury would agree the fire had not in fact started where investigators White and Reynolds claimed it had and could not in fact have started in the manner they decided it had.

But Taylor understood that without Bauer as a witness, those exhibits would have left Warne's team with a dry, logical presentation of evidence, whereas seeing and hearing him—and seeing and hearing Josh White and Dave Reynolds try to justify ignoring Bauer—would make vivid all the other details in the jurors' minds. Whether Ryan Bauer could be proven to have had anything to do with the fire, or whether he was completely innocent, wasn't in and of itself relevant. But why had the investigators intentionally disregarded him? And why, when the prosecutors learned that the investigators had been either corrupt or inept, had they not dropped the case? In short, Bauer represented the face of a failed and possibly dishonest investigation and prosecution. Removing him from the mix would rob Warne's questioning of perhaps its most powerful element. Without Bauer the jury could not so easily be led to conclude that the investigators hadn't done their jobs and that this case should never have come to trial.

It's fair to assume that Taylor's wanting to exclude Bauer from court meant that she agreed with Warne's strategy. And by extension, it also suggests that she recognized what a flimsy case she was prosecuting.

In her motion filed May 31, 2012, Taylor represented to the court that there was nothing to connect the Bauers to the fire, and she argued that the defendants ought to be prevented from presenting evidence that someone or something besides the defendants were responsible for starting the fire, either accidentally or purposefully. She wrote:

> Without a shred of physical evidence or expert support, Defendants intend to convert this trial into an arson witch hunt, spending weeks delving into the personal lives and transgressions of several individuals who they claim fit an arson profile. Given that there is no evidence of arson, this evidence is irrelevant. Further, any tenuous probative value this evidence may have is substantially outweighed by the risk of confusion of the issues, misleading the jury, wasting time, and unfair prejudice.
>
> A court may exclude evidence, even if relevant, whose probative value is substantially outweighed by the risk of unfair prejudice, confusing the issues, misleading the jury, undue delays, and wasting time. Fed. R. Evid. 403. Thus the Supreme Court recognizes that the evidence of an alternate perpetrator of a crime is 'frequently' so remote or lacks such connection to the matter at hand that it is excluded.

Now, to bolster her argument, Taylor cited a famous criminal case: Timothy McVeigh, the Oklahoma City bomber, whose attorneys were prevented by the judge from introducing into evidence "an alternate perpetrator—i.e., a white supremacist group that had a similar motive to bomb the federal building."

In Warne's fifty-five-page response, he noted that the issue wasn't whether Ryan Bauer had committed arson. The issue was that the government had failed to investigate Ryan Bauer,

> be it through arson, a chainsaw mishap, or smoking. But there is a train of interconnected evidence regarding Bauer which, if believed, will cause the jury to reject the government's conclusion. Indeed, this evidence is stronger than the plaintiff's evidence against these defendants. Since investigators ignored or failed to investigate this evidence, we may never know how the fire was actually started or by whom. Defense experts Gary White and Steve Carman, two respected and experienced ex-federal employees, have confirmed the government's investigation is deeply flawed, opining that the inves-

tigators discarded their training, abandoned science, settled for assumptions, and ignored contrary evidence, or worse. In light of this, the government's assertion that 'many experts have investigated this fire, and not one—not a single one—has concluded the fire was arson' wildly misses the point.

63

In late 2010 Sierra Pacific had tracked down a video shot for personal use by an observer in one of the borate-dropping planes that had been dispatched to extinguish the Moonlight Fire just after it was spotted and called in.

The video, time-stamped 3:09 that afternoon, was studied by SPI's own foresters and surveyors before being submitted to independent forestry experts, who confirmed their conclusion: Two hours after the dozer had allegedly sparked the fire, the smoke plume had not yet reached the area that Josh White had insisted, and now the United States and California Attorney General were insisting, was the fire's point of origin. Had the aerial photo been taken an hour earlier, the distances would have been even wider. But there was no mistaking that at 3:09, the two points were still at least a hundred yards apart.

This new evidence conformed to aerial photographs taken of the area in the days after the fire that showed the plume at the bottom of the classic V fire pattern wherein every tree inside the V looks torched—but the alleged point of origin is not at the apex of the V; it is on its perimeter.

What could account for the discrepancy between where the fire appeared to begin and where it was alleged to have begun? White's explanation, ratified by the continuing prosecution, was that the dozer had thrown a superheated fleck into a small pile of brush, where it smoldered for more than ninety minutes before finally running up the hillside to the point of origin, not unlike a slow dynamite fuse.

That theory was granted scientific credence by the prosecutors' chief fire expert, Kelly R. Close. His detailed report, based on the results of proprietary modeling software called FARSITE, concluded that the fire had indeed begun in the alleged area of origin.

Bill Warne's team gave Close's report to their own experts for analyses. The experts filed reports that disputed the findings in detail, and they were also deposed so that the prosecution could try to find holes or flaws in their methodology and conclusions.

One of those experts was Christopher Lautenberger, a PhD whose professional proficiency encompassed combustion and meteorology. Lautenberger studied the scene himself, measured the hillside's slope, used GPS coordinates of the culprit rocks, geologic records of the surrounding terrain, and other necessary data, including wind speed and direction, for his report, which concluded that Close had mistakenly increased the hill's slope by thirty degrees over its actual angle. This was a significant mistake in that it multiplied by seventeen times the speed at which the fire could have spread uphill under those specific conditions.

"Mr. Close," Lautenberger told Bill Warne in his deposition, "conducted FARSITE modeling in an attempt to support the general area of origin as a valid origin. His FARSITE modeling used a slope raster, a slope layer, that greatly over-exaggerated the slope and caused the fire to spread to the west much more rapidly than it would have, and, to date, this is the only simulation that I've seen or the only analysis that I've seen that purports to corroborate the general origin area as a valid point of origin. After correcting that slope error that Mr. Close had made, and rerunning the simulation, his own simulation shows that the point of origin—the *alleged* point of origin—is inconsistent with the air attack video. . . . To the best of my knowledge, there is no explanation provided for why there's no smoke at the alleged point of origin in the 3:09 air attack video."

Close himself was deposed in early March 2012. Bill Warne asked him whether now—having read Lautenberger's report and the reports of two other SPI-hired experts—he would like to amend anything in his own written findings. Close said he did not. Warne asked if Close understood that, under Rule 26 of the Federal Rules of Civil Procedure, he was required to correct known mistakes to his own report.

"I'm not aware," Close said, "that I have an obligation to actually make changes to the report. I do have an obligation to be truthful and clarify anything you'd asked me to clarify."

"And your testimony here today," Warne responded, "is you have found no mistakes in your reports, correct?"

"That is not correct."

"Okay, what mistakes have you discovered?"

"Since submitting my original report, at some point after that—I believe it was during the process of rebuttal reports—I did discover there was a data error in some of the information that I used for fire behavior modeling." He said he "looked into the matter and discovered that in fact there was an area in that slope layer that caused some of the slope values to be somewhat exaggerated in some parts of the terrain that I was examining."

This was a significant admission of error that Close brought to the attention of the U.S. attorneys, who did not ask him to alter his report. Still, for his own "edification," he said, he'd run projections using the correct slope. The source of the incorrect slope angle, he explained, had been another government expert witness, Chris Curtis, employed as a consultant for both Cal Fire and the U.S. attorney.

Warne interpreted the government's ignoring Close as an extension of everything that had happened so far in the prosecution of this case. The evidence, he said, strongly suggested that the two investigators had all along intended to pin the fire on SPI, and to do so had worked backward from their conclusion by conducting an investigation that was anything but scientific. Having had exclusive access to the site, he said, they may well have suppressed physical evidence that would have proved a different cause for the fire. Ever since, the government had covered the investigators' malfeasance no matter the evidence. Now that it was clear that the Department of Justice would not abandon the case in the interests of justice, it would be up to a jury.

Warne was eager to show the jurors an aerial photo, dated a week after the fire had begun, whose V-pattern of torched trees is nearly congruent with the classic V printed in FI-210 textbooks' discussions of how to determine an area of origin. On the same photo, Warne's team circled in red the government's alleged point of origin, which had been determined by surveyors using the government's own coordinates. The distance between the red circle and the heel of the fire (that is, the apex of the V) is some 250 feet—and whatever flame might have existed in the red circle would have had to travel against the wind.

As damaging as that the photo and the testimonies of Lautenberger

Heinbockel and, 185, 186, 188, 189;
deposition of Joshua White and,
208; document dump of, 173, 176,
210; exchanges e-mail with Warne,
127–29; meets with Reynolds, 231;
motions of, 237–38, 245, 251; as officer of the court, 225; Overby and,
127, 130; replaces Wright, 125
Taylor Lake, 2
Tehama County, Calif., 51
Terry, Andrea. *See* Jackson, Andrea
Terry
Theobald, Rod, 51
Thorpe, Emily Aebischer Emmerson
(Mrs. Harry Thorpe), 15, 30, 34, 60;
relationship with son Red, 41; re-
marries, 35
Thorpe, Harry, 35, 40, 47, 60
Tillamook Forest, 15
timber rights, 159
timber sales: environmentalists and,
179–80; on federal lands, 199
Tomascheski, Bud, 164–65
topography, fire paths and, 37
Trinity National Forest, 146
Truckee, Calif., 194
Turner, Ted, 7

Union Pacific Railroad, 19, 126
United States: lumber industry in, 121;
in 1960s, 114; wildfires in, 250
United States v. Jones, 27
University of California, Berkeley, 243
University of California, Davis, 125,
243
University of California Hastings Col-
lege of Law, 254
University of San Diego, 125
Upper Columbia Academy, Red Em-
merson at, 41, 46–47, 52–54
U.S. Bureau of Land Management, 145
U.S. Constitution, 171; Fifth Amend-
ment to, 156, 247, 253; Fourth
Amendment to, 27
U.S. Department of Defense, 126
U.S. Department of Justice, 13, 118,
125, 130, 158; antitrust division, 196,

197, 198–200; corruption of, 174;
Moonlight Fire suit and, 3
U.S. Department of the Interior, 146,
175
U.S. District Court for Eastern California, 125
U.S. Fish and Wildlife Service, 179
USFS (United States Forest Service), 3,
13, 90, 145, 179, 233; bulldozers of,
33; cutting permits and, 7, 18; fire
lookouts and, 11; government lawyers cover up misconduct of, 172;
Gunn Fire 2 and, 202; investigators of, 19; lands of, 1; Lief and, 174,
176–78, 186–87, 190; personnel from,
17; Reynolds retires from, 224, 227;
standard-issue protective gear of,
65; sued by Seattle Audubon Society, 180; supervisors of, 98. *See also*
Moonlight Fire
U.S. Interstate Commerce Commission, 158
U.S. Marines, Red Emmerson in, 75–
76, 131
U.S. National Weather Service, 249
U.S. Ninth Circuit Court of Appeals,
265
U.S. Secretary of Agriculture, 165
U.S. Secretary of the Interior, 146
U.S. Supreme Court, 26, 138, 236, 238

virtual cone, 37–38; of Moonlight Fire
origin, 43–44
voice recorders, 89, 120
Voth, Dan "Hippie Dan," 50–51; Ryan
Bauer and, 109, 110–12, 151–52

Wagner, Ben, 250
Wallace, Benny, 32, 50–51, 86; arrests
Ryan Bauer for drunken assault,
115–18; assaulted by Ryan Bauer,
147; stops Ryan Bauer, 79–80
Walnut Creek, Calif., 193
Warne, Bill, 137, 261; anticipates jury
trial, 265; Ryan Bauer deposition
and, 147; brief of, on prosecution's
bad faith, 235–36, 252–53;